Top Ten

THE IRREVERENT GUIDE TO MUSIC

ALEX OGG 35p

4 BOOKS

First published 2001 by Channel 4 Books
an imprint of Macmillan Publishers Ltd
25 Eccleston Place London SW1W 9NF
Basingstoke and Oxford

www.macmillan.com

Associated companies throughout the world

ISBN 07522 1975 8

500 594353   1 3 5 7 9 8 6 4 2

A CIP catalogue record for this book is available from the British Library.

Designed and typeset by Jonathan
Printed and bound by Mackays of Chatham, plc, Chatham, Kent

This book accompanies the television series 'Top Ten'
made by Chrysalis Television for Channel 4.
Senior Producer: Steve Gowans
Producer: John Quinn

This book is dedicated to Bill and Marion Ogg,
with apologies for Christmas,
and congratulations on their Ruby wedding anniversary

ACKNOWLEDGEMENTS

I'd like to thank the eternally wonderful Dawn Wrench first and foremost for her continued lack of judgement in men. And my beautiful baby boy Hughie, for being so damned compliant, especially on Daddy Days.

I'm grateful to Emma Tait and Verity Willcocks at Channel 4 books for deeming me worthy of the task and seeing it through to completion. Copy editor Rob Dimery deserves credit for a contribution above and beyond his role. My profound thanks to Steve Gowans and John Quinn at Chrysalis. John in particular unflappably answered all too frequent e-mails and phone calls and gave me a lot of encouragement when, frankly, I needed some. All while having to deal with the equally pressing task of getting the series to air. Thanks.

A few other people contributed. Among them Andrew Dineley (who checked the Eurovision chapter), Stewart Osborne (who helped with a bit of punk fact-checking), the amazing Joe Standerline and Mark Greaves (from whom I co-opted, with permission, a line in the introduction to Love Songs). Then there's the usual suspects who provided support, be it moral, fraternal, historic or alcoholic; Chris Taylor and the Winterton boys (Evan, Andy, Jon, Rich), the Scunny connection (Phil, Sarah), the Leytonstone posse (Mel, Phil, Colin), the Cambridge contingent (Rick and Sophie, the two Andys and Alan). From no specific time or place: Sue and Michael, Katelyn Adler, Mal and Pauline, Doug and Dawn, Helen and Serge, Caroline and Alice, Alice and Harry, James and Sarah, Tim and Lucy, Richard Bull and the Huggies, Abi and John, Amy Quinn (who loaned me a copy of one of the shows long before I knew I'd end up working on it), Jim and David Ogg, Nick Mason, Paul Cobley, Steve Smith, Victoria Smith (for her patience). Thank you one and all.

Contents

Sixties Soul

The term soul was first applied to music by jazz musicians, indicating a movement to take jazz back to its roots and make it 'more black'. Soon it came to represent the hybrid of R&B and gospel music that we recognize today. Most of the early soul acts had previously performed in R&B, doo wop or gospel groups, and soul emphasized the emotive aspects of each, marrying technical precision to bravura performances. Berry Gordy's Motown Records assembled a production line of hits (mirroring the car industry of its native Detroit) whilst consistently issuing classic records.

The artists that make up this list comprise some of the greatest acts in popular music. Each story is entwined with the kind of personal tragedy that underpinned the heartbreak expressed on their records – just as soul encapsulated the optimism and tragedy of the civil rights movement it served as a soundtrack for.

10/Sam And Dave   Points: 60

Recommended album: *Sweat 'n' Soul: Anthology 1965–1971* (1993) ● Top 20 hits: 6

Soul was never just melody and sweetness, it was also about sweat and conviction. No-one exemplified the idea of performance quite like Sam Moore and Dave Prater. Trading vocal lines using gospel call-and-response techniques, their spontaneous debut came at Florida's King Of Hearts nightclub in 1958. They subsequently became the greatest double act in soul, and in manager Phil Walden's eyes, 'the most incredible live act in the history of music'. Under Jerry Wexler's guidance, Isaac Hayes and Dave Porter were recruited to write material for the duo, with added musical potency provided by the Memphis Horns. Their first hit, 'Hold On! I'm Comin'', was inspired by Porter's bathroom plea as he was hurried into the studio. Further hits followed, including 'Soul Man', which topped the R&B charts, and 'I Thank You'. Sam Moore was somewhat dismissive

of much of the duo's material, and remains so today. It wasn't just the material that was lacking, however. Moore puts it down to relations between him and Dave souring after Dave shot his wife in May 1968. Despite receiving a facial gunshot injury, Prater's wife forgave him. Sam Moore did not. He claims to have told his collaborator that he would sing with him, but he would never talk to him again, either off stage or on. They didn't speak for the next ten or eleven years. In 1970 they split up but reunited a year later, by which time both were drug addicts. The duo's memory was revived when the Blues Brothers scored with a cover of 'Soul Man' in 1979. It did little to ease the duo's plight. Prater was caught trying to sell crack to an undercover police officer in 1987, and died in a car crash a year later.

9/Martha And The Vandellas

Points: 80

Recommended album: *Motown Milestones* (1995) ● Top 20 hits: 8

The Vandellas built on Motown's success with girl groups the Supremes and Marvelettes and left behind two of the most infectious singles of the sixties. Martha Reeves was spotted by Motown executive Mickey Stevenson at a talent contest. Initially she worked as secretary and typist to Stevenson, occasionally recording songs so backing singers could learn their lines before entering the studio. Eventually she was signed, along with high school friends Annette Sterling and Rosalind Ashford, to Gordy's Motown label as Martha And The Vandellas. A couple of ballads disappointed. Then, in the stifling summer of 1963, they recorded the Holland-Dozier-Holland composition 'Heat Wave'. After Sterling was replaced by Betty Kelly, 1964's 'Dancing In The Streets' became

> **Mickey Stevenson on the inspiration for 'Dancing In The Street':** 'In the city of Detroit in the summer, they would open the fire hydrants and let the water come out, so the kids could play and all that. And to see that was a joy. That song came out of that.'

the group's biggest hit, reaching number two. 'I thought it was fabulous,' recalls Reeves. 'I asked if I could sing it my way, and I gave it my all.' The backroom staff at Motown gave her a rapturous reception. 'The engineer phoned and said, "Hey, the machine wasn't on." So I had to do it again. That's why "Dancing In The Street" sounds live.' Like the Supremes, success produced disputes about the group's billing. 'I don't feel like a group, because I sang all the songs,' deadpans Reeves. 'Nowhere To Run' in 1965 featured one of the first conceptual pop videos, as the trio sat astride a car moving down a Detroit production line. In the afterglow of their success, Reeves went to Berry Gordy chasing unpaid royalties. 'He was indignant. He didn't want to talk to me any more. He said, "You can't run my company." I, being outspoken, said, "Looks like you can't either, 'cos you can't tell me where my money is."' Gordy settled out of court, but Reeves's career stalled.

8/Otis Redding
Points: 90

Recommended album: *Otis Blue* (1965) ● No. 1 hits: 1 ● Top 20 hits: 7

At the start of the sixties, Otis Redding was dominating talent shows at Georgia's Douglass Theater. 'The other talent on the show was good,' recalls his brother Rodgers Redding. 'But everyone waited on Otis Redding. He won every week.' Redding's burgeoning reputation reached Phil Walden, but he wasn't allowed to attend the performances, due to segregation. 'I would listen outside across the street in my car on the radio. When he came on stage they would just *scream*. It didn't take long to add Otis and Redding together equals success in this business.' Walden and younger brother Alan took

Alan Walden: 'To me, Otis Redding was soul music.'

on Redding as their client in 1961. However, as Alan recalls, their inter-racial friendship wasn't a straightforward deal in the Deep South. 'Otis said, "You know what they're calling me on the street? They're calling me a white man's nigger." I sniggered and laughed. "Hey, since the day I started working with you, I've been a nigger-loving white man."' Otis immediately dazzled on his vinyl appearances, scoring with 'These Arms Of Mine'. He went from strength to strength, releasing the epic 1965 album *Otis Blue*, and cutting singles 'Mr Pitiful', 'I've Been Loving You Too Long (To Stop Now)', 'Respect' and the indelible 'Try A Little Tenderness'. In June 1967, he appeared at the Monterey Pop Festival. Michael Lydon covered the event for *Rolling Stone*: 'Monterey pop festival – hippies, long hair, beads, pot, scruffiness. Up came Otis Redding and Booker T and the MGs – lime green suits, very spiffy, the shoes polished. It was like something from another planet. They were fantastic.' At the height of his powers, Redding wrote '(Sittin' On) The Dock Of The Bay', a journey's end ballad that some felt predicted his own imminent demise. Three days after cutting it, he died in an air crash after his private jet dived into a Wisconsin lake. He was just 27. Alan Walden was among many who felt the loss keenly. 'The world stopped for me for about three years. It affected me so badly, at one time I contemplated suicide. I still cry over Otis Redding, there are times when I still cry.'

7/Ray Charles
Points: 170

Recommended album: *The Best Of Ray Charles: The Atlantic Years* (1994)
No. 1 hits: 4 ● Top 10 hits: 17

Ray Charles Robinson is universally credited with the creation of soul music, singing secular songs but adapting the vocal expression of gospel music to R&B. It proved a powerful cocktail, too powerful for many, who felt that Charles was misapplying the religious fervour of gospel. Blind from the age of eight after contracting glaucoma, Charles taught himself to compose by Braille while at a school for the blind in Florida. By the mid-fifties, he was recording for Atlantic, cutting a series of successful sides beginning with 'It Should Have Been Me' in 1954. Throughout, his natural intelligence and sharp wit shone through. Biographer Michael Lydon considers him the most intelligent human he's ever met, while his valet Dave Simmons recalls being routinely beaten at chess by a man who

had to memorize the position of each piece on the board. Charles's breakthrough came in 1959 with 'What'd I Say'. Jerry Lee Lewis, Elvis Presley and Bobby Darin all had hits in the sixties with revivals of the track. 'Georgia On My Mind', 'Hit

Ray Charles: 'I don't want to do nothing but do what I'm doing, just leave here like Duke Ellington, just leave here playing my music. That's it, that's my contribution to the world.'

The Road, Jack' and 'I Can't Stop Loving You' all subsequently topped the US charts. Charles was also proving a hit with the ladies, as Lydon recounts: 'How he does it, I don't know. It's not like having a few affairs and feeling guilty about it. He's like a sultan with his harem.' His backing band the Raelettes comprised his core following. As Lydon elaborates, 'to be a *Raelette*, you've got to *let Ray*.' Charles was also addicted to narcotics. 'People want you to say that somebody coerced you into it,' he confides. 'But I can't lie like that. I *begged* my way into it.' He was busted for a second time in December 1966 and threatened with a huge jail sentence. Showing commendable strength of character, he opted to go cold turkey rather than be weaned off drugs gradually. Charles has since led an exemplary life, charming fellow musicians and audiences alike as *the* gentleman performer.

6/Smokey Robinson And The Miracles   Points: 210

Recommended album: *The Best Of Smokey Robinson & The Miracles* (1995)
No. 1 hits: 4 ● Top 20 hits: 21

William 'Smokey' Robinson is one of the great romantic songwriters, an effortless, uncomplicated singer, a master producer and arranger, and one of the figureheads of Motown's success. Bobby Womack likens Smokey to good wine, while Bob Dylan has called him America's greatest living poet. Berry Gordy first spotted Robinson at an audition he'd failed. Gordy helped the young songwriter structure his embryonic 'poems' into fully fledged songs. Their first collaborative success was 'Shop Around', Motown's first million-selling single, recorded after a middle-of-the-night studio session convened by Gordy. After that Robinson's name became a fixture on the R&B charts, the Miracles enjoying a decade-long purple passage in the sixties. However, the touring was playing havoc with the group's health. Robinson had married backing singer Claudette, who miscarried twice on the road. When they eventually had two healthy children, their names Berry and Tamla testified to Smokey's dedication to the house of Gordy. 'The Tracks Of My Tears', though only a minor hit on its original release in 1965, became an instant soul standard. So too 'The Tears Of A Clown' at the turn of the seventies, which temporarily delayed his decision to leave the Miracles. Although 'Being With You' was a huge solo hit in the early eighties, the squeaky-clean Robinson succumbed to crack addiction after his father died; the experience of being hooked on the drug was one that he has subsequently likened to becoming one of the walking dead. However, religion, as it is wont to do with errant soul singers, saved him, and his abiding passion these days is golf. Bobby Womack:

Bobby Womack: 'Every time you hear his voice on the radio, you feel that they're playing music again.'

'Someone who can write as many songs as he's written over the years, not just for himself, but for everybody, and made 'em happy, shouldn't he be able to go off and play a little golf if he wants to?'

5/Four Tops

Points: 300

Recommended album: *Anthology* (1988) ● No. 1 hits: 3 ● Top 20 hits: 30

A quartet formed spontaneously at a Detroit birthday party nearly half a century ago, the Four Tops comprised lead vocalist Levi Stubbs, Lawrence Payton, Abdul 'Duke' Fakir, and Renaldo Obie Benson. After a spell with Chess Records in Chicago, Mickey Stevenson signed the exuberant quartet to Motown. He teamed them with producers Holland-Dozier-Holland, and they hit immediately with 1964's 'Baby I Need Your Loving'. 'I knew it was a hit', smirks Benson, 'when they loaned us money to play poker with them.' But it was 1966's 'Reach Out I'll Be There' that catapulted the Four Tops into the international limelight. Fakir claims the group had no idea it was going to be a hit. Stubbs simply 'didn't like it', though Gordy insisted it would be the biggest hit of their careers. The song's exquisite harmonies and rhythmic drama, which framed Stubbs' lead vocal beautifully, proved Gordy correct. Everyone

Renaldo 'Obie' Benson:
'Our hearts have never left Motown. We are Motown to the day we die.'

expected Stubbs to go solo as a result. He refused all offers, because the Four Tops 'were about loyalty, friendship, honesty'. A run of hits followed, though the group's impetus slowed when Holland-Dozier-Holland left Motown in 1967. The Four Tops stuck it out for another five years. 'Loco In Acapulco', the theme song to 1988 hit film *Buster*, gave them their last Top 10 hit. That year, the Four Tops had reservations for the American flight that crashed at Lockerbie. A TV producer had delayed them, insisting they complete a recording. In 1997 Payton died of liver cancer. 'I miss him even now,' says Benson. 'I think about him all the time. We all do. And if you notice, we never talk about him. Know what I'm saying? It's painful.' Theo People came in as his replacement. Stubbs's health is also failing, but he still wants one more number one record before he goes.

4 /Aretha Franklin

Points: 320

Recommended album: *I Never Loved A Man (The Way I Loved You)* (1967)
No. 1 hits: 3 ● Top 20 hits: 32

Franklin was the daughter of a world-famous Detroit minister who sold albums of his sermons to his international parishioners. Singer Kim Weston remembers after leaving church, 'you'd go home and listen to the radio. And one of the highlights of a Sunday was listening to Rev C.L. Franklin. And you'd be waiting to see if Aretha would sing.' Aretha soon proved herself an independent spirit, and by the time she enjoyed secular success with 'Today I Sing The Blues' in 1960, she had two illegitimate children. Her father was not best pleased. Angrily asking her why she wasn't helping to clean the house, Aretha said she was a star – stars didn't do that kind of thing. After what was mostly a fruitless six-year association with Columbia, producer Jerry Wexler lured Franklin away to Atlantic Records in 1966. 'It was my notion to take her to a small town in Alabama called Muscle Shoals, just the quiet sleepy ambience of the Deep South, no distractions.' Together, they found the right groove in which to locate Franklin's fiery

gospel bawl. The Muscle Shoals sessions produced 'I Never Loved A Man (The Way I Love You)', 'Respect', 'Baby I Love You' and '(You Make Me Feel Like A) Natural Woman'. Wexler believes her destructive marriage to Ted White powered some of those stellar performances. 'If she's being abused or not comfortable, that's when she sings her heart out.' 'Lady Soul' achieved no fewer than sixty Billboard hits between 1961 and 1982, although subsequent image changes never quite gelled. 'I said, "Aretha, you do not have to sing one more song to prove that you can still sing,' recalls Wexler. 'All you have to do is play one of your old records against what all these people think is good.' In 1987,

Renowned engineer Tom Dowd, who worked at Muscle Shoals with Franklin: 'Musicians, when they walked in, they'd say, "Man, you have to hear this chick. She sings like a bird."'

she teamed up with George Michael for the British chart-topper 'I Knew You Were Waiting (For Me)', but then became progressively more reclusive, typically spending the hours between twelve to three or four watching soap operas. These days, Lady Soul is a keen gardener.

3/Temptations

Points: 325

Recommended album: *Anthology* (1995) ● No. 1 hits: 4 ● Top 20 hits: 32

As sole remaining founder member Otis Williams admits, 'We've done more harm to ourselves than any outside faction could ever do to us.' Yet their public image was conversely that of clean-cut, youthful charmers. Their combination of good looks and stunning vocals was a sure-fire winner: 'If I was gay', observes Bobby Womack, 'I'd have wanted one of them.' The group was drawn from existing Detroit doo wop outfits and featured lead singer Eddie Kendricks alongside Dave Ruffin, Paul Williams, Melvin Franklin and Otis Williams. They enjoyed a succession of hits for Motown with Smokey Robinson-written material beginning with 'The Way You Do The Things You Do'. It was the release of 'My Girl', with its sumptuous lead vocal from Ruffin, that changed the course of the group's career. Robinson

Manager, Shelly Berger: 'The Temptations could have come from Central Casting. Here you had five great-looking men, all over six foot tall, and they did it all.'

remembers that he wrote 'My Girl' specifically for Ruffin's voice. The acclaim went straight to Ruffin's head. 'He'd gone out and bought his own limousine,' recalls manager, Shelly Berger, 'and he had a sidekick, who we were informed one day was David's manager.' Brother Jimmy Ruffin argues: 'He had four, five, six hit records. Why should he now still be just a member of the group?' Otis Williams was having none of it. 'He felt that by being on the hits he was on, it should be David Ruffin and the Temptations. I said, "Well, *that* won't happen."' Ruffin didn't go quietly, bizarrely turning up at shows where he wasn't billed to play. 'Because this was happening', states Berger, 'we started beefing up our security, to make sure David didn't get into the building.' Paul Williams, meanwhile, was so dependent on alcohol, an off-stage vocalist was regularly singing his parts. Sacked in 1971, he committed suicide two years later. Ruffin, a crack addict, finally overdosed in 1991. Michael Jackson paid his funeral expenses (pallbearer Kendricks, who died of lung cancer a year later, was arrested at the funeral for failing to pay child support).

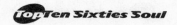

Franklin died of heart failure in February 1995. Despite personnel tragedies along the way, sole survivor Otis Williams has stubbornly kept the Temptations flame alive. Their 1998 album *Phoenix Rising* has been certified platinum. As he says, 'we have been able to survive in spite of ourselves.'

2/Marvin Gaye

Points: 330

Recommended album: *Superhits* (1970) ● No. 1 hits: 4 ● Top 20 hits: 33

The sixties career of complex, introspective singer Marvin Gaye saw the most expressive voice in soul adorn some of the most beautiful and enduring songs of the decade. The son of a minister, Gaye arrived at Motown as a session drummer with a history in doo wop groups such as the Moonglows. In 1961 he signed to Motown subsidiary Tamla and married Berry Gordy's sister, Anna. A year later he charted with 'Stubborn Kind Of Fellow' after being encouraged by Mickey Stevenson to drop ambitions to croon like Nat King Cole and 'get down' with a little R&B. The song's title underscored the independent and pugnacious way Gaye would pursue his career, although brother Frankie Gaye claims Marvin was not so much a rebel as simply unable to tolerate being ordered around. In 1964 he co-wrote 'Dancing In The Street' for Martha And The Vandellas (who backed him on 'Stubborn Kind Of Fellow'), and by the year's end his own '(How Sweet It Is) To Be Loved By You' established him as a bona fide pop star. According to friend Elaine Jesmer, the attention caught him unawares; beneath the surface were layers of insecurity. 'I don't think Marvin enjoyed performing then at all,' Jesmer maintains. 'He was skinny, he had acne medicine on his face at night. He was kind of innocent.' Barrett Strong and Norman Whitfield's 'I Heard It Through The Grapevine', previously a hit for Gladys Knight, confirmed Gaye's status when it topped the American charts for seven weeks in 1968. At the same time Gaye was enjoying success with his duet partner Tammi Terrell. Their natural chemistry and friendship produced a series of hits starting with 1967's 'Ain't No Mountain High Enough'. So close did they become that many assumed them to be lovers, a charge denied by Frankie Gaye, who puts their fascination with each other down to mutual respect and admiration. It was widely suspected at the time that the brain tumour Terrell suffered was caused by a hammer blow from boyfriend Dave Ruffin. Gaye, devastated, began to change as a man and an artist. Those changes acutely informed 1971's groundbreaking *What's Going On*, the most challenging and rewarding soul album ever released.

> **Elaine Jesmer:** 'When people wanted to yell and tear his clothes off, at that time, he was horrified. He'd get this panicky, wide-eyed look.'

1/Supremes

Points: 360

Recommended album: *Anthology* (1970) ● No. 1 hits: 12 ● Top 20 hits: 30

The Supremes patented a staggeringly successful formula, pairing the world's finest pop songwriting team (Holland-Dozier-Holland) with the breathless excitement of three glam-

orous but unashamedly girly singers. In 1959 Florence Ballard recruited Diana Ross and Mary Wilson to her fledgling vocal group, eventually signing to Motown. Thomas 'Beans' Bowles, Motown road manager, remembers 'laughing our cans off' listening to Ross's first efforts at singing. Wilson believes that Ballard was comfortably the most talented singer at the outset, and seemed destined to front the group. But for Berry Gordy there was no question who the lead singer was and he chose to push Diana, with whom he was *f*ally linked, to the forefront. With over thirty Top 10 hits, it's hard to argue with his judgement. While the group topped the charts with a sequence of classics beginning with 'Where Did Our Love Go', Gordy and Ross grew closer, eventually conceiving daughter Rhonda together. Martha Reeves remembers the switch in Gordy's focus. 'He had the habit of coming to different shows and critiquing everyone. He stopped critiquing anyone but Diana.' Gordy hatched plans to change the group's billing to Diana Ross and the Supremes. As Wilson recalls, this had a dramatic effect on Florence Ballard, who became depressed, resorting to alcohol to assuage her depression. Manager Shelly Berger insists she was simply too difficult to work with. 'Everybody thinks of this great pushing out of Florence – it wasn't a question of pushing Florence out, it was a question of Florence becoming unmanageable.' Ballard was expelled from the group in July 1967 and subsequently married Gordy's chauffeur Thomas Chapman. Her daughter Michelle, who has her mother's name tattooed on one of her breasts, protests that her mother only got angry because Motown made her so – she felt that they had cast her aside. Ballard attempted to sue Motown, was defeated, and died in 1976. Lookalike Cindy Birdsong took her place. The group split in 1970, Gordy guiding Ross to become the mainstream diva he'd always wanted her to be. The Supremes left behind an unmatched collection of precociously sweet pop hits, though for some there remains a bittersweet taste to their success.

Ten More Great Soul Performances From The Sixties

Sam Cooke: 'It's All Right' (1961)
Booker T & The MGs: 'Green Onions' (1962)
Joe Tex: 'Hold What You've Got' (1964)
Ike and Tina Turner: 'River Deep, Mountain High' (1966)
Eddie Floyd: 'Knock On Wood' (1966)
Junior Walker: 'Road Runner' (1966)
Robert Parker: 'Barefootin'' (1966)
Arthur Conley: 'Sweet Soul Music' (1967)
Wilson Pickett: 'Mustang Sally' (1967)
Edwin Starr: 'Oh How Happy' (1969)

Girl Groups

The story of women in music was once synonymous with exploitation and the satisfaction of male expectations and agendas – or, just occasionally, what men *perceived* women wanted. However, since the Andrews Sisters topped the charts with 'Boogie Woogie Bugle Boy' in 1944, things have come a long way. When the Spice Girls sacked their manager half a century later, ostensibly on the grounds of being a fella, it was a significant departure from a time when women – as recorded in many of the stories here – were controlled by ruthless, often misogynist svengalis and record labels.

Few of the artists chronicled here ever had an agenda beyond making an appearance on *Top Of The Pops* or *American Bandstand*. It's doubtful that the Nolans were ever conversant with Germaine Greer, for sure. Some made great records, some patently did not. But each contributed, in their own way, to the feminization of popular music. So enjoy our list – based on UK chart success – of the spiritual granddaughters of Bessie Smith and Billie Holiday, who between them had everything but the bloke.

10/Ronettes

Girl Power points: 27

Definitive Song: 'Be My Baby' (No. 4, October 1963)

Veronica 'Ronnie' Bennett, sister Estelle and cousin Nedra Talley started out as dance group the Dolly Sisters. They became a local hit after accepting a residency at New York's Peppermint Lounge. Ronnie Spector remembers feeling like a goddess up on stage with all the men going wild for them. They released several singles, to little avail, before linking up with Phil Spector, maverick producer and owner of Philles Records. The originator of the girl group sound, his cavernous, multi-tracked compositions provided female singers with dramatic acoustic spaces in which to work. The Ronettes' first collaboration with Spector, 'Be My Baby', proved a global smash, as did follow-up 'Baby I Love You'. Spector was given the credit but Ronnie is keen to dispel the idea that he was their svengali noting that although he produced and wrote the songs, her role as

the all-important lead singer sealed the deal. Punk pioneer Joey Ramone sees the Ronettes as both extremely liberating and highly unique, while music journalist Donna Gaines compares Ronnie to a female Elvis. John Lennon was widely reported to have fallen head over heels in love with Ronnie by the mid-sixties, but by that time she had entered into a traumatic romantic relationship with Spector. In 1966, he stopped Ronnie touring with the Beatles, a lookalike cousin taking her place. When they married two years later, Ronnie became Spector's captive – he stopped her from singing, insisted she not leave the house, and even confiscated her shoes. Divorced in 1974, Spector has since refused to allow Ronnie to sing any Ronettes' songs, although she is still doing her best to keep her name in the public's mind.

> **Mark Ribowsky, Phil Spector's biographer, on Spector:** 'He's the control freak of all time. He doesn't care if it damages his own royalties if he's not able to collect from these songs on the radio, he's winning if he's controlling his music.'

9/Nolans

Girl Power points: 34

Definitive Song: 'I'm In The Mood For Dancing'
(No. 3, December 1979, No. 51, April 1995)

The high priestesses of post-disco pap, the Nolans were formed after the sisterhood had seen *The Sound Of Music* seventeen times – their business cards even touted them as 'Blackpool's own Von Trapp family'. The original line-up included two brothers and parents Maureen and Tommy. Sisters Maureen Jnr, Anne, Denise, Linda and Bernadette soon took centre stage. Later, youngest sister Colleen made the group a somewhat unsexy sextet. They wore floor-length green satin 'curtains' for their debut on Cliff Richard's show. From then on, their family identity became a collective curse, as they were instructed to wear the same clothes even off-stage. Denise decided to go solo. Colleen couldn't work school nights, so that left four. It was as a quartet they changed image from variety favourites to fully fledged pop stars and gatecrashed *Top Of The Pops* with 'I'm In The Mood For Dancing' in 1979. Suddenly, Maureen was a sex symbol, much to the chagrin of the rest of the group. Eventually, Colleen was able to rejoin, and the Nolans went on to notch up six further UK hits. After domestic success dried up, they became Japan's idea of UK pop sophistication. The Japanese bought 9 million Nolans records, which means roughly one in four Japanese households purchased a copy.

> **Maureen Nolan:** 'This image we had in England, that we hated, worked fantastically well in Japan. They marketed us as "five fresh and fruity girls".'

Linda went on to become 'the naughty Nolan' after some 'glamour' photography; her mother turned a blind eye to her daughter's new direction, arguing that if her husband of the time hadn't minded, then why should her family? Colleen married then split from the inimitable Shane Ritchie, a marriage made in celebrity hell. All the Nolans remain engaged in showbusiness to a greater or lesser extent. Mostly lesser, actually.

8/Go-Go's
Girl Power points: 39

Definitive Song: 'We Got The Beat' (did not chart in the UK)

In the late seventies Los Angeles was finally catching on to punk, though record companies were still refusing to buy into anything that wasn't poodle rock. The Go-Go's were put together by former cheerleader Belinda Carlisle on vocals, Jane Wiedlin on guitar and Charlotte Caffey on guitar and keyboards. Immersed in the DIY ethic of punk, Carlisle had formerly played with the Germs (LA's answer to the Sex Pistols), and at the outset they only had a limited grasp of their instruments. Caffey admits that the Go-Go's were 'truly awful', but people seemed to love them. Among their fans were the UK's Specials, who invited them to support them at the height of the UK ska revival. Carlisle, for one, toured in consider-

> **Drummer Gina Schock on Belinda Carlisle's post-Go-Go's success:** 'I was so jealous at Belinda, so pissed at her. She was doing really well, I was like – *bitch*!'

able trepidation, nevertheless a condition hardly alleviated by the spitting and yelling that passed for hospitality among post-punk UK audiences. Wiedlin believes the group had everything going against them as far as British audiences of the time were concerned: they were American, women, and *not* playing ska. They were also contesting record company prejudice, which held that rock 'n' roll was a man's game. Miles Copeland at IRS disagreed, reckoning the Go-Go's to be the first girl group who wrote and sang all their own songs and played their own instruments – and were good at it, too. His faith was rewarded when 'We Got The Beat' topped the US singles charts. A number one album followed. However, the attention they subsequently received drove divisions between band members; from being a lone LA girl group against the world, their success turned the Go-Go's against each other. In 1984 Wiedlin went solo and within a year the band was finished. Carlisle also went solo and married Morgan Mason, the son of actor James Mason. Mainstream pop singles such as 'Heaven Is A Place On Earth' saw her enjoy continued success, while Wiedlin also had a solo hit with 'Rush Hour'. The band have recently reunited and take comfort in the knowledge that the Go-Go's were instrumental, as it were, in getting girls to pick up guitars and form bands.

7/Three Degrees
Girl Power points: 40

Definitive Song: 'When Will I See You Again' (No. 1, July 1974)

Next to Camilla Parker Bowles, the Three Degrees were perhaps the love of not-so-bonny Prince Charlie's life. Formed in Philadelphia in the sixties, sequinned MOR soul trio the Three Degrees were managed by girl group specialist Richard Barrett – a man who admired Phil Spector's treatment of his charges and his talent for getting what he wanted. After years of club work, and what Barrett likes to call the 'business of show', statuesque lead singer Sheila Ferguson became the group's focal point. A revolving line-up left the group feeling as if any of them might be replaceable, but during its most successful years Ferguson was flanked by Valerie Holiday and either Fayette Pinkney or Helen Scott. Legendary songwriting team Kenny Gamble and Leon

> **Richard Barrett on HRH Prince Charles:** 'This guy is groovy, trust me.'

Huff wrote their first global smash, 1974's 'When Will I See You Again'. HRH Prince Charles became a fan, and old jug ears even joined the group on stage. Ferguson's romantic relationship with Barrett was deteriorating, and the group were dragged through the debris. Holiday remembers Ferguson's decline, during which she would mix pills and booze. After a drug overdose Ferguson recovered from her problems and left Barrett, quitting the band in 1986 to marry an aristocrat. Her former colleagues weren't best pleased by her defection, and Holiday, in particular, remains aggrieved at it. Cynthia Garrison is now the third Three Degree. Barrett sued the group when they severed relations with him and the judge decided he owned the right to the name in perpetuity. Thus the group can only use the name Three Degrees outside America. Ferguson, now a fixture of musicals, hasn't spoken to her former bandmates in a decade.

6/Salt-N-Pepa

Girl Power points: 42

Definitive Song: 'Let's Talk About Sex' (No. 2, August 1991)

Few groups harness affection and record sales in equal magnitude, but Salt-N-Pepa is such a band. Sandy 'Pepa' Denton and Cheryl 'Salt' James were working in the Sears New York department store in the mid-eighties selling washing machine insurance when they met producer and co-worker Herby Lovebug, who was looking for someone to rap over lyrics he'd written. Hip hop has produced female artists since its inception, but none possessed any commercial longevity. Salt-N-Pepa were colourful and kooky, but in a genre where competitiveness was everything, the real deal was whether they could cut it on record. Yet when Salt first heard the demo tracks for 'Push It', their breakthrough hit, she was not impressed, refusing to rap over it. Lovebug, however, is nothing if not persuasive. The group's defining moment came in 1991 with 'Let's Talk About Sex' – a plea for maturity around sexual issues in the wake of AIDS. Salt-N-Pepa (with long-time DJ Spinderella stepping from behind the decks to take the role of third MC) took hip hop from the street to the mainstream pop market. Still, they found it difficult to get the respect they felt they were owed, which can be linked to the fact that it was some time before they stepped from behind Lovebug's shadow to write their own lyrics. Whether or not you consider them an authentic hip hop act or a pop group, Salt-N-Pepa made the music of the early nineties a lot more fun to listen to.

> **Salt**, on first hearing 'Push It': 'I am not rapping over that!'

5/Sister Sledge

Girl Power points: 46

Definitive Song: 'We Are Family'
(No. 8, May 1979, No. 33, November 1984, No. 5, January 1993)

Philadelphia's Sister Sledge were originally intended as the female answer to the Jackson 5. Sisters Kathy, Kim, Joan and Debbie began recording in 1971. They enjoyed only minor success until 1979, when Bernard Edwards and Nile Rodgers, fresh from their success with Chic, persuaded Atlantic Records to let them take the band under

their wing and see if they could develop them into something big. They restyled the group as a disco act, and were rewarded with a UK number six placing for 'He's The Greatest Dancer'. 'We Are Family' was even better. As Kim recalls, they hadn't finished writing the lyrics on the day they recorded it. As the song took shape, Rodgers and Edwards took inspiration from the group's family vibe. The sisters added some *ad libs* in the background, and hey presto, a career-defining moment resulted. Further hits such as 'Lost In Music' proved Sister Sledge were staples of the disco movement, one of the least faceless groups in a largely anonymous genre. However, by the turn of the decade disco's moment had passed, and Sister

> **Kathy:** 'To have a song like "We Are Family", such a timeless song, it means so much. It's something I don't think we could ever try, or want, to top.'

Sledge were victims of a vicious backlash. Undeterred, the sisters persevered, and enjoyed their biggest hit in 1985 with saccharine chart-topper 'Frankie'. But, as Kathy admits, the group remains most closely associated with their definitive song. Sister Sledge still play together, a group untainted by the airing of dirty laundry that often accompanies such revivals.

4/TLC   Girl Power points: 57

Definitive Song: 'Creep' (No. 22, January 1995, No. 6, January 1996)

A group that sold 50 million records, redefined the model of the female R&B band. TLC's story is more full-blown *Carmina Burana* than merely *soap* opera. In 1991 three kids from Atlanta – Lisa 'Left Eye' Lopes, Tionne 'T-Boz' Watkins and a friend called Crystal – signed with one-time R&B singer Pebbles, wife of LaFace Records' boss L.A. Reid. There were encouraging early signs, but the combo clearly needed some work. Pebbles replaced Crystal with dancer Rozonda 'Chilli' Thomas, while LaFace updated the R&B template with hip hop production and a sassy group vocal style led by T-Boz. The debut single 'Ain't 2 Proud 2 Beg' was an instant US Top 10 hit. Just as newsworthy, however, were the group's extracurricular activities. T-Boz was hospitalized with sickle cell anaemia, and Lopes fell out with American footballer boyfriend Andre Rison. As well as smashing up a few of the wide receiver's cars, she hit on the idea of a little payback arson; she was arrested for her pains, but agreed to alcohol rehab and so escaped jail. In 1995, as *CrazySexyCool* was on its way to 10 million sales, the band filed for bankruptcy. TLC's alliance with Pebbles was, according to the group, a slave contract. They sued Pebbles, who sued them right back, angry that something she had worked hard to put together was now dragging her name through the dirt. The parties settled out of court after a year of wrangling and TLC were released from their contract. Although they've been through some rough times, Lopes – previously not a model of considered philosophy – feels that those times have brought them closer together and made them strong. They returned in 1999 with *Fan Mail*, another global smash, and they remain a commercial force to be reckoned with.

3/Bananarama

Girl Power points: 64

Definitive Song: 'Robert De Niro's Waiting' (No. 3, March 1984)

The supreme eighties girl group, Bananarama clocked up twenty-three Top 40 hits, despite exhibiting more enthusiasm than musical ability, a trick they'd picked up from the London punk milieu in which they formed. Sarah Dallin, Keren Woodward and Siobhan Fahey knew Sex Pistol Paul Cook, who produced their debut single, 'Ai A Mwana'. Fun Boy Three's Terry Hall saw a picture of them in *The Face* and asked them to perform backing vocals on his new album. The girls, however, weren't yet 'tutored' in their duties, and would regularly crack up in the studio when the engineer counted them in to start singing. They kept a straight face long enough to appear on the Fun Boy Three's 1982 hit, 'It Ain't What You Do, It's The Way That You Do It'. Bananarama's major label debut, a cover of the Velvelettes' 'Really Saying Something', followed in May. Colin Bell had signed them to London Records, and reflects that although they didn't have the pizzazz or professionalism of the Spice Girls, nobody was interested in that kind of thing in the eighties anyway. Julie Burchill admires them for having the sheer cheek to be so shambolic and not care about it. Despite a succession of hits, the media refused to take them seriously – an opinion that the girls did little to change by giggling through interviews, though this may have been as much to do with shyness as anything else. Hit factory Stock, Aitken

Producer Pete Waterman: 'They didn't want to sing about love or anything like that. It had to be their way and nobody else's.'

and Waterman transformed them (or tried to) from a punk afterthought into grown-up pop stars; the shambolic prefix was no longer applicable. After hitting the Top 10 with a version of Shocking Blue's 'Venus' and 'Love In The First Degree' in 1987, the group faltered. Fahey quit in 1988 to marry the Eurythmics' Dave Stewart and enjoyed a number one single, alongside Marcela Detroit, as Shakespeare's Sister. Jacquie O'Sullivan was recruited in her stead, but by then their time had passed. O'Sullivan is now a casting agent, while Woodward is shacked up with Andrew Ridgeley of Wham!. Fahey returned to hook up with her mates again, recording 'A Song For Eurotrash' in 1998, and tried, unsuccessfully, to shop a new demo around.

2/Spice Girls

Girl Power points: 79

Definitive Song: 'Wannabe' (No. 1, July 1996)

Originators of girl power – a kind of intellectually befuddled version of the punk doctrine of riot grrrl – the Spice Girls are now the definitive girl group blueprint. The original quintet of Mel B (Scary Spice Melanie Brown), Mel C (Sporty Spice Melanie Chisholm), Geri Halliwell (Ginger Spice), Victoria Adams (Posh Spice) and Michelle Stephenson (didn't-hang-around-long-enough Spice) were recruited via an advert run in theatrical newspaper *The Stage*. This was truly a heaven-sent lucky break for certain members of the group – Mel C was living on housing benefit and income support at the time. They moved into a semi in Maidenhead, until Stephenson left to take up a university place (and subse-

quently become a TV presenter). Emma 'Baby Spice' Bunton, an ex-Mothercare model, enrolled in her stead and vocal coach Pepi Lemer was hired to polish up their rough edges. A media blitz in 1996 culminated in the release of 'Wannabe', which hit number one in July. From then on, the Spice Girls were rarely out of the British Top 10. Throughout they kept up their mantra of female empowerment, though commentators like Julie Burchill wonder exactly whose rights they were fighting for – men have generally never denied women the right to walk along the street wearing bra tops and hot pants, after all.

> **Mel B, on the Spice Girls' success:** 'The whole thing is very friggin' freaky.'

By November 1997 the Spice Girls had dispensed with manager Simon Fuller's services, arguing that men sometimes simply failed to understand women, particularly regarding business matters. Six months later, Geri Halliwell also headed for the exit. As well as becoming a UN goodwill ambassador, she has maintained a successful solo career. Journalist John Robb believes 'she's the ultimate wannabe self-made star, a pop dream. No matter where you live in the world or how well you can sing, you can still be a pop star.' The remaining members are now Spice Women, with babies, films (*Spiceworld*) and celebrity marriages and divorces (variously to football players and dancers) to their credit. The ubiquitous four have established total control over an entity that has also spawned five solo careers. That Maidenhead semi must seem a long way away.

1/Supremes

Girl Power points: 100

Definitive Song: 'Baby Love' (No. 1, October 1964, No. 12, August 1974)

The Supremes' saga is classic rags to riches stuff – and, in the case of one member, back to rags again. Diana Ross, Florence Ballard and Mary Wilson formed the band as the Primettes in Detroit, Michigan, in 1959. They hung around the offices of their local record label, Motown, hoping to get noticed. Motown proprietor Berry Gordy duly took an interest and signed the group, renaming them the Supremes. They were immediately despatched to one Mrs Powell, an austere deportment tutor, to learn how to conduct themselves properly, picking up etiquette hints such as how to get in and out of limousines without showing their behinds. 'Where Did Our Love Go' was released in August 1964 and became the first of their twelve US chart-toppers. The subsequent roll-call of smashes includes some of the best-loved songs in history – 'Baby Love', 'Stop! In The Name Of Love', 'You Can't Hurry Love', 'You Keep Me Hangin' On', 'I'm Gonna Make You Love Me' – all of them twenty-four carat pop classics. However, the schoolkids who had grown up together were now growing apart. Berry, Diana's boyfriend, pushed her to the forefront, and when Ballard's only lead vocal was dropped from the live set, the group imploded. Others, like black music author Nelson George, believe that at the end of the day, Ross was always going to be the star

> **Tour manager Tony Turner:** 'You just heard from a darkened stage where the Supremes had been standing – 'That *bitch*!' She [Ballard] immediately went into ranting and raving that Diana Ross had purposely engineered [Ballard's only lead vocal in the Supremes' set] being taken out of that show. That was the day I saw these Supremes ain't like no sisters and kissing cousins like the publicity machine is churning out.'

of the show. In 1967 the name was changed to Diana Ross and the Supremes. Ballard was devastated, but, dependent on the group income to supplement her drinking binges, clung on. When her behaviour became even more erratic, she was replaced by Cindy Birdsong – in the middle of a show. In 1970 Ross finally left the most successful girl group of all time and Berry turned her into the Barbra Streisand of soul. Wilson and Birdsong still work together occasionally. Florence Ballard died in 1976, a penniless alcoholic. A Supremes reunion tour in 1999 was cancelled, allegedly due to poor ticket sales.

Other Indelible Moments In Girl Group History

Chantels: 'Maybe' (1957)
Shirelles:'Will You Love Me Tomorrow' (1961)
Crystals: 'Uptown' (1962)
Angels: 'My Boyfriend's Back' (1963)
Chiffons: 'He's So Fine' (1963)
Shangri-Las: 'Leader Of The Pack' (1965)
Marvelettes: 'I'll Keep Holding On' (1965)
Martha & the Vandellas: 'Jimmy Mack' (1967)
Slits: 'Typical Girls' (1979)
Girlschool: 'Hit And Run' (1981)
Bangles: 'Eternal Flame' (1989)
En Vogue: 'My Lovin'' (1992)
Luscious Jackson: 'Deep Shag' (1995)
All Saints: 'Never Ever' (1997)
Eternal: 'I Wanna Be The Only One' (1997)

Comedy Records

$\mathcal{C}$omedy records, bereft of musical value, are vehicles designed specifically to raise a smile on the face of the nation's most gullible citizens, and buffer the artist's bank balance. Often a speculative cash-in on the fleeting popularity of a character actor or television series of the day, they are generally not the noblest of artistic endeavours. But they are part of our heritage. There was a time when all music hall comics were expected to perform a song at the end of their 'turn'. If it's good enough for Noël Coward, George Formby and Tommy Cooper, then it's good enough for Brucie and Mike Reid.

Harry Enfield dismisses comedy songs as 'shite', and, with the odd exception, he's spot on. But there have been glints of genius among the detritus. To compile the following chucklesome chart, several critical criteria had to be met. The records had to be funny (to someone), must actually possess a tune, and pure novelty efforts or cheesy spoofs were ruled out of bounds. Oh, and the song must have registered on the British 'hit parade', as they used to call it.

10/Harry Enfield
Key hit: 'Loadsamoney (Doin' Up The House)'   Comedy points: 14

Chart Position: No. 4, May 1988 ● Laughter Tally: 1 hit single
Other comedy efforts from the same stable: Fry and Laurie: 'Rock 'n' Roll Star'

In the late eighties, Enfield's Loadsamoney character became an unlikely icon of Thatcherite greed, to the extent that Neil Kinnock once employed him as a metaphor for economic analysis, commenting that behind the loadsamoney economy would come 'loadsatrouble'. Hmm. The obnoxious Cockney plasterer's own take on left versus right was more simplistic: 'All you need to know about politics is that Mrs Thatcher's done a lot of good for the country, but you wouldn't want to shag it.' The character was incubated as Paul Whitehouse and Harry Enfield were waiting on Caledonian Road station. That's according to Enfield. Whitehouse claims it was based on a Geordie friend who'd been on

holiday to Portugal who'd met some Chelsea fans who waved money at him for being a poor northerner – as was the wont of certain London football fans during the eighties. Loadsamoney first appeared on *Saturday Night Live*, a breeding ground for comic talent including Stephen Fry, Hugh Laurie, Rik Mayall and Ben Elton. The resultant single was produced by William Orbit – subsequently behind many of Madonna's late nineties hits. A follow-up effort featured another Enfield character – kebab shop proprietor Stavros – performing a pastiche of Wham!'s 'Last Christmas'.

Simon Mayo: 'If there's ever a William Orbit greatest hits album, I suspect that "Loadsamoney" by Harry Enfield won't sneak on.'

9/Windsor Davies & Don Estelle
Key Hit: 'Whispering Grass'   Comedy points: 25

Chart Position: No. 1, May 1975 ● Laughter Tally: 2 hit singles
Other comedy efforts from the same stable: Follow-up single 'Paper Doll'

The boys are here... allegedly to entertain you. *It Ain't Half Hot Mum* was another wartime sitcom from Jimmy Perry and David Croft, creators of *Dad's Army*. Documenting an entertainment troupe in India, it was unburdened by considerations such as a politically correct agenda. The linchpin performance came from Windsor Davies's Sergeant Major 'Taffy' Williams. Scripts usually found him intimidating Gunner Lofty Sugden, a cherubic pintpot unsuited to the rigours of jungle combat, and his ragbag detail of out-of-touch officers, intellectual misfits and khaki queens. In the mid-seventies it was considered hot entertainment, and Davies's bellicose shout of 'Shut Uuuuuup!' was much imitated in school playgrounds by wannabe bullies. Estelle always held ambitions to record, and persuaded his agent to organize a cast recording. Estelle sang most of the songs, out of which came 'Whispering Grass' – a sweet-voiced revival of the Ink Spots' standard. It was also released as a single. Melvyn Hayes, aka Gunner 'Gloria' Beaumont almost fills up as he recalls the song's impact, commenting that it went 'straight to the nation's hearts'. Indeed, it certainly performed commercially, topping the charts in May 1975. However, saccharine follow-up 'Paper Doll' stalled outside the Top 40. Windsor Davies does 'proper' acting these days, most recently in the BBC's *Vanity Fair*. Don Estelle appeared in *The League Of Gentlemen* (fetchingly curating a zoo on a mini-roundabout) and released a version of 'The Lonesome Pine' with heavyweight Rochdale politician Cyril Smith.

Don Estelle: 'I remember the first copy [of the single] coming to me at my house in Whitworth. I dragged the postman in. I said, "This is going to be a number one, this."'

8/Rolf Harris
Key Hit: 'Tie Me Kangaroo Down Sport'

Comedy points: 26

Chart Position: No. 9, July 1960 ● Laughter Tally: 3 hit singles
Other comedy efforts from the same stable: 'Stairway To Heaven' (No. 7, 1993)

Beatles producer Sir George Martin considers him to be a multi-talented fellow; by contrast, broadcaster Michael Grade describes him somewhat dismissively as 'a gifted amateur'. Rolf Harris has become the definitive ex-pat Australian, exhibiting fearless goodwill to allcomers – be they men, women, small furry animals or miniature electronic keyboards. 'Tie Me Kangaroo Down Sport' remains his greatest 'work'. It was originally titled 'Kangalypso' after Harris's initial attempts to write an Australian calypso. Being unashamedly Australian, the song was a huge hit in Oz. Easy to hum and readily adaptable, it later became the template for the rugby drinking song 'Bestiality's Best'. Harris had arrived and his distinctive follow-up, 'Sun Arise', was only kept off the top in 1962 by Elvis Presley. A version of the song was later recorded by Alice Cooper, while Leo Sayer confided to Rolf that 'Sun Arise' was the song that got him into showbusiness. 'Two Little Boys', a parable about fraternity in the playroom and the battlefield during the American Civil War, became the last number one of the sixties. In the following decade, Rolf gave the world the Stylophone (the poor kid's Steinway) and showed a nation of schoolchildren his etchings on *Rolf's Cartoon Show*. These days he can be found repairing broken down hedgehogs on *Animal Hospital*, though he was also reborn as a student favourite after appearances at Glastonbury and Rolfed-up versions of Led Zeppelin and Queen classics.

7/Young Ones
Key Hit: 'Living Doll' (featuring Cliff Richard and Hank Marvin)

Comedy points: 48

Chart Position: No. 1, March 1986 ● Laughter Tally: 3 hit singles
Other comedy efforts from the same stable: Neil: 'Hole In My Shoe' (No. 2, July 1984)
Alexei Sayle: ''Ullo, John Got A New Motor?' (No. 15, February 1984)

The Young Ones was an atypical TV sitcom about a student household knee-deep in grime, pretentiousness and failed promiscuity. Its roots lay in *The Comic Strip*, a Soho revue hosted in a converted porn cinema. As Nigel 'Neil the Hippy' Planer remembers, the place proved a favourite haunt for a host of TV producers, and shortly thereafter the idea of a group of characters sharing a house was born. The resulting televisual explosion of anarchy, cartoon violence and humour hasn't dated well, but at the time it seemed the sitcom revolution had begun. Alexei Sayle, who played an occasional character in the series, observes that the writers undercut the sitcom form in that they created unsympathetic characters and constantly broke up the narrative of the show with bands and other distracting elements. The first hit record spin-off

Alexei Sayle on the Young Ones' 'Living Doll':
'I'm very anti-charity – where it helps your career. I hated the idea and told everybody that they were sell-out shites for having anything to do with it.'

came from Sayle himself, ''Ullo, John Got A New Motor?'; Sayle's ill-fitting suit and pork pie hat raised a few eyebrows on *Top Of The Pops*. Neil then hit the charts with a deeply dippy version of Traffic's 'Hole In My Shoe'. The Cliff Richard connection had always been strong, his 1962 song giving the show its title. Producer Paul Jackson recalls that the idea of combining Cliff with the cast from the TV show arose when the first *Comic Relief* was being set up. A revival of 'Living Doll' with the Young Ones hollering inanities in the background topped the charts in 1986. Old school socialist Alexei Sayle wasn't impressed by what he took as a move to further certain comedians' careers as well as doing something for 'charidee'. Planer is now Grandpa Grimley on TV, Sayle still does stand-up, and Ade Edmondson and Mayall still do knock-down, *ad infinitum*, in *Bottom*, single-handedly keeping alive the fart gag. Ben Elton's a successful novelist and recently worked with Andrew Lloyd Webber.

6/Chef
Key Hit: 'Chocolate Salty Balls'   Comedy points: 51

Chart Position: No. 1, December 1988 ● Laughter Tally: 2 hit singles, 1 hit album
Other comedy efforts from the same stable:
Mr Hankey: 'Mr Hankey The Christmas Poo' (No. 8, December 1999)

Isaac Hayes is a legend in soul, and thanks to some Americans' scatological cartoon creations, he's now a legend in schoolyards across two continents. Hayes remembers his agent telling him he'd found a voice-over for him. Eagerly, Hayes asked if it was Disney. In somewhat of an understatement his agent apparently said 'No, not quite.' *South Park* creators Matt Stone and Trey Parker met Hayes at the studio and showed him the script. A quick flick through was enough to start the soul legend laughing uncontrollably. Parker and Stone were Colorado college kids who'd put together a simple animation sequence in college seen by a Fox TV executive.
He gave them $700 and they came up with a five-minute short, *The Spirit Of Christmas*, which could be sent as an internet Christmas card. Cartman *et al* soon became cyber celebrities, with 700 fan sites formed on the web. Within three months, *South Park* had become a networked TV show. Central to the series was the char- **Robert Peters, head of campaign to ban *South Park*: '**I respect creativity, I'm not against, you know, art, and all that stuff...'
acter of Chef, a well-meaning but sex-obsessed agony uncle whose basso profundo interpretations of Parker and Stone's lyrics invariably descend into explicit themes. The song produced heaps of good old-fashioned outrage. The Morality In Media network sent out pamphlets suggesting ways of protesting in order to get *South Park* taken off the air. It cited sections of Cartman's more colourful dialogue alongside passages from the Bible. 'Chocolate Salty Balls' featured a lead vocal by Hayes who was, unsurprisingly, reluctant to take it on at first. It was infantile, but the follow-up single was even more so. 'Mr Hankey The Christmas Poo' was inspired by a story Parker's father told him aged two. Bathroom detritus would, his father said, jump out and kill him if he didn't flush after doing his number twos. It obviously had a lasting effect on Parker...

5/Ray Stevens
Key Hit: 'The Streak'
Comedy points: 53

Chart Position: No. 1, May 1974 ● Laughter Tally: 3 hit singles
Other comedy efforts from the same stable: 'In The Mood' (No. 31, March 1977)
'Bridget The Midget (The Queen Of The Blues)' (No. 2, March 1971)

Ray Stevens was an established singer-songwriter in Nashville, recording dozens of country albums, long before he started charting oddball hits in Britain. In 1962 he'd moved from Atlanta to Nashville to record 'Ahab The Arab', a novelty single that featured dialogue, impersonations and mime sequences. He enjoyed more conventional hits, too, including 'Everything Is Beautiful', his first Top 10 British hit. More successful still was 1971's 'Bridget The Midget', on which he impersonated a chipmunk. Don't laugh – British punters sent it all the way to number two. In 1974 he had hit upon his greatest stroke of genius. The streak – the new craze of dashing onto the field of sporting events flaunting one's pink bits – deserved its own tribute. Stevens was flicking through a weekly news magazine when he came across an article about a Californian college student who had disrobed and streaked through a crowd. A bell rang in Stevens' mind and he decided that the subject was a good basis for a song. Others may have debated this but the song still worked. Bolstered by a rather incongruous and irritating party whistle played throughout, the single somehow topped the charts. The follow-up, the bluegrass-styled 'Misty', almost claimed the top spot too. He soon returned to novelty records, however, and 1977's 'In The Mood' consisted entirely of chicken noises. British audiences had it easy. Our American friends had to cope with efforts including 'Jeremiah Peabody's Polyunsaturated Quick Dissolving Fast Acting Pleasant Tasting Green And Purple Pills' and 'Harry The Hairy Ape'. Stevens' more recent efforts to resurrect his novelty career include 1989's 'I Saw Elvis In A UFO'.

4/Goodies
Key Hit: 'Funky Gibbon'
Comedy points: 61

Chart Position: No. 4, March 1975 ● Laughter Tally: 6 hit singles
Other comedy efforts from the same stable: 'The Inbetweenies' (No. 7, December 1974);
'Black Pudding Bertha' (No. 19, June 1975); 'Nappy Love' (No. 21, September 1975);
'Make A Daft Noise For Christmas' (No. 20, December 1975)

The Goodies was a much-loved British TV comedy serial that was more easily digestible, and more popular, than *Monty Python's Flying Circus*. Both shows were products of the Cambridge Footlights, which only increased the rivalry between them. Tim Brooke-Taylor, Bill Oddie and Graeme Garden put together a show that can best be described as surreal slapstick. By the mid-seventies, it had become a flagship BBC entertainment show, which allowed Oddie, an accomplished musician, the licence to branch out. Released in 1974, 'The Inbetweenies' served as a dry run, a conscious adoption of the

Graeme Garden: 'Bill always wanted to be a pop star. Tim is fearless, he'll just go for it. But me, I just felt such a fool.'

football chant approach to songwriting as practised by Slade and the Glitter Band. And it worked. Soon the Goodies had parallel careers as pop stars and entertainers. Their biggest hit was 1975's 'Funky Gibbon' – a song written about seeing a monkey at the zoo and featuring a dance step that replicated his movements. By the end of 1975, Oddie was the fifth most successful songwriter in the country. And the comedy act was still slaying them, literally: one

Comedy historian Robert Ross: 'Bill Oddie always said he was never a frustrated rock star, he *was* a rock star because he had so many hit records.'

audience member actually died laughing at *The Goodies*. The show lasted nine years and seventy episodes, before moving to ITV. But, in former boss Michael Grade's view, the trio's best work was behind them by that stage. They blew the budget on their one and only series for the opposition and that was that – the programme has never been screened on terrestrial TV since. Today, Oddie makes ornithology programmes back at the Beeb, while Garden and Brooke-Taylor do voice-over work and are regulars on Radio 4's *I'm Sorry, I Haven't A Clue*.

3/Benny Hill
Key Hit: 'Ernie (The Fastest Milkman In The West)'   Comedy points: 63

Chart Position: No. 1, November 1971 ● Laughter Tally: 5 hit singles, 1 hit album
Other comedy efforts from the same stable: 'Gather In The Mushrooms' (No. 12, February 1961); 'Transistor Radio' (No. 24, June 1961); 'Harvest Of Love' (No. 20, May 1963); ('Ernie' re-entered the charts in 1992)

The Benny Hill Show first aired on the BBC in 1955, spending some thirty-five years on TV until Thames pulled the plug in the late eighties. At its peak, it was syndicated in more than 100 countries, attracting fans from Snoop Doggy Dogg to Clint Eastwood. An essential element of the shows – as well as the sight of Hill being chased by scantily clad females around parkland and slapping short bald blokes on the head – were the 'saucy' songs, over 100 of which were recorded in total. It was no surprise when some of these were released as singles at the peak of Hill's popularity, but it was 'Ernie' that turned the clown prince of British slapstick into a pop star. Inspired by Hill's pre-fame career, it told the story of Ernie's conquests in an era when, alongside window cleaners, milkmen were routinely portrayed as cravenly opportunistic sexual predators. Walter Ridley, the record's producer, loves it to this day. Dennis Kirkland, the show's producer, remembers Benny coming over all coy when the song became a hit, and so a promotional film was made, to be screened on *Top Of the Pops* and thereby avoid giving Hill the embarrassment of walking out on a stage in front of massed ranks of teenagers. By the eighties, Hill was on the scrapheap, unable to understand why he was being pilloried by the politically correct lobby. Old friend Nicholas Parsons maintains that Thames threw away one of British comedy's great institutions when they dropped *The Benny Hill Show*. Shunned in his own back yard, Benny Hill died within twenty-four hours of the death of fellow comic Frankie Howerd.

Nicholas Parsons: 'He was very British, he loved this country [...] His humour stemmed from the old traditional music hall, bawdy, vulgar, outrageous humour, and the old seaside postcards.'

2/Monty Python
Key Hit: 'Always Look On The Bright Side Of Life'
Comedy points: 69

Chart Position: No. 1, November 1971 ● Laughter Tally: 5 hit singles, 8 hit albums
Other comedy efforts from the same stable: Rutles: 'I Must Be In Love' (No. 39,
April 1978); Rutles: 'Shangri-La' (No. 68, November 1996); Eric Idle with Richard
Wilson: 'One Foot In The Grave' (No. 50, December 1994)

Monty Python's Flying Circus is a British institution – not only in comedy, where it
rewrote the rules governing the humble joke for ever, but also in respect of the songs
composed by Eric Idle. As Idle recalls, coming from the Cambridge Footlights, music was
always an integral part of the package, and the team was well versed in coming up with
erudite, witty lyrics. Some of the songs featured in the series have become as immortal as
the ubiquitous dead parrot sketch – especially 'The Lumberjack Song' and 'Sit On My
Face'. Ex-Yes keyboardist Rick Wakeman regarded Python's knack of producing songs
that people sang even though they hadn't been hits as nothing short of an art form. Monty
Python did go on to reach the charts, finally, in 1991. Prompted by repeated plays from
Radio 1 DJ Simon Mayo, 'Always Look On The Bright Side Of Life' was re-released and
hit number three. An unlikely party piece, it was originally the bitterly sarcastic closing
song from Python's 1979 film *The Life Of Brian*, accompanying a tableau of foot-jiving
crucifixion victims. Suddenly it was being sung by relegation-facing football supporters
throughout the country. Between that surprise success and the end of Python, Idle worked
with Bonzo Dog Doo-Dah Band member Neil Innes on *Rutland Weekend Television* for
the BBC. Out of this sketch show came an affectionate Beatles parody that blossomed into
a full-grown band, The Rutles. The Rutles enjoyed some minor chart action while their
film, *All You Need Is Cash*, featured a guest appearance from George Harrison. Innes pays
tribute to Idle's knack of putting together extremely witty lyrics, placing him in the same
bracket as Noël Coward. It's a shame we haven't heard more from him recently, the odd
TV signature tune aside.

1/Goons
Key Hit: 'Ying Tang Song'
Comedy points: 215

Chart Position: No. 9 (on reissue in July 1973) ● Laughter Tally: 9 hit singles, 3 hit albums
Other comedy efforts from the same stable: Goons: 'I'm Walking Backwards For
Christmas' (No. 4, June 1956); Goons: 'Bloodnok's Rock 'n' Roll Call' (No. 3,
December 1956); Peter Sellers: 'Any Old Iron' (No. 21, August 1957); Peter Sellers and
Sophia Loren: 'Goodness Gracious Me' (No. 4, November 1960); Peter Sellers: 'Bangers
And Mash' (No. 22, January 1961); Peter Sellers: 'A Hard Day's Night' (No. 14,
December 1965); Harry Secombe: 'On With The Motley' (No. 16, December 1955)

Heroes of Prince Charles, the Goons were the missing link
between dreary forties music hall and modern comedy.
Peter Sellers, Harry Secombe, Michael Bentine and Spike

Harry Secombe: 'He wrote some
very good stuff when he was in the
nuthouse. We'd send him back.'

(31)

Milligan boasted the greatest comic wits of the post-war period. Although they started simply as four friends having a laugh on air, their radio shows, first broadcast in May 1951, soon had a huge following, inspiring many future generations of comics, including the Monty Python team. Despite being the most

Terry Jones: 'There's absolutely no doubt in my mind that the Goons are the gods – they're my comedy heroes. Spike Milligan, in particular, was breaking the medium up and finding something new.'

prolific and lateral writer among the quartet, Milligan was continually plagued with debilitating depression. Eventually Bentine left, going on to host *Michael Bentine's Potty Time*. As he had been the only non-musician, the remaining trio decided to make a record together – the towering 'Ying Tang Song' of 1955. Milligan recalls writing the song in about ten minutes on the Tube while he was on his way to work. It only has two chords: C and G7. The single gave *Goon Show* fans a permanent reminder of their heroes' genius without having to wait until the next episode of the radio show. A few more singles crept out, before Sellers departed for a film career. He too enjoyed musical success, performing 'Goodness Gracious Me' alongside Sophia Loren in 1960. Sellers died in 1980 at the age of fifty-five, leaving behind over seventy films. Bentine was struck down by cancer in 1996. Sir Harry Secombe presented religious programmes until retiring in the nineties. And the mercurial Milligan is still with us, despite all the odds.

We Are Not Amused
some other comedy records that didn't make the cut

Mike Reid: 'The Ugly Duckling' (No. 10, March 1975)
Jasper Carrott: 'Funky Moped'/'Magic Roundabout' (No. 5, August 1975)
Billy Connolly: 'D.I.V.O.R.C.E.' (No. 1, November 1975)
Hylda Baker and Arthur Mullard: 'You're The One That I Want'
(No. 22, September 1978)
Monks: 'Nice Legs, Shame About Her Face' (No. 19, April 1979)
Firm: 'Arthur Daley ('E's Alright')' (No. 14, July 1982)
Kenny Everett: 'Snot Rap' (No. 9, March 1983)
Commentators: 'N-N-Nineteen Not Out' (No. 13, June 1985)
Spitting Image: 'The Chicken Song' (No. 1, May 1986)
Spinal Tap: 'Bitch School' (No. 35, March 1992)

Punk

Punk was contemporary music's year zero – a rewiring of possibilities and attitudes that continues to inform much of Britain's musical output. Historians still argue whether its origins lie in New York or London, but in terms of attaining critical mass, its most precipitous moments arrived in the British capital in 1977. Fired by the Sex Pistols' horrified vision of urban society in meltdown, punk faced down the progressive rock dinosaurs who bestrode the early seventies. It wasn't just Emerson, Lake and Palmer (aka ELP) and Yes who were running scared. Hence the footage of newscasters declaring that punk rock may be 'more of a threat to our way of life than Russian Communism or hyper-inflation'. Punk's very name became synonymous with shock value.

Ian Dury on England in the seventies:
'A septic isle – grey, boring, shitty. The inner city kids weren't all right.'

Punk was a lifestyle for some, a fleeting fashion statement for others. But in musical terms it was an explosion of creativity fuelled by frustration and boredom with existing entertainment values. The movement has been theorized to death by academics as well as participants. Similarly, it has been lampooned beyond recognition. The punk rocker, resplendent in safety pins and technicolour mohican, can now be found working the King's Road tourists with a stoicism that would earn the admiration of a seasoned Beefeater at the Tower of London. But for a time in 1976 and 1977, when everything seemed possible, punk changed lives.

10/Damned

Punk rock points: 42

Biggest hit: 'Eloise' (No. 3, 1986) ● 2 Top 40 singles ● 3 Top 40 albums
Recommended album: *Damned Damned Damned* (1977)

The Damned were the jokers in the pack, the clown princes of punk. They were also the first at everything – first punk single ('New Rose'), first punk album, first punk band to break up, and the first to reform. Wilfully shambolic and a compelling live draw, they symbolized everything your grandmother recoiled against in punk – bad language, wanton stimulant binges and silly costumes notwithstanding. A succession of line-up

shuffles have failed to obscure the identities of the band's four unusual suspects – madcap bass player-turned-guitarist Captain Sensible, irascible drummer Rat Scabies (whom Sensible had met while cleaning toilets for the council), prolific songwriter and guitarist Brian James and vampire-fixated lead singer Dave Vanian. Punk was their vocation, even before they knew its name and wherever they set foot, mayhem ensued.

Rat Scabies: 'This is the problem of being the most raucous punk rock band in the world. You get your accounts and it says – miscellaneous damages, £28,000....'

Captain Sensible later recorded a number one single, a version of cheesy musical standard 'Happy Talk' that left the rest of the band and many Damned fans dumbfounded. Sensible's eventual defection cemented the Damned's mid-eighties decline as they changed personnel more often than their underwear. However, they did manage a hit version of 'Eloise' (the original had been a number two hit for Barry Ryan in 1968) by which time, Scabies admits, they had allowed themselves to become sanitized. The current line-up features the Captain and Vanian, but not Scabies, with whom the others have fallen out over royalties. Afforded scant recognition from punk critics, their apparent inability to take themselves seriously has diminished their reputation. A sorry state of affairs, given that many consider them to be among the most gifted songwriters of the punk movement.

9/X-Ray Spex
Punk rock points: 68

Biggest hit: 'Germ Free Adolescents' (No. 19, 1978) ● 4 Top 40 singles ● 1 Top 40 album
Recommended album: *Germ Free Adolescents* (1978)

Poly Styrene (aka Marion Elliott) wanted to take the toys from the boys – writing with heartfelt eloquence, through glinting, brace-lined teeth, about the way women were portrayed as commodities by society. She lists her influences as the Artful Dodger, Johnny Rotten and her singing teacher. After placing an advert in *Melody Maker*, she was joined by a youthful band of musicians who tackled Poly's subject matter with amateurish enthusiasm – a mess of guitar and drums embellished by the rude hoots of Laura Logic's saxophone. Poly's lyrics attacked the synthetic materialism gripping Britain, and in 'Oh, Bondage! Up Yours' the sexual stereotypes ('Little girls should be seen and not heard') women still laboured under. By the time the group dissolved in 1979, they had become far more sophisticated. Their finest hour, the achingly cynical 'Germ-Free Adolescents' became a substantial hit,

Poly Styrene: 'We rehearsed a few times, played at the Roxy and became famous instantly.'

and an album of the same title followed. Thereafter Poly saw a UFO, left punk behind and joined the Hare Krishna movement for that old spiritual re-evaluation gig, recording one notable solo album – 1980's *Translucence*. Punk revivals have drawn Poly out for occasional reunion shows since the mid-nineties. So, pretty much still saying up yours to that bondage lark, then.

8/Stiff Little Fingers

Punk rock points: 123

Biggest hit: 'At The Edge' (No. 15, 1980) ● 4 Top 40 singles ● 3 Top 40 albums
Recommended album: *Nobody's Heroes* (1980)

Alongside the Undertones, Northern Ireland's finest punk export. Their name taken from a song by the Vibrators, Belfast's SLF were a thrilling live act who recorded a brace of LPs – *Inflammable Material* (1979) and *Nobody's Heroes* (1980) – that were brutally taut chronicles of growing up in troubled times. As singer Jake Burns acknowledges, 'There was nothing for us in Belfast. It was sheer tedium. Up till then I'd been in cover bands singing 'Sweet Home Alabama' when I hadn't been further west than Donegal'. They got some stick for engaging journalist Gordon Ogilvie as co-writer, which wasn't considered punk rock. But if it resulted in a run of singles as powerful as SLF produced, spanning debut effort 'Suspect Device' (1978) to their last Top 40 entry, the 'Listen' EP (1982), then the complaints were groundless. With Jake Burns' ravaged vocals at the forefront, SLF were first-rate songwriters with the musical competence to branch out beyond punk. Sadly, as soon as they tried (as on 1982's 'Now Then') their audience deserted them. Burns got a gig working on production for Dave Lee Travis's radio show. SLF reformed in the late eighties (initially so they could afford plane tickets home to see their folks) and then permanently in the nineties – with the addition of former Jam bass player Bruce Foxton.

7/Buzzcocks

Punk rock points: 152

Biggest hit: 'Ever Fallen In Love (With Someone You Shouldn't've)' (No. 12, 1978)
7 Top 40 singles ● 3 Top 40 album
Recommended album: *Singles – Going Steady* (1981)

The Buzzcocks delighted in breaking one of punk's golden tenets – writing a series of songs that, in sometimes twisted fashion, addressed the age-old concepts of love and romance that other punk bands rejected out of hand. Pete Shelley and Howard Devoto met at the Bolton Institute of Technology, forming the Buzzcocks early in 1976 with the addition of bass player Steve Diggle and drummer John Maher. They made their debut as the support act to the Sex Pistols at Manchester's Lesser Free Trade Hall – the gig that legendarily inspired the careers of half a dozen bands, and inspired Shelley and co. to radically over-haul their wardrobe as well as their musical tastes. Their debut

Broadcaster Tony Wilson: 'Real punk was saying "fuck you". With all the simplicity, energy, delight and youthfulness of punk, Pete Shelley was saying, "I love you".'

release, the 'Spiral Scratch' EP, broke new ground for punk – being entirely self-released and self-promoted. Devoto's final involvement with the band before he left to form

Pete Shelley: 'I got a pair of salmon pink jeans and ran 'em up on my mum's sewing machine. They used to stop traffic....'

Magazine, the four tracks were edgy, visceral and compelling, setting a high watermark for all subsequent 'independent' music. That the Buzzcocks continued to prosper in Devoto's absence is testament to the songwriting of Shelley and Diggle – both of whom proved capable of

marrying pop sentiments and convention to euphoric guitar playing, and the jagged rhythms of punk's finest percussionist, John Maher. The result was a string of superb singles that peaked with the much-loved 'Ever Fallen In Love (With Someone You Shouldn't've)' – its title inspired from a line in the film *Guys And Dolls*. Eventually,

Steve Diggle: 'The joints, then the coke, then the acid – you end up thinking – "What will that fire extinguisher sound like with a bit of delay on…?"'

however, the plot was well and truly lost. The Buzzcocks reformed in the late eighties in the glow of punk nostalgia but, to their credit, released a succession of high-quality original material in addition to repackaging the hits.

6/Undertones

Punk rock points: 176

Biggest hit: 'My Perfect Cousin' (No. 9, 1980) ● 6 Top 40 singles ● 3 Top 40 albums
Recommended album: *Hypnotised* (1980)

The Undertones' story is as affecting as it is unlikely. They were led by Feargal Sharkey – a vision of youthful awkwardness in his crumpled Parka, his voice a brittle and quavering presence in the backdraft of the O'Neill brothers' guitar combustion. Punks in Parkas? Well, as bass player Mickey Bradley remembers, you wore whatever your mum bought you in those days. Formed in Derry as a covers band, they were about to pack it all in when local label Good Vibrations released their 'Teenage Kicks' EP ('True Confessions' was actually intended as the A-side). John Peel considered it the most moving pop song he'd ever heard, and played it continuously on his Radio 1 show. Suddenly, the Undertones were on the phone to Seymour Stein of Sire Records demanding a £100,000 advance (apparently the first figure that came into their heads). The story goes that Stein offered £30,000 and they all but bit his hand off. It resulted in a brief but always enchanting career of sublime hit singles ('You've Got My Number', 'My Perfect Cousin', 'Wednesday Week') that gradually revealed the group's pop spine. The press never quite took them seriously (a problem addressed in the self-mocking 'More Songs About Chocolate And Girls' – the lead-off track on 1980's *Hypnotised*) but they wrote about male schoolyard desire – and the perennial lack of girlfriends – in a manner unequalled by any band since. Two further albums failed to impress the masses, though both *Positive Touch* (1981) and *The Sin Of Pride* (1983) possess moments of quiet genius and charm. The band had all but imploded on the release of the latter, Feargal going on to a nationwide solo number one with 'A Good Heart' while the O'Neill brothers formed That Petrol Emotion.

5/Sham 69

Punk rock points: 206

Biggest hit: 'Hersham Boys' (No. 6, 1979) ● 5 Top 40 singles ● 3 Top 40 albums
Recommended album: *Tell Us The Truth* (1978)

It may surprise some that Sham 69 – much derided by critics at the time and since – were

such a commercially powerful phenomenon. But that's a testament to the connection Jimmy Pursey's working-class adju-
tants made with a huge section of the British populace. Sham's
raw politics and knees-up-Mother-Brown geezerdom didn't
appeal to everyone, but to their core supporters, their message
of unity and class pride was an
article of faith. The songs were
so simplistic you didn't have to
read much beyond their title –
'If The Kids Are United', 'Tell Us The Truth', etc – yet
they were delivered with indisputable power and conviction. However, some lumberheads managed to confuse
even such straightforward political sloganeering, and as the late seventies progressed, the
group became mired in problems caused by a growing right-wing fanbase. Pursey did
everything he could to prevent it, but the rising tide of hatred that engulfed the band led
to its dissolution in 1980. Like many of their peers, Sham have reformed sporadically
ever since.

Jimmy Pursey: 'We were the dustmen of punk. We'd write about things that no-one else would, because those were the things that really were going on in everyday life.'

Mary Perry of punk fanzine *Sniffin' Glue*: 'They were what punk rock was all about. They were working-class kids from a really boring part of the suburbs, Hersham. They were angry, they had something to say and they wanted to say it loudly.'

4/Siouxsie And The Banshees

Punk rock points: 264

Biggest hit: 'Dear Prudence' (No. 3, 1983) ● 5 Top 40 singles ● 3 Top 40 albums
Recommended album: *The Scream* (1978)

Sussed and stylishly spiteful, the effortlessly iconic Siouxsie Sioux (Susan Dallion)
and her long-standing sparring partners Steve Severin and Budgie have produced some
of the most elegant and challenging songwriting within the 'punk rock' canon – though
in truth they were stretching the boundaries of the genre from their birth. Siouxsie was
a Pistols' camp regular (part of the famed Bromley contingent, a group of suburbanite
punks that followed the Pistols and also included future Generation X singer Billy
Idol) before putting together her band for a momentous first gig at the 100 Club (which
featured future Sex Pistols bass player/zombie Sid Vicious on drums and Marco
Perroni, later of Adam and the Ants, on guitar). They
performed a raucous twenty-minute version of 'The
Lord's Prayer'. Widely perceived to be 'troublesome',
nobody was signing the Banshees. Chris Parry, their
eventual A&R man, notes that there was something a bit
unhinged about the group, and that people avoided
getting too close to Siouxsie thinking she might nut
them. A fan-led graffiti blitz around the capital eventu-
ally persuaded Polydor to offer them a contract – with the band all but ready to sign to
the BBC after John Peel's continued support. Nobody could have anticipated just how
good their first single, 'Hong Kong Garden', would prove to be. The inspiration for the
song was a Chinese restaurant in Chislehurst that Siouxsie frequented; unfortunately,
it was also frequented by right-wing skinheads, who would turn up *en masse* and

Siouxsie Sioux, on The Banshees' debut gig: 'It was a real gauntlet. We knew we couldn't play. I had ideas of people being nauseous, or dying from the horrible noise of it all.'

harass the Chinese owners. Siouxsie wrote the song as a tribute to the victimized restaurateurs. The Banshees' main themes revolved around childhood, madness and escaping the limitations of suburbia. But don't blame them for Goth, which they invented as a by-product. A prolific and quality-conscious career terminated in 1996 after *The Rapture* flopped commercially, though Siouxsie and Budgie continue to work together as The Creatures. They are one of the few bands to retain vigilance over their recorded output – maintaining a posthumous quality control that others here should envy. Siouxsie's strutting stage persona – dark intent and childlike devilment creating a presence that was somehow older and wiser than her years – remains one of the defining images of punk.

3/Clash
Punk rock points: 270

Biggest hit: 'Should I Stay Or Should I Go' (No. 1, 1991) ● 5 Top 40 singles
4 Top 40 albums ● Recommended album: *London Calling* (1979)

If some punk artists are more talked about than played, that is a charge that could never be levelled at the Clash – famously described by *Rolling Stone* as the best band of the eighties. The reason for that longevity as a listening experience lies in the rock 'n' roll spirit that coursed through their songs. Not only did the Clash most satisfyingly embody this ancient heartbeat, they also skilfully mixed and matched from everything else they heard – be it hip hop, salsa or reggae. As contradictory as they were compelling, singer Joe Strummer had previously served time in pub rock artisans, the 101ers, and swerved questions about his public school background (at the time, a childhood of tower blocks and poverty were considered *de rigueur* for the well-heeled punk rocker).

Don Letts, band confidante: 'They didn't get hung up on that stupid label [punk]. They realized the world didn't end at the end of their street.'

And while the Clash began life clutching at the Sex Pistols' coat-tails, their legacy (especially in musical terms) is of at least equal import. Like most of the punk bands discussed here, they were a fantastic singles band, but their run of albums is the greatest single body of work in the punk canon. Despite the acclaim heaped on the group's eponymous debut and the mighty *London Calling*, even the, some would say poorly produced *Give 'Em Enough Rope* and patchy, over-expansive *Sandinista* boast incredible moments. Today Strummer regards that much-berated triple album as magnificent and states that he wouldn't change a thing about it even if he could. Sadly, by the time Strummer's songwriting partner Mick Jones was sacked in September 1983 (he went on to form Big Audio Dynamite), the group had burned out. A posthumous number one in 1991 when 'Should I Stay Or Should I Go' accompanied an advertising campaign was scant consolation. After years of slow contractual death, Strummer finally re-emerged as a solo artist at the turn of the millennium, still dismissing rumours of an imminent Clash reunion. As drummer Topper Headon explains, the Clash were a one-off nuclear explosion – no-one truly believed they could recreate the moment again.

2/Stranglers

Punk rock points: 396

Biggest hit: 'Golden Brown' (No. 2, 1982) ● 10 Top 40 singles ● 5 Top 40 albums
Recommended album: *Rattus Norvegicus* (1977)

Make no bones about it, people were a little suspicious of, and intimidated by, the Stranglers. They were older than the other punk groups, with whom they never socialized, and much nastier. Moreover, they relished projecting an image of menace and violence. The Stranglers had a keyboard player (albeit a very good one, Dave Greenfield, he of the worst rock 'n' roll hairstyle since Slade's Dave Hill was at the summit of his powers). And as far as cementing your place in the history books goes, beating up on punk's main chronicler, Jon Savage, isn't going to win you any brownie points. That the Stranglers proved such a force had everything to do with a unique schism between main songwriters Hugh Cornwell (a chemistry graduate who was almost regally dismissive of his peers) and the cosmopolitan bass player Jean-Jacques Burnel, a lithe punk sex symbol who practised karate kicks while punishing his bass. The debate about whether these grizzled old sweats from Guildford were punk or not is academic. They were seen as

Jean-Jacques Burnel:
'We weren't misogynistic.
We were misanthropic.'

such by the people who bought their records in huge numbers – usually against the advice of critics. But you couldn't really blame the press for taking a dim view of the band, given some of the treatment they received. Jean-Jacques recalls taking one music journalist who had dissed the band up to the first floor of the Eiffel Tower (that's about 200 feet up), stripping him, tying him to one of the girders and leaving him there. On another occasion they hired strippers to accompany a show at Battersea Park – no way were they attempting to inflame those already accusing them of sexism. The marvellously vitriolic *Rattus Norvegicus* announced a sound that the Stranglers gradually mollified over the ensuing years until they hit a commercial watershed with 'Golden Brown', widely acknowledged as an exquisite paean to heroin use that featured harpsichord and was played in 3/4 waltz time (not very punk, that). Although drummer Jet Black still maintains it was about toast. Eventually their loyal and passionate fanbase began to dwindle, before Cornwell left for a solo career at the end of the eighties. The decision surprised Burnel for one, who admits that he hadn't realized how pissed off, or ambitious, Cornwell was. After almost twenty years as a unit, everyone expected the Stranglers to disappear. Much to the horror of many fans, they recruited youthful singer Paul Roberts instead, and continue to tour and record sporadically.

1/Sex Pistols

Punk rock points: 422

Biggest hit: 'God Save The Queen' (No. 2, 1977) ● 10 Top 40 singles ● 4 Top 40 albums
Recommended album: *Never Mind The Bollocks* (1977)

The catalysts of punk rock, the Sex Pistols were arguably responsible for the greatest cultural upheaval of the post-war period. As befits such a band, their history is now

shrouded in myth. The story begins with Steve Jones single-handedly rejuvenating the classic rock chord progression, providing Johnny Rotten with a platform for his wilting sarcasm. That alchemy begat punk rock. The original Pistols – Rotten, Jones, drummer Paul Cook and bassist Glen Matlock – were put together by McLaren, the owner of the Sex boutique in King's Road, London, in the musically moribund mid-seventies. They played a few gigs and caused a minor stir – though one that paled in consequence to the heat generated on 1 December

John Lydon: 'I don't know what made me so awful. Parents quite liked me. People still say I'm completely hateable and detestable. The old nightmare – you created the monster, not me!'

1976 when they appeared on a local news programme hosted by Bill Grundy (who, Lydon admits with relish, did wonders for their career) as a replacement for EMI labelmates Queen. Fuelled by free booze, the Pistols entourage proceeded to rise to Grundy's provocation with a 'torrent' of four-letter words. The nation was shocked, etc, and McLaren had his moment of infamy – though he had Freddie Mercury to thank for it. From then on the Pistols featured regularly on tabloid front pages as the establishment depicted them as corrupters of the nation's youth. The game was afoot, and the Pistols responded with the epochal 'Anarchy In The UK'. A succession of labels got cold feet over the group before they finally washed up at Virgin. Then came their masterstroke – they released 'God Save The Queen', a

Broadcaster Tony Wilson: 'They were musically, culturally, in every way, the best thing in the world.'

scathing assault on the previously untouchable British monarchy – at the height of the Jubilee celebrations. Lydon came up with the lyrics, which he later likened to a piece of bad poetry, while he was eating baked beans in his father's kitchen. Some drew their own conclusions about Lydon's missive to the monarchy not reaching the number one spot in Jubilee week. The Pistols' debut album *Never Mind The Bollocks* became the subject of a farcical court case over the legality of its title. By now Matlock had been replaced with the gormless, self-destructive Sid Vicious, which proved a bad portent for the group's all-too-brief career. On tour in America they self-destructed, Rotten famously leaving the stage of their

John Lydon on the Pistols after his departure: 'They wanted to continue without me. Quite frankly, the talent had gone...'

last gig with one final taunt – 'Ever get the feeling you've been cheated?' Sid went on to be charged for murdering his junkie girlfriend in the Chelsea Hotel then predictably overdosed on heroin, as McLaren tried, and failed, to keep the Pistols afloat minus Lydon. The original Pistols regrouped for the self-explanatory 'Filthy Lucre' tour in 1996, but you could hardly begrudge them the desire to cash in a little on their glorious past.

The Argumentative Punk Rock Influence Matrix

Motörhead < **Damned** > Anti-Nowhere League
Patti Smith < **X-Ray Spex** > Au Pairs
Who < **Stiff Little Fingers** > Naked Raygun
Beatles < **Buzzcocks** > Smiths
Ramones < **Undertones** > Wedding Present
Slade < **Sham 69** > Cockney Rejects
Velvet Underground & Nico < **Siouxsie & The Banshees** > Madonna
Little Richard < **Clash** > Pogues
Doors < **Stranglers** > Elastica
New York Dolls < **Sex Pistols** > Everything

Love Songs

Birds do it, bees do it, and at least a million songwriters have attempted to capture the magic of 'falling in love'. The love song is the staple currency of popular music – despite the era or the musical fashion, the charts are the province of serial romanticists. This love stuff has proved most adaptable to the cause. According to the Four Aces it was 'a many splendoured thing'. Over the years songwriters have decided it is like oxygen (Sweet), a killer (Vixen), a wonderful colour (Icicle Works), contagious (Taja Seville), and even 'like a violin' (Ken Dodd). In short, there is no definitive recipe for the love song. Most are daft, nonsensical exercises in remedial wordplay that would shame a Christmas card writer. But each of those selected here have touched a nerve with the masses.

There are too many broken hearts in the world, Jason Donovan once said. And too many bad records about the condition. For the lovers out there, there's a good chance one of the following will constitute 'our song'. A reminder of what you first felt for your life partner and soul mate. A time when everything was innocence and shared discovery (Mills & Boon-speak for 'frantic early relationship shagging'). And, most likely, before they ran off with your best friend and got custody of the dog. So dim the lighting, change into something silky but gently chafing and uncork a bottle of fine wine as we get it on with the nation's ten all-time smoochies.

10/'You're The First, The Last, My Everything'

Passion points: 190

Weeks in chart: 14 ● Weeks at No. 1: 2 ● Chart appearances: 1

The love walrus, the bedroom behemoth, ladies and gentlemen, Mr Barry White. It's thought more babies have been conceived to White's honey-coated purr than in the blackouts of the Second World War. Born in Los Angeles, he was incarcerated for car

theft before embarking on a musical odyssey that led to a more legitimate source of spare tyres. He began his career as a producer. While recording a demo he discovered, on playback, that his voice was perfect for the sound he was trying to achieve and thus began his singing career. In 1974 he topped the charts in Britain and America with his signature tune 'You're The First, The Last, My Everything' – adapted from a country composition. From then on White, backed by the Love Unlimited Orchestra, became the musical elixir of love, not only reaching parts others could not, but massaging them into grateful reverie while he was there. Even Anne Diamond, visibly moistening on breakfast TV, was moved to request a cold shower after reading out a list of Barry's song titles. That's the power of the lurve man.

> **Barry White:** 'Guys come up and say, "I was with this terrific lady last night, and I couldn't move her. She wouldn't move till I put on your CD, man, and it's *banging*!"'

> **Barry White, on the discovery of his distinctive vocals:**
> 'I was fourteen years old, I went to bed like any other night. I was planning on getting up the next day and going to school. But I woke up the next morning and spoke to my mother and I scared the hell out of both of us.'

9/'The Lady In Red'   Passion points: 220

Weeks in chart: 15 ● Weeks at No. 1: 3 ● Chart appearances: 1

'The Lady In Red' topped the UK charts in July 1986 and continues to mop up dance-floors populated by leching forty-somethings everywhere. The author of the song himself, Chris De Burgh, sees the song as something in the way of musical foreplay, to get people in the mood for the main event. He also cites the fact that it has been voted the song women most like to have on in the background while making love. Over the years, the debate over whether the song was written about De Burgh's wife has, if not raged, at least flickered. In the past, De Burgh has gone on record as saying that he'd been away in London recording and when he first saw his wife Diane again, dressed in red needless to say, he didn't recognize her at first, although he found her stunningly attractive. But fast forward to the present day, and he says it wasn't about her at all. It seems 'The Lady In Red' will be with us for eternity. A De Burgh impersonator (a lab assistant in real life) won the champions heat of *Stars In Their Eyes* with 'The Lady In Red'.

> **DJ David Jensen:**
> 'People like the song a lot, it's an easy song to dance to or sing along to. Outside of that context, it's maybe something you wouldn't want to be caught playing with the car windows down.'

> **Journalist Stuart Maconie:**
> 'Most people like having controversial opinions. I'd like to say – "That's where you're wrong, Chris De Burgh is a fine man and an excellent singer, and the course of pop music would be very different without him." But I can't.'

8/'Nothing Compares 2 U'

Passion points: 250

Weeks in chart: 15 ● Weeks at No. 1: 4 ● Chart appearances: 2

The song that made Sinead O'Connor a bona fide pop star in 1990 was written by Prince for his protégés the Family in 1985. The Family's St Paul Peterson recalls the song being written for fellow group member Jerome Benton, who had recently split up with his girl-friend. Five years later, Peterson, who now plays with the Osmonds, heard Sinead's version on the radio and was less than impressed. But, as Chris Hill of Ensign Records notes, the fact that Prince wrote the song ceased to matter after Sinead made it her own. Sinead's manager Falconer O'Ceallaigh, who some believed had something beyond a merely professional relationship with the singer, brought Sinead's version of 'Nothing Compares 2 U' to Hill's office one day, as Hill remembers: I was on my own in the office. I put the tape on, and my heart nearly stopped. There was a tear rolling down my cheek. He rang Sinead up and said, "Hill is crying! Must be a good record!" I was so embar-rassed.' Before the single's video was filmed, Falconer and Sinead broke up, adding an extra poignancy to the song's history. Sinead herself is one of the great puzzles of our time, her immense talent overshadowed by seemingly perpetual conflicts with record companies, the fathers of her children, religious institutions and Frank Sinatra. Not to mention her own demons. The story came full circle when Prince realized that a song he'd neglected may have been ripe for commercial harvest after all; a duet version with Rosie Gaines resulted. Gaines recalled how moved people had been at the first live performance of their version, but critics believe that their highly-strung take had little of the dignity or clarity of O'Connor's definitive rendition, still one of the most emotional pieces in pop history.

7/'Hello'

Passion points: 280

Weeks in chart: 15 ● Weeks at No. 1: 6 ● Chart appearances: 1

His former group the Commodores once played raunchy funk tunes, but by the early eighties Lionel Richie had embarked on a solo career based on syrupy emotional ballads and slick party tunes. A respected producer and writer, in November 1980, Lionel provided Kenny Rogers with 'Lady', a US chart-topper. He then topped the charts with the Diana Ross duet 'Endless Love' for nine weeks in August 1981. There was no hotter commercial property in America; Lionel himself puts a lot of his success down to his abiding faith in God. He'd begun to write ballads because none of the other Commodores were interested in slow songs, and that guaranteed him two tracks on each album. DJ David Jensen remembers Richie telling him that a songwriter had to come up with ballads to be covered by other artists and, thus, to be remembered. In 1984 Richie enjoyed his biggest hit with 'Hello', a song that was built around memories of his own frustrations with the female sex as a youngster. Without the babe-magnetism of the football, baseball or basketball players, Richie was too shy to approach the ladies. The single topped UK and US charts on the back of a video featuring a blind woman who had produced a near-

perfect sculpture of her fellow teacher – Richie. The songwriter himself felt that he had produced a lowest common denominator ballad, until video director Bob Giraldi decided to mess around with the narrative by making the subject of the song blind. Many considered the video trite, and the song overbearingly sentimental, a claim that Richie himself accepts. However, as he says, his experience in the music business has taught him that it's the simple songs that people remember and sing.

6/'When A Man Loves A Woman'   Passion points: 390

Weeks in chart: 36 ● Weeks at No. 1: 0 ● Chart appearances: 3

One of the most enduring romantic statements of all time was a classic rejection song. Singer and hospital orderly by day, Percy Sledge had been dumped for someone with a bigger car. He poured his heart into performing 'When A Man Loves A Woman' on-stage. DJ and producer Quin Ivy was at the show and made a beeline for Sledge and asked him where he had found a song with so much feeling. When Sledge replied that he had just made it up, Ivy signed him up imme-

Jimmy Johnson, sound engineer on the recording: 'The first record I ever remember, from the first time it was played, that the phones rang off the hook.'

diately. The original recording of 'When A Man Loves A Woman' came out in 1966. The arrangement, underpinned by Spoon Oldham's sepulchral organ, deserves equal credit. As Stuart Maconie comments, it makes the record sound as though somebody is testifying in church. A Top 5 UK hit, the song topped the charts in America, Percy remembers the moment that he got his first cheque for $35,000. It's fair to say that Sledge's career afterwards was something of

Quin Ivy: 'We were working with antiquated equipment, and the bass was bleeding over into the other mics. It gave it that muddy sound. As it turned out, that was great.'

an non-event as he played the chicken-in-a-basket circuit. But the one great song he left behind has kept his name alive. It charted again in 1987 at number two when it was featured on a jeans advert. More ignominiously still, Michael Bolton took his version into the charts in 1991.

5/'I Will Always Love You'   Passion points: 580

Weeks in chart: 36 ● Weeks at No. 1: 10 ● Chart appearances: 2

Dolly Parton, the quintessential country star, wrote this heartfelt 'Dear John' about showbiz partner Porter Wagoner. Parton had been a fixture on Wagoner's show from 1967, but had tired of his jealousy at her growing popularity. Parton says it was a love-hate relationship: she was doing all the loving, he was doing the hating. Frustrated that Wagoner wouldn't listen to her opinions, or her songs, a broken-hearted Parton penned an emotional *cri de coeur* to tell him, and the world, how she was feeling. The song was later resurrected for the 1992 Hollywood blockbuster *The Bodyguard*. A vehicle for Whitney

Houston's celluloid debut, co-star Kevin Costner suggested she record the Parton oldie as the theme. A major international hit resulted, including a record-breaking fourteen-week stay at the top of the US charts (ten weeks at number one in the UK). It won Houston a Grammy for best vocal performance, though not everyone was a fan of her technique, including journalist Terry Staunton, who stated that the ability to hold a note for a very long time, at a high volume, did not constitute great singing as far as he was concerned. The song nevertheless became a karaoke standard. Bizarre trivia point: 'I Will Always Love You' has proved to be the most effective flab-buster on a calorie-counting karaoke machine in Japan. Statistically, it is also the most requested song at UK funerals. The song hit the news again in 1993 when a twenty-year-old Whitney wannabe was jailed for a week after deafening her Stockton neighbours by playing the song at full volume.

4/'Everything I Do (I Do It For You)'   Passion points: 650

Weeks in chart: 31 ● Weeks at No. 1: 16 ● Chart appearances: 2

Bryan Adams topped the UK charts for a record sixteen weeks in July 1991 with this ode to Sherwood Forest's golden couple. Soundtrack specialist Michael Kamen (*Lethal Weapon*, *Die Hard*, *Licenced To Kill*, etc) recalls that the melody had been knocking around for twenty-five years – he'd first come up with it when he'd been a keyboardist and singer in a band. However, his fellow band members wearied of Kamen endlessly playing it, apparently threatening him with physical violence unless he stopped. It was only when Kamen was sent a rough cut of *Robin Hood, Prince Of Thieves* that he was reminded of the tune. He first envisaged Maid Marion as the singer, but Kate Bush, Annie Lennox and Lisa Stansfield all turned him down. So in the end the male lead got to wear the tights. Adams, a dedicated no-frills Canadian rocker, hadn't recorded much of note recently. He added lyrics and cut a version of the song that opened with piano and electric guitar. Kamen fought to put

Michael Kamen: 'This couple were getting married in America, and they asked the band they'd hired if they could play the music from *Robin Hood*. The band said, "Yeah, OK". As the bride walked down the aisle, they started up – "Robin Hood, Robin Hood, with his band of men...."'

strings on the arrangement, eventually bullying Adams into compliance despite a considerable amount of disagreement. It's fair to suggest that Adams considered Kamen to be stubborn. After the discussion Adams sent Kamen a symbolic mule. However, the duo prospered in partnership, and have collaborated on further films including *The Three Musketeers*. 'Everything I Do' became the wedding song of the nineties.

3/'Without You'   Passion points: 660

Weeks in chart: 46 ● Weeks at No. 1: 9 ● Chart appearances: 2

Under the patronage of Paul McCartney, Badfinger were signed to Apple Records in 1968. By the time of their first major success, 'Come And Get It', the line-up featured Pete Ham

(vocals), Tom Evans (guitar), Joey Molland (bass), and Mike Gibbons (drums). During sessions for debut album *No Dice*, they were struggling to lay down a final track. Ham and Evans were working on two different songs – Ham had the verse part and Evans had the chorus. Ham's girlfriend Beverley Tucker remembers the night they put them together. Ham had promised her that he wouldn't go into the studio that night, and told her to get dressed up to go out. As they got to the front door, Evans appeared with an idea for a song. Ham retorted that he'd promised Bev a night out, at which his girlfriend said, 'No, go work with Tom. I don't mind, I'm smiling.' Ham replied,

Producer Richard Perry on Nilsson's version: 'Right from the very first take, it was goosebumps time.'

"Yes, your mouth is smiling, but your eyes are sad."' It was a line that was transposed onto the finished song. In the studio the band were somewhat less impressed, and Evans thought the song 'corny'. A year later Harry Nilsson (of 'Everybody's Talkin'' fame) walked into their studio. He played what Molland remembers as an epic production of the song, as if he'd made a motion picture out of it. Nilsson had heard the song at a party and brought a vocal-and-piano take to producer Richard Perry. Perry chivvied Nilsson into doing a new version (a process that he later likened to pulling teeth) with proper orchestration. The song shot to the top of the charts and won Nilsson a Grammy and Ham and Evans an Ivor Novello award. Sadly, royalty disagreements soured the success. On 24 April 1975, Ham hung himself in his garage. Evans was devastated. Eight years later, he too was found hanged. Nilsson died of a heart attack in 1994. He had just returned to songwriting after thirteen years of alcoholism. Mariah Carey released her take on the 'cursed' ballad within a month of his death. It went straight to number one.

2/'Love Is All Around'   Passion points: 830

Weeks in chart: 51 ● Weeks at No. 1: 15 ● Chart appearances: 2

The Troggs made their name in 1966 with the basic, raucous garage rock of 'Wild Thing', later covered by Jimi Hendrix. It was all a little bemusing for a bunch of in-fighting yokels from Hampshire. 'Love Is All Around', released just over a year later, was their unlikely attempt to forge a link with the West Coast psychedelic movement. Bizarrely, former bricklayer Reg Presley (aka Reg Ball) was inspired to write the song after seeing Salvation Army band, the Joystrings, on TV. Mike Mills of R.E.M. believes 'Love Is All Around' to be one of the best-ever love songs, in that it succeeds in being sentimental without descending into schmaltz and features a classic chord progression. The song reached number five in 1967 and was the Troggs' last substantive hit. Recriminations and a decline in their musical ability proved their downfall, both aspects captured amid glorious profanity on the hilarious *Troggs Tapes*. That document of an abortive studio session would have been the band's lasting legacy had 'Love Is All Around' not been resuscitated for the 1994 comedy *Four Weddings And A Funeral*. Wet Wet Wet keyboard player Neil Mitchell admits that the band had always wanted to do film music, be it a soundtrack or a song in a James Bond movie. Alongside the Troggs' 'Love Is All Around' came the options of tunes by Barry Manilow or Gloria Gaynor. The Wets liked the simplicity and obscurity of the Troggs song, although as Marti Pellow notes, if he had approached the

rest of his band with a lyric like the opening line he would have been escorted from the studio amid gales of laughter. The song was recorded hastily over a few cans of lager. Back in Andover, Reg, now a dedicated UFO-watcher, received the demo, which he pronounced 'brilliant'. Bolstered by the film's success, the song took root at the number one spot; the band played *Top Of The Pops* fourteen times in a row. Naturally, the phenomenal success of the record generated huge amounts of money. As writer, Reg took the lion's share, and admits to spending a little of it on crop circle research. After fifteen weeks at number one, the Wets themselves admitted that they could not work out who was still buying the record. In the end, Phonograph issued a statement saying it would stop manufacturing the single at the close of business on 13 September 1994.

1/'Unchained Melody'   Passion points: 1,260

Weeks in chart: 96 ● Weeks at No. 1: 14 ● Chart appearances: 7

It may beggar belief, but 'housewife's favourite' Jimmy Young was once a pop star. In 1955 his A&R man invited him to hear a ballad he'd found. Young recorded it in Decca's Hampstead studio suffering from acute stomach pain. The recording session was at ten past one; at two o'clock Young was undergoing an emergency operation in University College Hospital, something that he feels may account for the emotion on the record. Young's version of the track, originally written to accompany prison film *Unchained*, went straight to number one. As was the custom in the fifties, several competing versions soon populated the chart. While Young was at number one, Al Hibbler was at number two and versions by Liberace and Les Baxter also registered Top 20 entries. Ten years later the song was given its definitive treatment by the Righteous Brothers (Bill Medley and Bobby Hatfield). The record was more or less a solo performance by Hatfield. It stalled outside the Top 10 on release, but in 1990 it was memorably employed in hit movie *Ghost* and leapt straight to number one. Then, in a 1995 episode of *Soldier Soldier*, actors Robson Green and Jerome Flynn thrilled their TV audience with a new version. As Simon Cowell of the record company BMG recalls, record shops had been inundating the company, claiming that zillions of people were trying to buy a record by Robson and Jerome that didn't exist. Cowell put in about forty calls to the show's producer and eventually managed to get Robson and Jerome's numbers. However, no one would talk to him – apart from Robson's lawyer, who allegedly informed him that if he continued to harass his client, he would be sued. Eventually Green asked how much was on the table and eventually agreed. 'Unchained Melody' has now been a hit in every decade since the fifties (Leo Sayer also had a hit with it in the eighties). Its position as the nation's favourite love song is assured, the quality of the original composition outshining its treatment by less worthy hands down the years.

Bill Medley: 'We started out as two Little Richards, and thank God someone came along and said shut up and sing a ballad. Worked out pretty good for us.'

Some Less Romantic Ditties

Alternative TV: 'Love Lies Limp'
Freshies: 'If You Really Love Me, Buy Me A Shirt'
Gloria Estefan: 'Go Away'
Michael Jackson: 'Leave Me Alone'
Only Ones: 'Why Don't You Kill Yourself'
Peter Shelley: 'Love Me, Love My Dog'
Police: 'Don't Stand So Close To Me'
Quireboys: 'I Don't Love You Anymore'
Toy Dolls: 'Ron Dixon Dumped D-D'
Yardbirds: 'Evil Hearted You'

One-hit Wonders

One-hit wonders are the shooting stars of pop, burning brightly on the charts and exciting the imagination of their record companies before disappearing into communes, taxi driving or sundry other less-celebrated pursuits while their careers are written off as tax losses. Reasons for their demise range from mental instability to fickle fate to audiences catching on to their wholesale lack of talent. Some gimmicks were never going to endure for a second single. For other acts, it was sheer luck that they ever broke their Top 20 cherry in the first place. They are a colourful and varied bunch. Step forward Deee-Lite, Chesney Hawkes, Aneka, the Floaters. Line-dance this-a-way Billy Ray Cyrus and your 'Achey Brakey Heart'.

In an industry when musicians now bombard us with their every waking thought over a catalogue their mothers would gag at listening to in its entirety, brevity is too readily mocked. Those listed below embraced the concept with unequalled vigour and determination, though some of them were not wise to the fact while they were doing so. So then, a list of ten of the greatest moments in pop history that remained just that – momentary.

10/Jilted John

Points: 24

Chart position: No. 4, August 1978 ● Failed follow-up: An 'answer' single by Gordon

In the seventies the chip shop was the amphitheatre of dreams and the romantic crucible for urban youth. Jilted John's self-titled hit used the chippie as the scene of the crime to document the defection of his girlfriend Julie to a trendy Johnny-come-lately – called Gordon. Gordon's undemanding part (he was instructed on stage to 'dance without moving' while being branded a moron by the lyrics) was taken by Bernard Kelly. At the time the record broke, its author (Jilted John turned out to be one Graham Fellows) was at a Christian youth camp. He wasn't a Christian – he went because there were a lot of

'nice girls' there. The song's conversational delivery was inspired by John Otway's 'Cor Baby That's Really Free'. Its success enabled Fellows to appear on *Top Of The Pops* alongside heroine Debbie Harry of Blondie. As a tribute, he composed a song, 'Debbie Debbie' (to the tune of 'Denis Denis'). Kelly laments the moment he read the lyrics, which apparently featured lines such as 'Every time I see your face, I get an erection' (at which, today, he holds his head in his hands and moans, 'Oh, my God!'). Unable to follow-up the song's success, Fellows could later be found attempting to pick up Gail Tilsley (then Gail Potter) outside a cinema in an episode of *Coronation Street*. Needless to say, he got the brush-off. However, he did achieve success of some kind under a new persona, Radio 4's John Shuttleworth. The latter has made him considerably wealthier than Jilted John ever did, and he now looks back on that youthful creation with affection. His former partner, Kelly, writes for TV. 'I've had twenty years of having, "Oi! Gordon! Mr Moron!" shouted at me, Kelly laments. 'It's not so bad being called Jilted John, but being known as a moron for 20 years….'

9/Crazy World Of Arthur Brown   Points: 31

Chart position: No. 1, June 1968
Failed follow-up: Never released, as the band broke up after their disappointing debut album. With later recordings including lyrics likening a ghost to a piece of toast, he has failed to deprive chart compilers of their beauty sleep.

'Fire' remains one of the most distinctive records of the sixties, its powerful intro still a masterpiece of theatrical pop. If the fiery first line didn't grab your attention, its author's flaming headpiece did. Arthur Brown (aka Arthur Wilton), a very prosaic name for such a demonic presence, got the idea after someone left a crown of candlesticks outside his room. He lit the candles in a basement club and got an immediate reaction (not least from the fire wardens, one would imagine). Over the years the headgear evolved from a vegetable colander with candles (the wax would drip through and stick to his head) to a metal pie dish filled

Arthur Brown: 'If I was in a restaurant, everyone thought I was suddenly going to leap up on a table and shout "Fire!" in the middle of my kebab. It got to be a little overwhelming.'

with petrol. His bizarre act attracted the attention of Joe Boyd, co-founder of the UFO club, which Pink Floyd made their spiritual home. After a series of noteworthy performances there, Brown was offered a recording contract, of sorts: an advance of £375 and a 3.5% royalty rate. Despite the success of 'Fire', he became disenchanted with the world of pop. He retired from commercial music to live on a commune, claiming that he needed to find out who he really was. Nowadays he is occasionally tempted from semi-retirement (recently joining Kula Shaker on stage in 1999), but you're more likely to encounter him practising outdoor Tai Chi. It's impossible to say whether or nay his bald patch resulted from years of wax burns.

8/Althea And Donna

Points: 43

Chart position: No. 1, December 1977
Failed follow-up: The aforementioned, lamentable 'Puppy Dog Song'

The only number one single to emerge from Britain's seventies fixation with reggae actually came from two Jamaican schoolgirls, whose 'Uptown Top Ranking' topped the charts in 1977. Althea Forrest and Donna Reid adapted their song from Trinity's 'Three Piece Suit'. Trinity himself was apparently less than chuffed with the result, and remains embittered by the whole experience, arguing that the duo didn't deserve their success because, as far as he is concerned, it was his record. The girls met on a beach the summer after graduating from high school, and talked producer Joe Gibbs into recording them. When Radio 1 picked up on the single it charged up the charts, aided by a farcical appearance on *Top Of The Pops*. The BBC Pops orchestra, required to play songs live at the time, audibly struggled to recreate the Jamaican mood. Althea maintains that the horn player was on the point of hitting her with his instrument because she persistently hassled him to get the vibe right. In his defence, the unfortunate journeyman may have been blinded by Donna's frightening Afro. The record had been made without contract, allowing Richard Branson to step in and sign them to Virgin. After their breakthrough, the group elected to write their own material and came up with the 'Puppy Dog Song'. They retired from music to raise families thereafter, but promise to return to the studio soon. Pedantic footnote: Althea's name was mis-spelled Althia on the record.

7/Our Kid

Points: 49

Chart position: No. 2, May 1976 ● Failed follow-up: 'Romeo And Juliet'. Could have been a hit – but they didn't have enough 'work days' left to promote it.

Few artists could claim to have had their careers stymied by their local authority, but that's the fate that befell Liverpool's Our Kid. In the mid-seventies, the Osmonds were the dominant teenybopper force and, as Paul Gambaccini notes, it was only a matter of time before people looked for British kids – *kids*, not teenagers – to do the same. Our Kid were lead vocalist Kevin Rowan, Brian Farrell, Terry McCreith and Terry Baccino and were put together in 1974 by Francis Davis, a veteran impressario on the northern working men's club scene (think Michael Caine's character in *Little Voice*). Enter songwriter Barry Mason, responsible for hits including Tom Jones' 'Delilah'. He wrote 'You Just Might See Me Cry' for their appearance on seventies talent show *New Faces*. 'There were some great acts', Baccino claims, 'and we won. I felt so guilty about winning that I burst out crying.' 'You Just Might See Me Cry' went on to reach number two in May 1976 and sold half a million copies. When Our Kid played the Liverpool Empire the road had to be blocked off with mounted police, in scenes reminiscent of Beatlemania. Davis booked them a summer season in Great Yarmouth – a career-ending mistake. The boys played two shows a night, six nights a week, then returned at the weekends to record in London. Then the offer of a TV series materialized. Unfortunately, they couldn't take it up: Mason had to sit down with the group in the Polygram boardroom and tell them that because they were so young, they were only allowed to work for a restricted number of days in the year. And, due to an error of judgement that Davis today admits was his biggest mistake, they'd already used up all their work days for that year on

Terry McCreith: 'We did get some money out of it, but mostly it was soaked up by recordings and albums we made, staying in big, swanky hotels. There was just enough left for a Flake and an *Echo* at the end of the day.'

those small gigs. Mason still believes the band would have been a world smash had they got the TV series. McCreith is now an actor, Farrell a sports shop manager, Rowan a painter and decorator. Baccino is the only one to remain working as a (struggling) musician.

6/Men At Work
Points: 78

Chart position: No. 1, January 1983
Failed follow-up: 'Overkill' reached No. 21 in April 1983. They had two further Top 40 hits that year without ever breaking the Top 20 again.

If ever a song came to define national identity, it was Men At Work's irreverent tribute to Australia, 'Down Under' – even though its co-author was a Scottish ex-pat, Colin Hay. He formed the band, initially as a duo, with guitarist Ron Strykert. The song was a fixture of rowdy sets that the expanded quintet (with the addition of keyboardist Greg Ham, bassist John Rees and drummer Jerry Speiser) played in and around Melbourne at the turn of the eighties. Hay remembers that when they played it in pubs they played it for six minutes and no one would notice because they were all too busy getting trollied. A demo found an initially lukewarm response from local DJ Russell 'Rusty Nails' Thorpe, but the song was released following the group's Australian breakthrough 'Who Can It Be Now?' and took off. It was partially influenced by Barry Humphries' caricature of Sir Les Patterson – Australian cultural ambassador – and its lyric captured the optimism, fraternity and informality with which the Aussie psyche is associated. It went straight to number one, but Men At Work were soon under attack from a spiteful British press; Ham had to endure being called 'the ugliest man in the ugliest band in the world'. However, their success continued outside Britain for several years. All of which has made Colin realistic about their appeal. He reasons that the punters are out there and a band has to physically get out and find them and play in their town to draw a following. 'Down Under', meanwhile, was employed as something of an *ad-hoc* national anthem at the closing ceremony of the 2000 Olympics in Sydney.

5/Toni Basil
Points: 101

Chart position: No. 2, February 1982 ● Failed follow-up: 'Nobody', peaked at 52 that May

Toni Basil was offspring to a bandleader and an acrobat, so being 'conventional' was hardly in her nature. She proved it by working as a choreographer while appearing in

several cult movies – including the Monkees' *Head*, *American Graffiti* and, divested of her garments, *Easy Rider*. Simon Lait, head of Radialchoice Records, met her in a Chinese restaurant on Sunset Boulevard and immediately saw her as a star waiting to be discovered. Lait contacted Nicky Chinn – half of the hugely successful Chinn/Chapman hit factory, which had been behind Mud and many other teenybopper delights. Chinn played Lait a series of tracks, one of which was a song called 'Kitty' by seventies good-time popsters Racey. Basil changed the words round to 'Mickey' and added – she claims against the advice of her record company – a series of cheer-leader chants. The single proved an instant success, aided by a deftly choreographed video. When it topped the US charts and reached number two in the UK, it seemed Basil was set for a long career. The BBC certainly thought so, affording her a TV special, where she worked alongside voguish celebrities such as dog trainer Barbara Woodhouse. But when the too-similar follow-up 'Nobody' laid down and played dead, Basil's career possibilities narrowed. While acknowledging that hers is not an unusual music biz story, Basil states that since 1982, she has probably received less than $3,000 in worldwide royalties. Not bitter at all, then. Chinn maintains that if she had found the right follow-up, she would have had another hit. The video to 'Mickey' left a big impression, however. Basil is rightly proud that an image taken from it currently resides in the Museum of Modern Art.

4/Charles And Eddie   Points: 134

Chart position: No. 1, October 1992 ● Failed follow-up: 'NYC (Can You Believe This City?)' tested record company credulity when it stalled outside the Top 30

The publicity 'scoop' on soul duo Charles Pettigrew and Eddie Chacon was that they met on a New York subway train and started chatting because Eddie was holding a copy of Marvin Gaye's 'Trouble Man'. Their producer, Josh Deutsch, is apparently sceptical about that, assessing the chances of someone carrying a record finding a 'soul mate' by chance on the subway as minimal. The duo, however, have stuck by the story. Deutsch *was* convinced by the duo's talent, particularly Charles' falsetto and flamboy-ant stage presence (especially in his previous band, Boston's Down Avenue). With Hall & Oates as his inspiration, the producer found a song demo, 'Would I Lie To You?', from a British writing team. Both the Fine Young Cannibals and Maxi Priest wanted the song, but co-author Mick Leeson was persuaded to give it to the duo by Deutsch. Leeson argues that sometimes the enthusiasm someone displays for a song virtually guarantees future hit-status, and Deutsch's fervour won the day for Charles and Eddie. The follow-up single '(NYC) Can You Believe This City?' was written about the duo's fabled introduction (or according to which story you believe, its lyrics *inspired* the publicity story), and they enjoyed a few further lowly chart entries. However, the group never replicated the success of 'Would I Lie To You?'. Charles became a solo performer while Eddie wrote hit material for acts including the UK's Eternal. They are currently considering a rekindling of their musical partnership.

3/Nena
Points: 156

Chart position: No. 1, February 1984
Failed follow-up: 'Just A Dream', peaked at 70 in May 1984

Nena Gabriele Kerner was the voice behind one of the surprise international successes of 1984, an anglicized version of her eponymous German band's hit, '99 Luftballons'. The song, retitled '99 Red Balloons', was allied to a vaguely punky backbeat and symbolized Cold War paranoia – though that lost something in translation. It was powered by a vocalist who outraged the British tabloids with her unshaven armpits, part of her 'wild rock chick' image, and drew lascivious comments from TV stalwart Frank Bough ('That Nena, she's something, isn't she?'). Keyboardist Uwe Fahrenkrog-Petersen maintains that Nena had something special. According to him, even

Nena: 'We all had our childhoods, and we all know how important the balloon was.'

if the band was only playing to five people, she would inspire some kind of reaction. Uwe notes, without a hint of jealousy, that the group got its major break on television because allegedly the guy in charge preferred pretty young girls to less marketable male musicians. The single's overnight success in Germany led to the international release of '99 Red Balloons'. Touring Britain was a bemusing experience, as Nena was confronted with a host of signs that read 'We love your unshaved armpits'. Some of the press the band received was far from charitable. One headline claimed Nena was the 'biggest attack on England since the V2'. But when the follow-up single – which some, including Esther Rantzen considered 'very boring' – got nowhere, the group's fleeting fling with British pop was over. Nena the band broke up in 1987, but Nena the delightful Deutscher pop star is still a big pull in Germany. '99 Luftballons', we are assured by Uwe, remains 'a must' at any decent Germany party – if that isn't an oxymoron.

Manager Alex Grob: 'I always told her, one of these days you're going to get arrested for looking like that.'

Keyboardist Uwe Fahrenkrog-Petersen: 'They did not like us because we were not so hip leader as the Londoner of the moment. So what?'

2/Doctor And The Medics/ Norman Greenbaum
Points: 177

Chart position: No 1, May 1986 (No. 1 for Norman Greenbaum in March 1970)
Failed follow-up: 'Burn' reached No. 29 in August 1986

If ever a band were conversant with their own lack of ability, it is Doctor And The Medics. So when their lucky moment came, courtesy of a revision of Norman Greenbaum's hippy classic 'Spirit In The Sky', they grabbed it with both hands and partied. With a true chancer's grasp of logistics, they decided fate was never going to smile so kindly in their direction again – were they right about that... Doctor (Clive Jackson) recalls that they toured the world for three years on the back of 'Spirit''s success. Greenbaum, having been there and bought several variations of the T-shirt, could sympathize with their opportunism. He'd worked as a dairy farmer since leaving Dr West's Medicine Show and Junk Band (one hit: the novelty single 'The Eggplant That Ate Chicago'). Written as a kind of new age spiritual, his version of the song had reached the top in March 1970, before he refused to stop there and recorded the esoteric follow-up, 'Canned Ham'. 'Spirit In The Sky' quickly became an albatross and few fans were interested in listening to anything else. The situation reached ridiculous heights. At one date in Santa Cruz, Greenbaum's entire forty-minute set was composed of the song. Then he had to play it as an encore for another fifteen minutes. Doctor And The Medics' version simply cranked up the original

Clive Jackson (Doctor):
'If you look at the band at the present, it's mainly influenced by age. The fact is, we look like a bunch of old c***s.'

a bit, according to Jackson. When their career began to follow a similar trajectory to Greenbaum's, they set up a snail farm in Wales before the commercial limitations of such an exercise dawned on them. Nowadays they're fixtures on the free festival circuit – possibly because few would countenance paying to see them grow old disgracefully.

1/Carl Douglas   Points: 215

Chart position: No 1, August 1974
Failed follow-up: 'Dance The Kung Fu' stalled at number 35 in November 1974

Jamaican-born but Finchley-based, Douglas was just a common-or-garden struggling soul singer when he wrote 'Kung Fu Fighting' after seeing a couple of kids in Soho practising their Bruce Lee-inspired chops and windmill-kicks – martial arts being all the rage at the time. He suggested it as a B-side to his producer, Biddu, in the studio, humming the opening melody then explaining how he wanted instruments to 'answer' each part of the vocal. Biddu played the song to Robin Blanchflower at Pye, after the commissioned A-side, 'I'm Going To Give You My Everything'. He wasn't optimistic. However, Blanchflower liked the opening bars and by the end of the song, he thought an 'absolute smash' was on the cards. He proved right, as the single motored to the number one spot in August 1974 – the soundtrack to a summer in which Bruce Lee gave the zeitgeist an Oriental seeing-to. From there, things went downhill with 'Dance The Kung Fu'. Douglas, however, remains proud of his achievements with 'Kung Fu Fighting', stating that it's one of the songs people always remember. Carl returned to the charts with a remix of the song in May 1998. Even if a good royalty stream has ensured the 'cat' no longer looked as if he'd be as 'fast as lightning' should there be any argy bargy, it was nice to have him back.

Bubbling Under
some other one-hit wonders with
a particularly low-quality threshold

Animotion: 'Obsession' (No. 5, May 1985)
Archies: 'Sugar Sugar' (No. 1, October 1969)
Chippendales: 'Give Me Your Body' (No. 28, October 1992)
Joe Dolce: 'Shaddap You Face' (No. 1, Feb 1981)
Paul Gardiner: 'Stormtrooper In Drag' (No. 49, July 1981)
Garry Lee and Showdown: 'The Rodeo Song' (No. 44, July 1993)
Mike Reid: 'The Ugly Duckling' (No. 10, March 1975)
Jimmy Shand: 'Bluebell Polka' (No. 20, December 1955)
Sherbet: 'Howzat' (No. 4, September 1976)
Video Kids: 'Woodpeckers From Space' (No. 72, October 1985)

Heavy Metal

Named from a line in Steppenwolf's 'Born To Be Wild', heavy metal emerged as a form of back to basics rock 'n' roll in the mid-seventies, its musicians (overwhelmingly male) schooled on the truism that rock stardom offered them their only chance of being desirable to the opposite sex. The formula was one of screaming guitar leads and trebly solos while the rhythm section pounded out a blunt distillation of the blues. A primal shriek rather than a primal scream, metal bands gave themselves points not just for technical virtuosity but also volume, clubbing listeners via the intensity and conviction of their performances. The songs, meanwhile, explored the entire vista of human experience – or at least those human experiences involving fast cars, large-chested women and Norse gods of war.

A byword for testosterone-fuelled masculinity and male bonding, heavy metal found a ready adolescent audience of pasty young men anxious about their sexuality. They had their own unique dance craze: headbanging. This is best described as a circle of spotty teenagers ritually jerking their heads back and forth in time with the music, their lanky hair flaying clouds of dandruff across youth club floors. It was the only place and time in history that the sleeveless denim jacket was considered high fashion. The only firm and fast rule of heavy metal is that each album should feature one corny ballad, for the ladies, you understand, and that lead singer and lead guitarist should be warring factions intent on convincing the world they are the real talent. And while contemporary hard rock has fractured into subdivisions such as death, thrash and even, God forbid, funk metal, the following British acts were the commercial bastions of the movement, and are scored on domestic chart success. For those who have rocked, we salute you.

10/UFO

Metal points: 38

Recommended album: *Lights Out* (1977) ● 4 Top 20 albums

Formed in the late sixties as a quasi-psychedelic rock act led by singer Phil Mogg, UFO achieved little until they recruited German guitar genius Michael Schenker in 1973, after they spotted him playing with support act, the Scorpions. 'If I look back,' Schenker offers, generously, 'I realize how much impact I had. Because I was so focused, I think I would have left my mark with any band on the level that I did.' His playing added an extra dimension to the band on a run of exemplary hard rock albums beginning with *Phenomenon* in 1985. Bass player Pete Way and Mogg spent much of their time taking the Michael out of Schenker, whose English didn't extend much beyond yes and no. He would quit and rejoin the band almost weekly. Gary Bushell toured with UFO, and remembers the chaos surrounding them, primarily due to the fact that they spent their considerable earnings, from their considerable record sales in the States, on drugs. Schenker had finally had enough by November 1978. In 1982 Way left too. Mogg kept the band going with sundry backing musicians before finally admitting defeat in 1988. In 1995 the band's classic line-up, featuring Way, Mogg and Schenker, recorded *Walk On Water* together. Schenker compares the UFO experience to chocolate. 'If you eat too much, oh, chocolate again. But if you stay away from chocolate and have it again, it's amazing.' Pete Way reckons the story would make a great soap opera. He's not wrong.

Michael Schenker: 'Someone in the band told me once, you're so lucky you don't understand what they're saying.'

9/Judas Priest

Metal points: 72

Recommended album: *Screaming For Vengeance* (1982)
3 Top 20 singles ● 5 Top 20 albums

The godfathers of contemporary heavy metal, according to veteran author Malcolm Dome, Judas Priest helped establish the Midlands as the crucible of the movement and gave aggressive hard rock its signature black leather look and twin-guitar roar. The group were formed when guitarist K.K. Downing and bassist Ian Hill decided former choirboy Rob Halford's piercing falsetto, which registered more high Cs than an examination board, would complement their new band. Alongside second guitarist Glenn Tipton and innumerable drummers, they matched cornball lyrics to simple but brutal power chords. And, allegedly, a sense of humour, which they brought to play in their videos in particular. At the peak of their domestic popularity they filmed the incredibly hammy promo for 'Breaking The Law' in a London office Barclays Bank – our leather-bound heroes pushing past security, guitars in hand, before Halford bent back iron bars to enter the safe. From then on, things simply got more extreme. Halford kept upping the ante with studded leather outfits, peaked caps and stacked boots. America loved them. *Screaming For Vengeance* went platinum there in 1982, though they were subsequently sued by the parents of two children who attempted suicide (one died) in 1986 after listening to *Stained Class*. Halford admits that

he was devastated to think that someone could be inspired to kill themselves because of his music. Halford left the band in 1993 and confirmed his widely rumoured homosexuality four years later. The faux macho metal community slammed their knuckles, freshly grazed from trailing along the ground, onto pub tables in outrage, much to Halford's astonishment that his sexuality could be an issue. His former bandmates continued with new vocalist 'Ripper' Owen, recruited from British Steel, a Judas Priest tribute band.

8/Saxon

Metal points: 84

Recommended album: *Wheels Of Steel* (1980) ● 4 Top 20 singles ● 6 Top 20 albums

They came bearing flying V guitars and trousers so tight they reduced circulation more effectively than certain celebrity editors. Barnsley's Saxon were born of the New Wave Of British Heavy Metal (a back-to-basics rock movement that adopted the independent creed of punk) alongside Iron Maiden and Def Leppard. Singer Biff Byford confirms their humble background, pointing out that the band was never into large-scale drug binges. Formed while on the dole, these were real men who wrote songs about real men stuff. They seemed obsessed at one point with transport – be it crashing planes or steam trains. And – big thematic, this – the glory that is rock music and its attendant lifestyle. Despite somewhat unpromising material, signposted by titles such as 'Sixth Form Girls' and 'Just Let Me Rock', Saxon gave audiences a good night out and were a little more tongue-in-cheek than some of their more precious contemporaries. Saxon's more unlikely fans included Sir Elton John, who played piano on *Rock The Nation*'s 'Party Till You Puke' in 1986. However, as contemporary American bands laid waste to trad rock values, Saxon disastrously attempted to crimp their hair and change direction with albums such as 1988's *Destiny* – featuring what some see as a less than adequate version of Christopher Cross's 'Ride Like The Wind'. Byford has since acknowledged the mistake and gone back to what he does best – singing about procuring sexual favours while touring timewarped provincial towns.

7/Motörhead

Metal points: 119

Recommended album: *Ace Of Spades* (1980) ● 4 Top 20 singles ● 6 Top 20 albums

Motörhead were the punks of heavy metal, disinterested in melodic niceties and dismissive of matters such as image or personal grooming. Instead they harnessed their energies to perform a brutal compound of rock 'n' roll at deafening amplification and feverish intensity. They were formed and led by the callused crown prince of rock, Ian 'Lemmy' Kilmister, after stints as a roadie for Jimi Hendrix and bass player for Hawkwind. He met drummer Phil 'Philthy Animal' Taylor in Portobello Road, which formed part of Lemmy's hunting grounds as a professional one-armed bandit player. Guitarist Fast Eddie Clarke's initial impressions on meeting Lemmy were that he was a speed freak with the single-minded notion that sleep was a waste of life. The noise the trio subsequently made was anything but soporific. They were a colourful, mishap-prone bunch. Especially Taylor, who acted like

Keith Moon's wilful younger brother. Lemmy remembers him hurting himself by trying to climb out of his bathroom mirror – he'd drunkenly thought it was a window. On another occasion they played a game which involved lifting band members above each other's head. Taylor fell and broke his neck. As Taylor recalls, 'The doctor said, "You're lucky. The reason you're not paralysed for life, or dead, is that you were so drunk when you hit the floor, you were relaxed."' Live shows offered unparalleled displays of power, Lemmy's ravaged vocal lines powered by two musical likeminds turning in their own warp-drive performances. Motörhead's biggest hit came via a duet with Girlschool, but it was Lemmy's collab-

> **Lemmy:** 'Rock 'n' roll's supposed to take you away from the sh*t job you're in for an hour and a half and make you feel 100 feet tall.'

oration (a cover of 'Stand By Your Man') with punk exhibitionist Wendy O'Williams that pushed Clarke out of the band. Taylor was gone within a year too. Lemmy has persevered with numerous aides since, and he's still doing it to this day, as committed to the rock 'n' roll work ethic as he ever was. 'That's what rock 'n' roll bands are supposed to do, isn't it?' he argues. 'They're not supposed to be bloody political and environmentalist.'

6/Whitesnake

Metal points: 159

Recommended album: *Lovehunter* (1979) ● 6 Top 20 singles ● 8 Top 10 albums

Before leading Whitesnake, David Coverdale spent three years as lead singer for Deep Purple. His former bandmates Jon Lord (keyboards) and Ian Paice (drums) joined him at various points in Whitesnake, alongside guitarists Micky Moody and Bernie Marsden, but keeping track of line-ups proved a fruitless exercise in accountancy. However, Paice maintains that at that time, due in great part to the diversity of characters in the band, Whitesnake was a fun combo to belong to. As the group evolved, their lyrics became increasingly fixated with double entendres, while Jon Lord reckoned Coverdale's emphatically enunciated vocals had taken on a bizarre, Roger Moore-of-rock hue. Still, almost everyone focused on the sex angle, which wasn't hard given song titles such as 'Slide It In', the title track of their 1984 album. Coverdale explored his lusts to such a degree that even his band got restless at the 'crassness' of the lyrical content, criticisms Coverdale is happy to shrug off. He never claimed to be Shakespeare, is his riposte. The British press were rarely kind to the band. Coverdale is bemused by this, maintaining that he can't have slept with their wives, or anything. Soon the original members had left, and Whitesnake turned into a bombastic pop-rock act that sold millions of records in America. Dame serpent has drooped somewhat since, however, leaving Coverdale to work with guitarist Jimmy Page.

5/Rainbow

Metal points: 164

Recommended album: *Rainbow Rising* (1976) ● 4 Top 20 singles ● 9 Top 20 albums

As a child, Ritchie Blackmore had tried a number of pursuits before rapidly abandoning them, so when his father bought him a guitar, it came with a blunt imperative – if he didn't

learn to play it, Blackmore Senior would break it over his son's skull. Blackmore Junior's cranium has escaped parental rebuke, though he has retained his father's rigid sense of purpose. After leaving Deep Purple in 1975 the virtuoso guitarist formed Rainbow by recruiting Purple's support band Elf, minus the guitarist. In the process he got the singer he wanted, Elf's Ronnie James Dio. Blackmore then sacked everyone except Dio and hired a new team, including legendary drummer Cozy Powell. Former Deep Purple bass player Roger Glover was added, precipitating the dismissal of Dio, who claims that Roger was Ritchie's conduit, remembering Roger asking him on Ritchie's behalf if he could write some love songs instead of his more fantasy-oriented material. Dio left the band immediately. Blackmore defends the constant search for perfection that rendered Rainbow's line-ups so unstable, even suggesting that a dissatisfaction with his own abilities may have caused him to embark on a doomed search for perfection in others. New singer Graham Bonnet was a bit of a shock for diehard fans – he looked more like a marine than a rocker, and confessed he'd never heard of Rainbow. 'I was more into the R&B kind of thing and pop stuff,' he says. Despite big hits with 'Since You've Been Gone' and 'All Night Long', Powell and Bonnet were soon out of the band. Bonnet maintains he'd walked and wasn't sacked. Next up behind the microphone was Joe Lynn Turner. He sang on Rainbow's biggest hit, 1981's 'I Surrender'. Three years later, Blackmore sacked everyone again and reformed Deep Purple, temporarily. These days he's happy leading the New York renaissance music unit Blackmore's Night. Playing the lute.

4/Def Leppard

Metal points: 204

Recommended album: *Pyromania* (1983) ● 12 Top 20 singles ● 7 Top 20 albums

Beginning life rehearsing on the top floor of a Sheffield spoon factory in 1979, Def Leppard were the whippersnappers of the New Wave Of British Heavy Metal Movement. Singer Joe Elliott, whose father fronted the £150 to finance their first record, puts their success down to sheer blind faith in their own talent. After recording their debut disc, they placed an advert in a local music paper, 'Leppard Loses Skins', and drummer Rick Allen joined the band, which also comprised Pete Willis (guitar), Steve Clark (guitar) and Rick Savage (bass). Allen was amazed when his parents agreed to let him leave school early to join, but by his sixteenth birthday his career choice was vindicated as Def Leppard secured the support slot to AC/DC at Hammersmith Odeon. Their debut album reached the Top 20, but it was with second effort *High 'n' Dry*, produced by Mutt Lange, that they got the formula right. His input, acknowledged by the band as that of unofficial sixth member, helped them turn the corner. Willis was replaced by Phil Collen in time for 1983's *Pyromania*, again produced by Lange, which reached number two in the US charts. They'd 'arrived'. Then, on New Year's Eve 1984, Allen was involved in a high-speed accident in his Corvette Stingray that resulted in his left arm being ripped off. After deciding he didn't know how to do anything else apart from drum, he convinced a sceptical band to persevere with him. Elliot confesses that Allen's unbridled enthusiasm for continuing made the rest of them feel that they simply couldn't abandon him. Allen worked out a computer-enabled method of keeping time with his right arm, using his right foot on a conventional bass drum

and his left playing the snare drum or toms, as required. By August 1987 Def Leppard and Allen were a going concern again, and *Hysteria* surpassed everyone's expectations by selling 10 million copies. Four years later Steve Clark died after an alcoholic bender, aged just thirty. The remaining quartet pulled together to finish new album *Adrenalize* and looked for another guitarist who liked soccer and Monty Python. Their ideal replacement turned out to be Vivian Campbell, formerly of Whitesnake. And, despite their fair share of adversity, Def Leppard remain one of Britain's most successful rock exports.

3/Deep Purple   Metal points: 215

Recommended album: *Machine Head* (1972) ● 3 Top 20 singles ● 13 Top 20 albums

Ritchie Blackmore recalls seeing Robert Plant of Led Zeppelin for the first time and realizing that his band couldn't possibly compete unless they found a singer who could scream as well as the lion-maned one. Fortunately, they found someone who was a pretty nifty singer too: Ian Gillan. Deep Purple had previously been an underachieving (one US hit single aside) concern. But when Gillan and bass player Roger Glover arrived, their fortunes took a dramatic upswing. With Jon Lord on keyboards and Ian Paice on drums, the new line-up made their debut in the summer of 1969. They soon became the biggest rock act on the planet via albums such as *Deep Purple In Rock* (1970), *Fireball* (1971) and *Machine Head* (1972). 'The chemistry required to make a band work, would be the kind of chemistry that would be positively dangerous in a laboratory,' Lord muses. That wasn't the only chemistry going on, however. As Gillan notes, they were five guys off council estates with a lot of money in their pockets who'd had their egos inflated beyond reason. Purple's defining moment came when the band were watching Frank Zappa play his set in Montreux. Someone fired a flare gun into the ceiling, the casino was set alight and thick clouds of smoke crept out over Lake Geneva. The sight inspired 'Smoke On The Water', a song which subsequently became the first hurdle for any aspirant metal guitarist. However, tricky old Ritchie was proving problematic to work with. He admits that when he feels a band member is slacking, or he disagrees with them, he prefers to retire and sulk rather than thrash things out. Gillan detested the focus on hit records and left in 1973, followed shortly by Glover.

Ian Gillan: 'I literally had tears running down my face the first night at the Speakeasy [at Deep Purple's debut]. 'I thought, this is it. This is what I've been looking for.'

David Coverdale came in as singer, and the band went on to further success and excess. In 1975 Blackmore left to form Rainbow, the remaining members persevering for another year. They were offered $2 million a man to reform in 1984, did so, and have kept reforming on and off ever since.

2/Black Sabbath & Ozzy Osbourne   Metal points: 237

Recommended album: *Paranoid* (1970) ● 3 Top 20 singles ● 18 Top 20 albums

Black metal from the Black Country, the members of Black Sabbath grew up in grinding poverty. Not least singer Ozzy Osbourne, who remembers his parents having a can

of Heinz soup in a saucepan next to a pan of water to make it go further. In 1970 the band gave metal a dark twist, with Tony Iommi providing the bludgeoning guitar, backed up by drummer Bill Ward and bass player 'Geezer' Butler. Their eponymous debut album was littered with occult references and brain-smelting riffs. The follow-up, *Paranoid*, was even more ferocious – its title-track and the insistent 'War Pigs' being the other stand-out. By 1978, after five further albums, Ozzy increasingly dependent on drugs and drink, bust up with the band. He was replaced by Ronnie James Dio of Rainbow, who had the unenviable task of facing audiences who would hold up signs with 'Ozzy, Ozzy, Ozzy' written on them. Dio eventually walked after Iommi accused him of remixing a live album to highlight his own vocals. He was replaced by a succession of vocalists including Ian Gillan. Ozzy's solo career took off in grand style with 1980's *Blizzard Of Oz*, though he was already becoming increasingly erratic. Manager and wife Sharon remembers him disappearing for days on end on the pretext of popping out for a drink. Then came the notorious incident in which he bit the head off a live bat. This ill-advised act encouraged fans turn up at gigs with animal carcasses of every variety and throw them on stage. However, Ozzy changed his ways with the arrival of his family. (His son once asked him if was true he got everybody in his audience to spit in a bowl and then drank it on stage. Sadly, it was not.) In 1999 he rejoined the original Black Sabbath line-up. Thirty million record sales later, he's not finished with us yet.

1/Iron Maiden
Metal points: 441

Recommended album: *The Number Of The Beast* (1982)
20 Top 20 singles ● 14 Top 20 albums

West Ham's finest, and premiership graduates of the New Wave Of British Heavy Metal, Iron Maiden starting out playing small pubs in the East End of London A good night would result in a £25 fee and half a lager per band member. After several line-up shuffles, the group's first success arrived with 'Running Free' in 1980, which secured that vital first *Top Of The Pops* appearance (refusing to mime, they were the first band to play live on the show since 1973). However, just as the band began to establish itself, it became obvious that singer Paul Di'anno's interest was waning. In particular, he was unhappy with the constant touring – the main reason the other members formed the band. Bruce Dickinson of Samson, a private school-educated history graduate, didn't need to be asked twice. With Dickinson's cavalier vocals lending the band an extra dimension, plus astute marketing (a mention here for cartoon mascot Eddie), the group formed an indelible bond with their audience. They put a lot of personal money into supporting elaborate tours, and didn't blow their royalties on traditional rock 'n' roll lifestyles. Manager Rod Smallwood recalls that when *Number Of The Beast* was standing at the top spot in the UK charts, bass player Steve Harris came up to him at the Marquee and told him that they couldn't afford to buy a round; they were getting £60 a week at the time. Such fiscal shortcomings were soon atoned for as the band racked up worldwide sales in excess of 50 million. One of the reasons for their longevity could be their relative temperance. Rather than improving Bolivia's foreign trade

deficit, Iron Maiden simply ordered a couple of crates of Ruddles and had the football results phoned over. Steve Harris has never even tried a cigarette in his life. After twelve years, although their success was hardly slowing, Dickinson, with interests in fencing, flying and novels, called it quits in 1993. The rest of the band weren't surprised so much by Dickinson's decision as by his timing: they had a tour to complete. Dickinson finished the tour playing to bemused and distraught fans, before setting out on his solo career. In came former Wolfsbane singer Blaze Bayley, and while the band's activities continued unabated, their fanbase diminished steadily. It surprised no-one when it was announced that Dickinson (and guitarist Adrian Smith) would rejoin for a 1999 comeback tour. What no-one had expected was that Iron Maiden would raise $30 million in a bond issue of share certificates in its back catalogue.

Ten Who Missed The Cut & Their Finest Albums

Diamond Head: *Lightning To The Nations* (1980)
Demon: *The Unexpected Guest* (1982)
Venom: *Welcome To Hell* (1981)
Napalm Death: *From Enslavement To Obliteration* (1988)
Girlschool: *Screaming Blue Murder* (1982)
Thunder: *Back Street Symphony* (1990)
Magnum: *On A Storyteller's Night* (1985)
Gillan: *Glory Road* (1980)
Quireboys: *A Bit Of What You Fancy* (1989)
Little Angels: *Young Gods* (1991)

Boy Bands

Ladies of a certain age may have used their undergarments as tokens of esteem with which to acknowledge the inestimable brilliance of Tom Jones, but the sphere of hardcore, hysterical pop adulation has always been the preserve of the teenage girl. At various moments in pop history they have formed an audience so loyal, fawning and profitable that the systematic record company milking of them has become a modern art form. Indeed, the ingenuity of industry moguls in recruiting teenage consumers using good-looking but vacant youths as decoys is one of the foundation stones of contemporary capitalism, never mind the record industry.

As former *Smash Hits* editor Kate Thornton notes: 'Boy bands come along in a girl's life when she is at her most vulnerable and hormonal.' Not to mention at a point when her tastes are, if not completely indiscriminate, certainly wayward. Undeniably the artistic dregs of contemporary music, for boy band read pretty boy pop, a manufactured entity designed with the sole purpose of making money. That some of these unholy creations have gone on to exhibit charm or skill as songwriters is merely a by-product of the intensive farming of the country's stage schools and aspirations.

Pity, too, the adult that must eventually emerge from any boy band. Much as each is seduced by the idea of a secure fanbase, and a future cushioned by adulation, all ultimately fall fast and hard – destined to become the subject of mocking press reports as they slide down the celebrity ladder. Their final humiliations can be so absolute as to be almost biblical. But let's not forget that teenmania played a large part in forging the identities of rock and pop's two most lasting icons – the Beatles and Elvis Presley. To stretch the point, people may consider Gary Barlow's 'Back For Good' a pop classic to rival anything in the Motown canon in thirty years' time. And, if pop music ever stops concerning itself with libido and adolescence, it will cease to be pop music.

10/Curiosity Killed The Cat

Points: 92

5 Top 20 hits

First spotted at a King's Road pizza restaurant by manager Peter Rosengard (later an award-winning insurance salesman), Curiosity Killed The Cat were led by Ben Volpeliere-Pierrot. His tastes in headwear were as outlandish as his appellation, and predicted Jamiroquai's fashion sense by a decade. Julian Brookhouse, Nick Thorpe and Michael Drummond completed the line-up. Andy Warhol directed the video to 'Misfit' after the band gatecrashed his London exhibition and cheekily offered to work with him as fellow artists. Ben admits that their following comprised 'posh totty' (a group of West London girls) and 'posh whatnots' (West London guys). Pretty much a West London fanbase, then. After five Top 40 singles, CKTC's career slide was dramatic. They famously took acid on a Timmy Mallett kids TV show, and shortly thereafter bass player Nick left the band to pursue family life. The band all contributed to the songwriting and had made a pact that if one of their number left, they would no longer be Curiosity Killed The Cat. Instead, after Nick's departure they stumbled on as the abbreviated Curiosity. The absolute nadir followed on a *Jim'll Fix It* appearance: Ben shared the stage with a teenager called Caroline from Surrey who said that she wanted to dance like him. The whole band looked thoroughly embarrassed throughout. Curiosity departed the scene, only to re-emerge – Ben now shaven-headed – in the nineties playing the National Lottery show. But as he admits, nobody phoned up after their performance offering to help them stage a comeback...

9/Monkees

Points: 141

7 Top 20 hits ● 1 No.1

The Monkees were a pop confection created by producers Bob Rafelson and Bert Schneider in 1965 in order to steal some of the Beatles' thunder. There were 437 applicants for four roles. The rumour that Charles Manson was turned down may have been a hoax, but the story that Stephen Stills was rejected due to his bad teeth rings true. Instead, wool-hatted Mike Nesmith was joined by chirpy Brit Davey Jones, already a successful singer, ex-star child actor Mickey Dolenz and fellow folk troubadour Peter Tork. Don Kirschner was drafted in to oversee a production run of teen-friendly anthems, including 'Last Train To Clarksville' (like the Monkees' theme tune, written by Tommy Boyce and Bobby Hart). For a three-year period their sterling musical output (despite rumours they didn't play on the finished studio versions) belied their nerdy TV personalities. By 1968 they had fired Kirschner, electing to write more of their own material (Dolenz came up with the wonderfully titled 'Randy Scouse Git' – aka 'Alternate Title' – after watching Warren Mitchell's foul-mouthed character Alf Garnett on British TV) but the TV show was axed. Tork wanted to write 'proper' music (though his main gig these days is as a cabaret artist on cruise liners). Nesmith inherited his mother's liquid paper patent and the fortune that went with it. Dolenz produced a series of TV shows, including *Metal Mickey*.

And Davey Jones, formerly a failed jockey, achieved his lifetime's ambition by partnering the winner of the 3.15 at Lingfield on 1 February 1996.

8/Osmonds
Points: 155

6 Top 20 hits ● 1 No.1

The Osmonds left huge teethmarks in the pop pie of the seventies via the kind of overbite that would have kept the entire metalworking industry of America in overtime, should corrective braces have been employed. This strict Mormon concern from Utah sought to bring Christian values to the merciless exploitation of teenage girls that boy bands had previously conspired in. They were discovered on Andy Williams' US TV show, and were thereafter promoted as a white alternative to the all-conquering Jackson 5. Comprising brothers Alan, Wayne, Jay, Merrill and lil' old Donny, they were dedicated to wholesome family entertainment. What they couldn't have anticipated was the way fans hungered for their pop flesh – to the extent that security guards who came between them were subjected to bites, punches and gouges. Wayne remembers one occasion on which two girls attempted to nail themselves to the band in a coffin-shaped box. But as strict Mormons all, our heroes were never to be tempted by the sins of all that teenage flesh. Amazingly, authorities in South Africa banned their signature song, 'Crazy Horses', because they thought it was a eulogy to heroin. The band's success wound down when mums' favourite Donny – who scored a UK number one with the mushy 'Puppy Love' – also became the fans' favourite. Little Jimmy also scored his own number one. In the nineties Donny was to be found on stage in Broadway playing Joseph, while his brothers set up a family theatre in Missouri to promote God's own entertainment values.

7/New Kids On The Block
Points: 225

11 Top 20 hits ● 2 No.1s

Previously svengali Maurice Starr had achieved chart success with another quintet, New Edition. But when Bobby Brown and his bandmates splintered for solo careers he struck up a relationship with five white guys from a tough Boston neighbourhood. (In the process, he was called by the FBI, who asked him why he'd given his phone number to a young boy in a Massachusetts flower shop.) Donnie Wahlberg, Danny Wood, Joey McIntyre and brothers Jordan Knight and Jonathan Knight were duly recruited. PA engagements and a debut album for CBS that apparently sold only 5,000 copies failed to inspire interest, though Starr remained convinced of the group's long-term appeal. He was proved right in March 1989

Joey McIntyre: 'On the road we had a tape. When the tape went bad, we went to the store and bought another tape.'

when '(You Got It) The Right Stuff' reached the US Top 3 and the group became a teen phenomenon. However, the group members' contributions to the music they produced was openly questioned. McIntyre is adamant that the boys were on the records, although

conceding that they employed a tape for live performances. Bolstered by a stream of hits, the band split from Starr and thereafter hardly shifted a single record. Relaunched under the acronym NKOTB, like so many declining boy bands their demise was confirmed by a horrible children's TV reckoning – flummoxing Andi Peters with their drunken behaviour on the set of *Live And Kicking*. Jordan has a successful solo career, while Donny now earns a crust as an actor, recently appearing in *Sixth Sense* as the loony who shoots Bruce Willis at the start of the film.

6/Bros
Points: 227

10 Top 20 hits ● 1 No.1

If tabloid pop writer Rick Sky calls you 'naff', you know you've got problems. If your manager says his first impressions of you were that you were arrogant, illiterate, pompous and naive, your name is Bros. Formed by identical twins Luke and Matt Goss and augmented by unprepossessing schoolmate Craig Logan, the trio were rescued from obscurity by Tom Watkins, who moulded the blond twins into contemporary Aryan youths – though there was little anyone could do with poor old Craig, who ruined the group's symmetry. Watkins insisted that they perform a song called 'When Will I Be Famous?', written with his musical collaborator Nicky Graham. The hit that resulted gave birth to Brosmania and the group became the teen sensations of 1988. Some said Matt had a good voice (true) and that Luke was a good drummer (contested). But the boys themselves were very much secondary factors in the construction of the group's chart fodder. On the back of their considerable success they apparently became increasingly self-deluded about their own talents and decided they'd write their own songs for a projected second album. The story goes that when Tom Watkins heard the results of Matt's songwriting sessions, he balked and immediately started looking for the next teen sensation to mastermind. The two parties become embroiled in expensive court proceedings, a situation exacerbated by the fact that the boys seemed to have been spending like the clappers. Schadenfreude filled the air as tabloid headlines guffawed at Bros's inability to settle credit card bills. Craig, meanwhile, got a £1-million handshake and now runs a successful production and management company, thereby having the last laugh several times over.

Nicky Graham: 'Luke would come into the studio, hear how things were going, get into the little Jeep he'd just bought, go up the King's Road and pose for a bit, come back to the studio and say, "Wow!"'

5/East 17
Points: 276

14 Top 20 hits ● 1 No.1

From Walthamstow via the Bronx, or so they might have you believe, East 17 came bedecked in baggy clothes and ready-for-it attitude – this time round Tom Watkins had found charges of more substance than Bros. With the impish Brian Harvey providing lead vocals and Tony Mortimer the songs, everyone tended to overlook poor old Terry and John as anonymous stage-fillers. The quartet launched their career with 1992's 'House Of Love' – Mortimer's response to the Gulf War. He wanted to put some intelligence into

Tony Mortimer: 'No boy band ever, ever partied like we did.'

the lyrics, though Harvey was content simply to do some R&B. Watkins was determined to mould the group as the 'street' answer to Take That; *Smash Hits* editor Kate Thornton recalls that although East 17 were regarded by some as the 'mongrels' of the boy band

Tom Watkins: 'Take That went to bed with coathangers in their mouths to wake up with smiles the next morning. East 17 went to bed with any young lady that was available to them.'

world, they had an edge that Take That lacked. For a time, especially when they reached the Christmas number one spot in 1994 with 'Stay Another Day', it seemed they may even surpass the yardstick Watkins had set them. Mortimer was proving an able writer, although output was sometimes irregular. However, the band were never destined for the straight and

narrow path demarcated for boy bands. Harvey, prompted by a journalist, confessed to the ingestion of large quantities of ecstasy and called the drug 'safe'. The tabloids descended. Loyal to a fault, Watkins told the rest of the band that they had to choose between Harvey and him. Harvey left, then rejoined, but East 17's moment had passed. Mortimer wanted time away from the pressures of stardom – which he has surely attained – though both he and Harvey remain active in the music business.

Tony Mortimer: 'I prefer writing ballads. They're easy to write. They're slow, there are hardly any words, the melodies are drawn out and before you know it, you're at the end of three and a half minutes.'

4/Bay City Rollers

Points: 278

11 Top 20 hits ● 2 No.1s

Brothers Alan Longmuir and Derek Longmuir formed the Bay City Rollers in Edinburgh, under the patronage of manager Tam Paton, in 1967. Four years of ill-paid club slog finally paid off when they hit the Top 10 with 'Keep On Dancing' in 1971. Eric Faulkner,

Eric Faulkner: 'I was on the beach fishing once. I saw this guy in the water, and he was ready to jump. He looked like he'd had enough of it. I went in and pulled him back out. "You think you've got problems, mate. I used to be a Bay City Roller!"'

Stuart Wood and Leslie McKeown joined between 1972 and 1973. Apparently, even at the outset there were tensions; McKeown's first impression of his fellow band-mates was that they were all 'tossers', but the band hit its stride with 'Remember (Sha La La)'. The mid-seventies were dominated

Journalist Julie Burchill: 'They didn't look like humans. They looked like foetuses. I felt physically ill when I saw them on TV.'

by hoary rock bands and the only alternative for teenagers, previous to the Scottish five-piece, were the Osmonds. The Rollers' gimmick of trimming denim with tartan caught on with the nation's youth, who suddenly turned into extras from *Braveheart*. Their appeal was a mystery to many, but the hits continued to pour in and the boys even got their own

TV show – *Shang-A-Lang* – and secured an American number one with 'Saturday Night'. But then it all went horribly wrong. Faulkner took too many downers one night at Tam Paton's house and overdosed. Paton phoned the newspapers before he thought to contact the emergency services. Then, McKeown ran over a pensioner. The group trundled on until

Journalist Caroline Sullivan: 'They were soft and cuddly. You could imagine bringing them home to meet your mother. And while they were there, they'd probably help with your homework.'

Former manager Tam Paton, on the Bay City Rollers' ongoing attempt to recoup money from him: 'They can shove it where the monkeys shove their nuts.'

the tensions found release during an on-stage fist fight in Japan. That was it. Approximately 100 million records sold, nothing to show for it; they're still trying to recover the money from Paton.

3/Wham!

Points: 297

11 Top 20 hits ● 4 No.1s

Rick Sky thinks Simon Napier-Bell's intention with Wham! was to create a kind of Butch Cassidy and the Sundance Kid of Eighties pop; Julie Burchill thinks their appeal rested in the frisson of sexual tension created by young guns Andrew Ridgeley and George Michael. With the latter a fully-fledged mainstream pop star these days, it's easy to forget how important the launchpad was. Backing singer Shirlie Kemp recalls that George really needed Andrew, Pepsi De Marque (her fellow backing singer) and herself in those early days, because of his initial lack of self-confidence. In the face of expanding dole queues and economic austerity, Wham! showered fans in party invites. 'Club Tropicana' was the spiritual theme for the Club 18–30 generation, celebrating escapism and sexual indulgence – a song that rejoiced in the claim that there was enough for everyone when, in the Britain of 1983, there clearly wasn't. While Michael's role was readily apparent, some began to question just what contribution Mr Ridgeley was making beyond picking up royalty cheques and playing a guitar that roadies would routinely unplug on stage. Napier-Bell was holding back an old Michael/Ridgeley collaboration, 'Careless Whisper', perhaps realizing that its release could start the countdown on Wham!'s final dissolution, as it was clearly going to be dominated by a huge vocal from Michael, with little for Ridgeley to contribute. Wham! persevered for a while, becoming major pop stars in China. But by 1986 Michael had split the band. It's fair to say he's enjoyed by far the greater solo success since. Ridgeley leads a pleasant enough life with Keren Woodward of Bananarama as part of the Cornwall surfing community.

2/Take That

Points: 409

14 Top 20 hits ● 8 No.1s

The magic of Take That, according to manager Nigel Martin-Smith, can be attributed to the unique blend of personalities involved. He put them together after first encountering Curtis

Rush – aka songwriter Gary Barlow – playing the northern working men's club circuit. Gary was the solid one; Mark Owen was the small, pretty one; Jason Orange and Howard Donald were there to appeal to the older woman; and Robbie Williams was the naughty wisecracker. Martin-Smith remortgaged his house to finance a record called 'Do What You Like' which was accompanied by a risqué, buttock-baring video and Nick Raymond duly signed them up to RCA. The first three singles flopped, and they were apparently about to be dropped before recording a version of the Tavares' hit, 'It Only Takes A Minute'. The boys' female following was augmented by the 'pink pound' of a large gay constituency to produce a powerful commercial package. A succession of number one singles – 'Pray', 'Relight My Fire' and 'Babe' – ensued, before Take That became international stars with 1995's 'Back For Good', written very much with America in mind. It topped charts in 26 countries. Ironically, Barlow had by now realized that the group had served its purpose, and could envisage a split just around the corner. Robbie trumped any separation in July. The country went into a period of national mourning when, in February 1996, a press conference announced the split. The Samaritans were deluged with calls from suicidal teenage fans. Robbie became tabloid fodder before making the step from pop star to rock star. Barlow also put out an album, then sat back on his considerable royalties, but it's Robbie Williams who remains the people's choice of all the Take That graduates.

Nigel Martin-Smith on Robbie's departure: 'He got the sympathy vote that "I was in this horrible machine that made me millions of pounds and turned me into a star and gave me the opportunity to do what I've always wanted to do – but it's been *awful*." What b*****ks!'

1/Boyzone

Points: 525

17 Top 20 hits ● 6 No.1s

When Take That splintered in 1996, it left a big hole in the pop marketplace. Enter Boyzone. Louis Walsh – directly inspired by Take That – was determined to fill the void with a cast of good-looking Irish boys. Amazingly, they would go on to surpass the attainments of their inspiration. An audition of 150 boys unearthed Ronan Keating and Stephen Gately as the core of the group, around which the remaining three members – Shane Lynch, Mikey Graham and Keith Duffy – were built. Almost immediately, the fledgling group was booked on *The Late Late Show with Gay Byrne* – a now famous televisual debacle where the group did their best to 'exert' themselves to a backing track. Touring Ireland was hardly a peachy job either, as every night they faced not only the girls at the front of the stage, but also their boyfriends. They were not averse to throwing a bottle or two, or even spitting, at the pop hopefuls. The group were rescued by 'Love Me For A Reason', their 1994 breakthrough. It was the first of a sequence of hyper-successful cover versions. Jimmy Osmond regards the cover as a great piece of flattery, though the boys claimed they'd stamped their own identity on it. 'Baby Can I Hold You' (Tracy Chapman), 'Words' (the Bee Gees) and, most unlikely of all, Cat Stevens' 'Father And Son' followed. Critics scoffed that they couldn't write their own tunes; neither could Sinatra or Presley, came the rehearsed replies. Boyzone were, it was claimed, boring to a fault. Then came Gately's confirmation – allegedly under 'speak up or let us tell the story' tabloid thumb-

screws – that he was gay. Courageously, he did so and the group's success continued unabated, with a further cover version, 'When The Going Gets Tough' topping the charts in 1999. Since then the group has elected to pursue a variety of solo projects, as rumours about their imminent demise continue to circulate.

The Ringo Link

Every boy band is populated with pretty faces. But some distinctly ordinary Joes snuck in when no-one was looking, allowing temporary pauses for breath between fans' shrieking fits.

10 Curiosity Killed The Cat
That Caroline from Surrey was pretty frightening.

9 Monkees
Micky Dolenz looked like he'd come off the set of *Planet Of The Apes*.

8 Osmonds
Loveable Jimmy was always the most unforgivably toothsome.

7 New Kids On The Block
Danny Wood on a points decision.

6 Bros
Craig. By a country mile.

5 East 17
Brian Harvey. Looked like something you might find
in trap three at Walthamstow dog track.

4 Bay City Rollers
All five of them.

3 Wham!
Too close to call.

2 Take That
Sorry Gary.

1 Boyzone
Regardless of sexuality, Mr Gately would have been hard pressed to get a
snog at the office Christmas party, while Mikey would have been ugly as
a tyre-fitter, never mind a member of a boy band.

Electro-pop

In 1964 Robert Moog designed a 'transistorized machine', the first workable synthesizer, in collaboration with Walter Carlos. His *Switched On Bach* album was composed entirely on the instrument. Though the synth was employed extensively by several rock groups, it was Brian Eno of Roxy Music who realized the eponymously titled Moog offered possibilities beyond that of an adjunctive keyboard. So too did Stevie Wonder, while both the Beatles and Mick Jagger also purchased Moogs. The other principle forefathers of the electro-pop scene of the early eighties are Germany's Kraftwerk. Their 1974 hit 'Autobahn' predicted the accented melody and minimalist approach favoured by so many electro-pop outfits. But the genre only matured when drum machines (first effectively showcased in the disco idiom by George McRae's 'Rock You Baby') were added. Thereafter Giorgio Moroder's pioneering work on Donna Summer disco hits such as 'I Feel Love' brought the various threads together.

The term electro-pop, with its modernist implications, belies the fact that most of the artists here wrote in a classical songwriting vein, albeit with new instruments. Some argued that synthesizers compromised musical standards – the Musician's Union launched a facile 'keep music live' campaign to that effect. While it was certainly true you no longer had to 'learn' an instrument in a conventional fashion, the synthesizer also liberated musicians by allowing them to concentrate on basic songwriting principles. The artists are ranked according to UK record sales. See also our accompanying eighties new romantic chapter for bands such as ABC and Spandau Ballet, who straddled both genres.

10/Bronski Beat

Points: 95

Recommended album: *The Age Of Consent* (1984)

Led by diminutive Glaswegian Jimmy Somerville's distinctive soprano, Bronski Beat had an explicit sexual as well as musical agenda. Their breakthrough hit, 1984's 'Smalltown

Boy', documented the travails of a young man escaping homophobic thuggery in the provinces. The music borrowed heavily from the Euro disco innovations of Giorgio Moroder that were adored by the gay scene. And if anyone was in any doubt about where Bronski Beat were coming from, their label was called Forbidden Fruit. Backed by fellow Glaswegian Steve Bronski and Londoner Larry Steinbeck on synthesizers, the group followed its initial success with another didactic track, 'Why?', which brought them a second Top 10 hit. Again, it was notable for Somerville's piercing vocal track. Somerville's conviction for gross indecency in February 1985 further fuelled his accusations of hypocrisy levelled at Thatcherite society's curtain-twitching morality. Bronski Beat took the challenge further with *Age Of Consent*, the album's title addressing the glaring legal inequality faced by young homosexuals, but Somerville's political emphasis was beginning to alienate his musical collaborators. Bronski admits that the rest of the band wouldn't join Somerville on demonstrations, preferring instead to stay at home and smoke. After deliberately covering Donna Summer's 'I Feel Love' (a version that featured Marc Almond and also sampled Summer's 'Love To Love You Baby') in the light of her alleged comments about homosexuals, Somerville, who by now was beginning to look more and more like a miniature Phil Mitchell from *EastEnders*, left to form chart-toppers the Communards. Apparently the final straw was Bronski's admission that he intended to vote SDP at the forthcoming election. The remaining members recruited new vocalist John Jon and enjoyed a number three hit with safe sex song 'Hit That Perfect Beat' before sinking into obscurity.

9/Thompson Twins
Points: 159

Recommended album: *Into The Gap* (1984)

With a name inspired by characters from Herge's Tin Tin cartoon, this initially experimental trio was formed in Chesterfield in 1977 by vocalist Tom Bailey and friends Pete Dodd and John Roog. 'We were living in squats, we didn't have any money or any equipment apart from what we made or stole. It was ferociously alternative lifestyle statement stuff,' reflects Bailey. After relocating to London in 1980 they picked up drummer Chris Bell, then percussionist Joe Leeway and Alannah Currie on percussion and saxophone. The music was wilfully experimental, often improvised, and debut album *A Product Of Participation* in 1981 won glowing reviews but few sales. It was only when they secured the services of producer Steve Lillywhite that the group blossomed. Second album *Set* housed the minor hit single 'In The Name Of Love', which became a major dance hit in America. But before they travelled there to capitalize on its success, the group trimmed to a trio of Bailey, Currie and Leeway. It was in this formation that they enjoyed success as a singles band, a run that began with 'Love On Your Side' in 1983, taken from the number two album *Quick Step & Side-Kick*. That was the first of five Top 10 hits, which included 'We Are Detective' and more conventional offerings 'Hold Me Now', 'Doctor Doctor' and 'You Take Me Up'. Released over a fourteen-month period, the one thing each had in common was a hook line hammered home by repetition. Attendant album *Into The Gap* topped the UK charts. Frankie Goes To Hollywood cruelly rechristened them the

'Thompson Twats' on the door of their *Top Of The Pops* dressing room, and they weren't their only critics. 'It was just a really awful reaction, people saw it as a serious thing, they didn't see the irony, they didn't see it as a joke,' laments Currie. Thereafter they never caught sight of the Top 10 again, though Bailey did provide keyboards on Foreigner's chart-topper 'I Want To Know What Love Is'. He collapsed from exhaustion in the mid-eighties after two years of solid touring, while Leeway had left by December 1986. 'We were fighting for our ideas before, and the fight for your ideas wasn't there any more,' he surmises.

Tom Bailey: 'We had a strange paranoia that we'd be found out for the shallow charlatan that we really were. We really weren't good enough to be adored by so many millions of people.'

'We should have left when Joe left,' Currie admits. Currie and Bailey had their first child together in 1988, and by 1996 the duo had regrouped as Babble, after relocating to Currie's native New Zealand to share domestic bliss on a farm. Ahhh. 'We didn't really deserve to be that successful,' reflects Bailey today. 'It became an embarrassing thing.'

8/New Order
Points: 195

Recommended album: *Brotherhood* (1986)

Mancunians New Order rose from the tragic wreckage of Joy Division, the definitive post-punk band whose troubled singer Ian Curtis hanged himself in May 1980. After a stuttering start they went on to progress from moody, melodic electronica to dance-literate indie kids, a fascinating and often compelling journey. Founding Joy Division members Pete Hook (bass), Bernard Sumner (guitars) and Stephen Morris (drums) decided to recruit the latter's girlfriend, Gillian Gilbert, as keyboard player rather than opt for an established local musician. Rightly, they thought that would keep the group dynamic intact. After initial misgivings, Sumner took over as vocalist. Their debut single 'Procession' could have been ripped straight from Joy Division's songbook, but increasingly their material added buoyancy and texture, Hook's low-slung bass playing providing luxuriant melodies, aided by Bernard's frenetic washboard rhythm guitar. In 1983 they recorded what was then the best-selling 12-inch single of all time – 'Blue Monday' – an extraordinary marriage of yearning vocals (actually helped by Sumner's somewhat overreaching amateurishness), keyboards and an explosive drum break. From then on New Order perfected the disco sound it was OK for white indie kids to like, working with Arthur Baker on 'Confusion' (a song that reached the US R&B charts) and then cutting imaginative singles such as 'Bizarre Love Triangle'. They also collaborated on what many considered the first ever decent footy tune, 'World In Motion' – a number one single with the English football squad (including a John Barnes rap). Eventually the members split off to pursue personal projects – Sumner took up with Johnny Marr to form Electronic, Hook (who had married comedienne Caroline Aherne) to Revenge and Monaco, the other two forming, presciently, The Other Two. They reconvened to cut a track for the soundtrack to Leonardo DiCaprio's *The Beach*.

7/Gary Numan
Points: 197

Recommended album: *The Pleasure Principle* (1979)

There is a corner of the *Top Of The Pops* studio that will remain forever Numanoid, wise men say. A sanctuary where Gary Webb, of Hammersmith, London, is venerated as the leather-clad sci-fi sex god some maintain he truly is. Numan took his name from a telephone directory before forming punk band Meanstreet. Then he discovered synthesizers.

'A massive, thundering, huge bass sound came out of it. It just blew my head off. It was one of those Eureka! moments. Wow, that's it!' He subsequently founded Tubeway Army with the assistance of Paul Gardiner and his uncle, Gerald Lidyard. A self-titled debut album was released to little impact, until the

> **Gerald Lidyard, Gary Numan's uncle:**
> 'I distinctly remember him telling me when he was fourteen that he had this record that was going to make him very famous. It was called "Cars" but he didn't know what it was going to sound like yet.'

extracted single, the electronic alienation mantra 'Are Friends Electric?', was released. Densely atmospheric, without any hint of a pop sensibility, it was one of the least likely number ones in chart history. Thereafter Numan threw the Tubeway Army sobriquet aside and released signature song 'Cars' under his own name. Numan claims it was actually written about a road rage incident, and describes how he felt cocooned in his automobile during the ensuing fracas. Both the single and attendant album *The Pleasure Principle* reached the top of the UK charts. Numanoids, as his fans were collectively nouned, multiplied like laboratory mice. It wasn't all fun, however. 'People think you're surrounded by young girls that are falling over themselves all the time,' he says. 'It's not like that at all. You're surrounded by blokes who'd like to take a swing at you given half a chance.' Numan's success had somehow conjured a tidal wave of antipathy. At one point his father had a petrol bomb placed under his car and his mother required police protection. Further hits followed, but when he attempted to reinvent himself (from icy synthesizer lizard king to avant-garde funkster and beyond) only the hardcore remained interested. Luckily, Numan has always had fans of unsurpassed zeal, and they forgave him his support of Margaret Thatcher and rock star antics (a round-the-world trip in his Cessna plane that had to be aborted) when those less saintly might not. Throughout,

> **Moby:** 'It's difficult to be an electronic musician and not be a fan of Gary Numan. In addition to making remarkable electronic music, he's also a pop star.'

Numan maintained a prodigious output, averaging an album a year, and touring commitments. He does admit 'losing direction completely' in the eighties. He also faced bankruptcy, and had his credit cards withdrawn. Despite being the subject of widespread ridicule in the mainstream music press, the hip hop kids of the Bronx knew a star when they heard one – seminal artists such as Afrika Bambaataa decided that Numan was 'the man' when it came to nicking bits of synth riffs and drum patterns. Other fans include the Foo Fighters, Smashing Pumpkins and Marilyn Manson.

6/Tears For Fears

Points: 199

Recommended album: *The Hurting* (1983)

Formed in Bath by schoolboy friends Curt Smith and Roland Orzabal, Tears For Fears' origins lay in ska-pop group Graduate, who almost scored a novelty hit with 'Elvis Should Play Ska'. After that band sundered the duo stayed together and took their new name from a chapter in Arthur Janov's book *Prisoners Of Pain*. 'We were both from broken families,' explains Smith, 'we're both middle sons of three sons. Both grew up with our mothers rather than our fathers. So there are lots of similarities.' They were immediately signed to Phonogram by Dave Bates after recording two demo songs. Adding drummer Manny Elias and keyboard player Ian Stanley, they charted with third single 'Mad World', produced by Chris Hughes of Adam and the Ants. It eventually rose to number three in the British charts. Just as well, because, as Orzabal confirms, 'the record label were about to pull the plug'. After a second Top 5 hit, 'Change', debut album *The Hurting* topped the British charts; Orzabal responsible for the songwriting, Smith the singing. In 1985 they established themselves in America via two number one singles; 'Everybody Wants To Rule The World' (later revised to 'Everybody Wants To Run The World' as a benefit single to help the African famine relief as part of Sport Aid Week) and 'Shout'. The following year Orzabal was named Songwriter Of The Year at the Ivor Novello Awards. Increasingly, however, he was writing tunes suited to his own voice and not Smith's. 'Yes, we definitely had issues and fights about that,' confirms Smith. 'The older I got and the more robust the songs became, the more comfortable I became fronting them,' reckons Orzabal. After two years of substantial international success it was time for a breather. During the absence Smith successfully sued three tabloid newspapers for printing false-hoods about his schooldays (he had never even attended the St Albans' school in question). *The Seeds Of Love*, the 1989 album they'd spent eighteen months and over £1 million recording, entered the UK chart at number one, and featured guest artists Oleta Adams and Phil Collins. 'I wanted to get to that point that some musicians get to, where it's just world class,' reckons Orzabal. Some critics judged the record to be both highly derivative of the Beatles and hopelessly overblown. In October 1991 the duo announced the end of their partnership. 'At that point we had nothing in common,' says Smith, 'we couldn't talk to each other without fighting, so I just walked away.' 'I don't think he particularly cared for me too much,' admits Orzabal, diplomatically. He attempted to keep the band going, releasing 1993's *Elemental* as a solo project, the extracted 'Fish Out Of Water' being an obvious pay-off to his former partner. Smith retired to America to invest in real estate until returning in 1998 with new band Mayfield. The duo managed to heal the rift in 2000 and they're working on a new record. It's doubtful their label will allow such indulgence a second time around, though.

5/OMD
Points: 245

Recommended album: *Architecture And Morality* (1981)

Orchestral Manoeuvres In The Dark, to give them their full title, were formed in Liverpool by Paul Humphreys (synthesizers) and Andy McCluskey (vocals). Those who find their current appellation bizarre should consider some of its forerunners – like Hitlerz Underpantz and VCL XI (after the number pictured on a Kraftwerk album sleeve). They played their first gig at famed Liverpool post-punk haunt Eric's in October 1978, shortly after McCluskey gave up his job in the Customs office of Liverpool Docks. The backing tracks were provided by 'Winston', their tape recorder. Sounds pretentious? 'I was an incredibly serious, painful bastard when I was twenty years old,' confesses McCluskey. After switching from Factory to Virgin Records subsidiary DinDisc, they scored their first Top 20 hit in May 1980 with 'Messages'. But it was with the follow-up, 'Enola Gay', titled after the American warplane that dropped the atom bomb on Hiroshima, that they estab-lished themselves. 'One thing we didn't want to do was write songs with typical, stereotype lyrics,' states McCluskey. From then on the band's work became more reflective, as OMD dumped simplistic synth ditties for more elaborate, sensual compositions. The style was best exhibited on third album *Architecture And Morality*, which housed the dovetailing singles 'Joan Of Arc' and 'Maid Of Orleans'. Fourth album *Dazzle Ships* 'just killed us dead commercially,' says McCluskey, 'Everybody said "Enough! Sorry, we're not buying this. You can't have all these radio samples going on. This is not pop music."' The band's success dwindled, at least in the UK, but by the mid-eighties they were beginning to win over American audiences. However, Humphreys and McCluskey fell out before they could milk the land of opportunity. 'We were starting to get tired,' admits Humphreys. By 1989 Humphreys had bowed out, opting to work with former members Martin Cooper and Martin Holmes as the Listening Pool. 'I had a nervous breakdown,' admits McCluskey. 'I'd been writing songs with Paul Humphreys since I was sixteen years old. I got to the age of twenty-nine and the carpet was pulled out.' With McCluskey now the sole custodian of OMD, the band made an unlikely return to the UK Top 5 in 1991 with 'Sailing On The Seven Seas', with attendant album *Sugar Tax* reaching number three. McCluskey eventu-ally called it a day in 1996, though he still 'had the ego to believe I could write good songs, I just needed a different messenger'. The recipient? None other than Atomic Kitten.

> **Paul Humphreys:** 'We couldn't do any wrong. Every song we released was bigger than the one before. We started to feel like we had the Midas touch. Which was very dangerous.'

4/Human League
Points: 247

Recommended album: *Dare* (1981)

The Human League started life as a Sheffield experimental trio that wrote endearing but unsuccessful Kraftwerk-influenced singles. When Martin Ware and Ian Craig Marsh left to form BEF, then Heaven 17, remaining founder member and singer Phil Oakey faced an

immediate logistical problem. A tour had already been scheduled when the split occurred, and both Ware and Marsh as well as the remaining band members would have faced legal repercussions if they had failed to appear. Out of sheer desperation, therefore, Oakey trawled the Sheffield nightclubs and recruited Susanne Sulley and Joanne Catherall after spotting them at the Crazy Daisy disco. (Less celebrated is the fact that he also recruited former Rezillos songwriter Jo Callis on synth, who proved crucial in the act's future development.) Nowadays, the Human League have become synonymous with one song – 'Don't You Want Me', their number one single from 1981 that the band always thought was a bit naff. The song was their first collaboration with Martin Rushent. 'Martin understood us,' says Oakey, 'he was also very diplomatic, because we were fairly prickly characters in those days.' Sulley confesses that if it hadn't been for Rushent's ability to sooth the strife in the recording studio, the band would never have made their best-selling album *Dare*. Having been persuaded to issue 'Don't You Want Me' as a single by their record label they were left aghast by its subsequent success. But it was by no means the last of their hits. 'Mirror Man' and '(Keep Feeling) Fascination' both reached number two in the British charts, and they've kept popping up ever since, notably in 1995 with number six hit 'Tell Me When'.

3/Erasure
Points: 365

Recommended album: *Pop! The First 20 Hits* (1992)

If the Pet Shop Boys were naughty but, some felt, a little stiff-lipped, and Depeche Mode were too darned self-conscious, electro-pop's very own show-stopping show-off was Andy Bell – the voice and image of Erasure and a man who probably takes a bow when he opens the fridge at night. The duo was formed in 1985 when erstwhile Depeche Mode and Yazoo member Vince Clarke, who could probably produce a hit record paired with a telephone box, auditioned forty-two aspirant vocalists after placing an advert in *Melody Maker*. However, the Bell we know now was not the one he first encountered. Clarke remembers the singer being the epitome of shyness and barely speaking in the studio. Clarke, the engineer and his assistant spent much of the time trying to get Bell to laugh in order that he'd lighten up. But once his personality was unshackled, it was never going to go back into its box quietly. After a couple of flop singles, they reached number two in December 1986 with 'Sometimes'. It set the blueprint for all the group's subsequent releases: manicured synth-pop with accented melodies given lustre by Bell's dramatic vocal performances (and a dress sense that some might say recalled Liberace in a blizzard). By 1988 the duo were one of Britain's most popular bands, after first gaining a foothold with mainland European audiences. Their domestic popularity was confirmed when third album *The Innocents* entered the charts at number one. Critics carped that Erasure were Depeche Mode-lite, but by 1997 they'd registered no less than twenty-six Top 30 singles. The best of these included 'Blue Savannah' in 1990 and 1992's chart-topping 'Abba-esque' EP. The latter was Andy's idea, naturally. The song's five-week tenure at the top of the charts gave Bell ample opportunity to play dress-up, but this time, he also got Vince in on the act. After an uncustomary breather in their recording schedules, the duo returned to action in 2000 with the release of the largely unsuccessful *Loveboat*.

2/Depeche Mode

Points: 388

Recommended album: *The Singles 1981–1985* (1985)

They started out peddling fairly average electro-pop by numbers ('New Life' being critically acknowledged as the worst offender) and ended the millennium as the heroin-ravaged rock 'n' roll bad boys from Basildon. Vince Clarke put together the band, originally titled Composition Of Sound, in 1980, with Martin Gore and Andy Fletcher, bank and insurance clerks respectively. With Clarke uncomfortable in his role as singer they recruited David Gahan from Southend Technical College, who suggested their new name. They were signed to Mute Records by Daniel Miller (who'd rejected their initial demo as 'bloody awful') in 1981, earning their first Top 60 hit with the narcissistic 'Dreaming Of Me', followed by 'New Life' and 'Just Can't Get Enough'. However, principal songwriter Clarke had no intention of touring, and left to form first Yazoo with Alison Moyet and subsequently Erasure. Unsurprisingly, the remainder of Depeche Mode were less than enamoured at Clarke's departure, and he admits to feeling guilty at the time over his unexpected departure. Gore took over as songwriter and the band recruited a third synthesizer player, Alan Wilder, in Clarke's stead. Fortunately, the personnel swap didn't affect the group's popularity one iota, and by 1983 they'd enjoyed a run of seven consecutive Top 20 hits. They eventually translated their success to America, after two abortive attempts during which they'd been lambasted by the U.S. press to the extent that they'd nearly given up on the idea. Huge success ensued, with Depeche Mode out-merchandising Bon Jovi as a live act. By the mid-eighties, however, the group had torn up the script and turned just a little deviant; the S&M imagery of 'Master And Servant' providing a pointer to their future direction. 'Personal Jesus' (1989) and the following year's *Violator* upped the ante as Depeche Mode added rock bombast to the familiar melodic cunning of their electro-pop tunes. Their personal lives had also taken a dark twist. By 1995, Gahan was a fully-fledged heroin addict. His erratic behaviour saw off Wilder, while Fletcher increasingly handled the group's management rather than playing an active role in their performances (he was later financially embarrassed during the Lloyd's 'names' scandal). Gahan collapsed after an overdose in May 1996, an incident that forced him to confront his personal demons and take stock of his life. To his credit, Gahan pulled out of the nosedive. And nothing seems to dent Depeche Mode's popularity – the following year's *Ultra* album entered the charts at number one in Britain, Spain and Germany.

1/Pet Shop Boys

Points: 495

Recommended album: *Discography – The Complete Singles Collection* (1991)

Allegedly named after a controversial sexual practice involving hours of furry fun with hamsters, the Pet Shop Boys – Neil Tennant and Chris Lowe – were immediately branded as arch ironists on their arrival in the early eighties. However, they have maintained throughout their subsequent career that they are simply pop evangelists. Certainly, they were always in love with the notion of pop; Tennant had previously held down a day job with *Smash Hits* magazine. When he met Lowe, son of a jazz trombonist, in a hi-fi shop in London's King's Road, the two immediately embarked on demo sessions together. On assignment in America in 1983 (he was meant to be interviewing Sting) Tennant happened upon Bobby 'O' Orlando, who agreed to produce the duo's debut single, 'West End Girls'. After a couple of false starts the Stephen Hague remix of the song topped the British charts, after which the pair hooked up with manager Tom Watkins. 'I think they saw me as being strong-arm enough to go in there and bang a few desks, because I would not take no for an answer. I'm not claiming that any of these ideas were anything but theirs, what I'm claiming is that I made those ideas happen for them,' Watkins states today. A run of distinctive singles followed. 'It's A Sin' railed against Tennant's Catholic education, 'What Have I Done To Deserve This?' was a duet with sixties icon Dusty Springfield, while 'Rent' was the humblest of love songs. The Pet Shop Boys always pursued openly gay themes, Tennant implicitly singing to male subjects, but the band never made that the entire rationale or justification for their career. As Tennant protests, 'I don't think that your music is necessarily defined by your sexuality.' For a time in the eighties the Pet Shop Boys were justifiably considered 'the Smiths you could dance to', a tribute to the intelligence and wit their records displayed, but also to Lowe's nose for melody. Alongside their production line of hits, the duo collaborated with Liza Minnelli and produced an album for Springfield. Tennant also worked with ex-Smith Johnny Marr and New Order's Bernard Sumner as part of Electronic. They collaborated extensively with film-maker Derek Jarman on a series of elaborate stage shows, cheekily covered a U2 song ('Where The Streets Have No Name', spliced with Frankie Valli's 'Can't Take My Eyes Off You') and even wrote a pop hit for Patsy Kensit ('Eighth Wonder's 'I'm Not Scared'). Despite Tennant's admission that he was 'bored witless' by the pop star treadmill, *Bilingual* saw them move into Latin percussion while 1999's *Nightlife* included a tribute to the Village People, 'New York City Boy'. They're part of the furniture these days. Even Tony Blair's had British music's very own 'odd couple' round for tea.

Neil Tennant: 'We were never really concerned with pursuing the goal of being cool. When you're younger, being cool is the most important thing. Which tends to mean you just do what everyone else does.'

Ten Other Outfits Who Ran Amok With A Synth

Yazoo
(Introducing Genevieve Alison-Jane Moyet, or Alf as she understandably preferred)

Trio
(German one-hit wonders of 'Da, Da, Da' fame)

Talk Talk
(The best electro-pop band you've probably never heard)

Landscape
(Delivered 'Einstein A-Go-Go' and then diddlysquit)

Thomas Dolby
(The thinking man's Gary Numan)

Blancmange
(Wibbly wobbly synth-poppers found to be 'Living On The Ceiling')

Flying Lizards
(Dadaist multi-instrumentalists)

Fashion
(Lamentable Brummie 'electro-funk' band)

Fad Gadget
(Oddball Frank Tovey's nom de plume)

Blue Zoo
(More electro one-hit wonders, this time of 'Cry Boy Cry' fame)

Country

It's fair to say that country music has had a bad press. Its capacity to produce sentimental mush about donkeys dying in the road, horrific fashion accessories and the truly unforgivable line-dancing craze of the early nineties should not obscure the fundamental role it played in the development of American popular song. It is not an indigenous form of music in the UK, but that hasn't affected its popularity. As Bo Duke (someone who gets into their car via the *window*) says, it's uniquely American.

Country drew on the traditions of fiddle-based folk music and rustic (or 'hillbilly') songwriting. Through the thirties and forties, regional radio broadcasts of barn dances became hugely popular. Post-war, Nashville Tennessee and the Grand Ole Opry (which started as a barn dance programme in 1925) became the spiritual home of country, a position both retain to this day. Country is now variously considered to be 'white man's rhythm and blues', 'working-man's music' or 'the rural folk sound of America'. And, of course, it is all of those things and more, as proved by these ten acts who've enjoyed UK chart success but are ranked according to US sales.

10/Tammy Wynette
Country points: 13

5 husbands ● 2.5 million US album sales
Recommended album: *Stand By Your Man* (1968)

Tammy was an archetypal country gal – a teenager from Mississippi who married to escape the farm. She then threw her kids in the back of her station wagon, pram tied to the roof-rack, and drove to Nashville. While working as a beautician she hooked up with Billy Sherrill and recorded a series of hits, including 'Your Good Girl's Gonna Go Bad' and 'I Don't Wanna Play House'. The songs touched on fairly unromantic themes, but were

Tammy Wynette: 'Most people say it would make a wonderful soap opera. I'm sure it could, but to me it's just my life.'

topped by 'D.I.V.O.R.C.E.'. Conversely Tammy's next big single, 'Stand By Your Man', was a hymn to female fidelity, tolerance and, some would say, indulgence. Her 'man' was

third husband and country legend George Jones. They were Nashville's golden couple, until his drinking drove them apart. After a forty-four-day marriage to an estate agent, Wynette finally settled with George Richey. By now she was a superstar. As her publicist Evelyn Shriver recalls: 'You paid for hair and make-up, you paid for limousines, you paid for private planes, you paid through the nose if you wanted Tammy Wynette for something.' But despite her work rate, her health was brittle. As her career flagged in the eighties, Richey suggested she cut a pop hit. Britain's KLF offered her a lead vocal on their typically esoteric 'Justified And Ancient'; Shriver remembers Tammy saying: 'Where *is* Mu Mu land?' The song went to number one in nineteen countries. In April 1998 Wynette finally succumbed to long-term health problems. Her daughters requested her body be exhumed, believing that Richey may have had some involvement in her death.

9/Glen Campbell

Country points: 48

5 wives ● 9.5 million US album sales
Recommended album: *20 Golden Greats* (1976)

As a youth in Arkansas, Campbell was handed a $7 catalogue guitar by his father and thereafter never looked beyond music for a career. He joined session group the Wrecking Crew and played on albums by Dean Martin, Frank Sinatra, the Beach Boys and others. 'A marvellous variety I got to play,' he recalls. 'I don't remember not having a guitar in my hand.' His solo career took off when he recorded the Jimmy Webb composition 'By The Time I Get To Phoenix' in 1967. It was followed in 1969 by another Webb epic, 'Wichita Lineman'. Kenny Rogers recalls hearing Campbell's version. 'I'd go cut my little country stuff, and we'd compare records. I'd play mine, and I'd have steel guitar, a few guitars and strings. Glen would play "Wichita Linesman", which had eighty strings, and I'd go – "Never mind, let's listen to yours for a while." Mine sounded so simple by comparison.' Campbell became an international draw, outselling the Beatles in 1969, and starring opposite John Wayne in *True Grit*, though there were arguments on set when he stated he didn't want to die at the end of the movie. 'I wish I hadn't gone along with it.

Glen Campbell: 'I lived through "Rhinestone Cowboy". That whole song – it was the way I was when I was struggling on the road.'

But my manager said at the time to do what Hal Wallis and [Henry] Hathaway wanted me to do.' He dropped out of the hit parade for a few years thereafter, but 'Rhinestone Cowboy' brought him back to the top of the charts in 1975. It revitalized his career, but only temporarily. He hit rock bottom after a fling with singer Tanya Tucker and a full-blown romance with cocaine. As country boys do, he got to praying. 'Lord, deliver me from this and I swear I'll never do it again.' Born again, he left LA and moved back to Phoenix with a new family. 'I'm happier than I've ever been in my life, and more content,' he says now.

8/Johnny Cash

Country points: 49

44-year recording career ● 9.5 million US album sales
Recommended album: *Johnny Cash At San Quentin* (1969)

For purists, Johnny Cash represents the true heart of country music, and has never been surpassed as a performer. The man in black scored his breakthrough hit with the 1956 country chart-topper 'I Walk The Line'. He then recorded a series of hits with Sun Records, working alongside Jerry Lee Lewis and Elvis Presley. Colleague Porter Wagoner recalls their adventures: 'Elvis said, "Will you guys ride with me today?" And he had this pink Cadillac parked in the garage there, and the guy brought it around. Johnny Cash and I were standing there waiting. Cash said: "I'm not riding in *that* car." Presley said, "Why not?" Cash said: "That's a queermobile. I'm not riding anywhere in that car." He got in his own car and drove. But that shows you how naive that three country boys were.' Cash's name remains synonymous with his late sixties performances at the San Quentin and Folsom prisons. Singer Merle Haggard was a San Quentin inmate from 1957 to 1960. 'He was a rebel and they identified with him. And he was successful. Didn't give a shit if he was talented or not, they liked him personally because he had enough nerve to get up there and enough sincerity to come out there on New Year's Day and play music for those damned old men, these assholes doing time. Everybody appreciated it.' Married to singer June Carter, Cash eventually pulled out of a drugs-inspired nosedive, commenting: 'For a long time I took my chances and tried a little bit of everything there was to try.' Marty Stuart was Cash's guitarist from 1981 to 1985: 'The thing I learned from Johnny Cash is that he didn't compromise what he believed in. He never compromised his integrity.' In the nineties he signed with rap entrepreneur Rick Rubin as his health declined, but he remains country's inimitable prince of darkness.

7/John Denver

Country points: 51

1st US artist to play Vietnam ● 10.3 million US album sales
Recommended album: *Back Home Again* (1974)

John Deutschendorf, hopelessly short-sighted, always looked more like the Milky Bar Kid than a Nashville outlaw. The son of a war hero pilot, he moved to California to work as a draughtsman and play the region's folk clubs. Eventually he beat 250 applicants to join the Chad Mitchell Trio. In 1968 he was signed as a solo artist by RCA. 'Leaving On A Jet Plane', extracted from his debut album, became a US number one when Peter, Paul And Mary issued their version. His own breakthrough came with the pop-country ballad, 'Take Me Home, Country Roads' in 1971. Not everyone considered him a legitimate country act, but the sniping never troubled Denver. By 1975 he was the highest-grossing country act, with singles such as 'Sunshine On My Shoulders', 'Thank God I'm A Country Boy' (written by his guitarist John Sommers)

Annie Denver, John's first wife: '[John said that] his best and truest friend was the outdoors. It's the place I think that John was the most at home.'

and 'I'm Sorry' topping the US charts. The most memorable was 'Annie's Song' – written for his wife following a row. She recalls: 'John was leaving to go skiing and it was a snowy day. He said I'll go up, take a few runs, and I'll be back. And he came back within an hour and a half. He'd got on the chairlift, sat down, and wrote this song. Bam!' Thereafter his compositions moved gradually away from the country idiom. Moreover, Denver embraced a number of liberal causes, advocating environmental awareness, attacking censorship, and defending gay rights. He also became the first American artist to play Vietnam. John Denver was always proud to be called a country boy, but a redneck he certainly wasn't. His arranger Lee Holdridge remembers that Denver seemed to have a bottomless well of sympathy for the underprivileged and put his boundless energy to work for numerous good causes. On October 12 1997, after a round of golf, he took off in his private plane, which subsequently crashed into Monterey Bay in California, killing him.

6/Dolly Parton

Country points: 52

6 homes, 1 theme park, lots of wigs ● 10.4 million US album sales
Recommended album: *The Dolly Parton Collection* (1980)

Far from the dumb blonde persona some say she sometimes affects to be, or merely 'the best chest in the west' as Terry Wogan once described her, Dolly Parton is as witty, fun-loving and business savvy as any kid on the Nashville block. Singer Hank Wangford comments: 'Fantastic words, very perceptive songs, great melodies, what else do you want?' Parton grew up in a shack in Locus Ridge, Tennessee, and was composing songs before she even knew how to write them down; her mother, amazed by her little girl's talent, did it for her. Initially, her audience consisted of family and farmyard animals, but soon she was booked onto local radio. She graduated in 1964, though she'd been all set to break out for years, and headed for Nashville. It took her longer than she thought to make it, but not for the first or last time in her career, she demonstrated both courage and fortitude in pursuit of her ambitions. It was country TV star Porter Wagoner who gave her a break. They became a huge success together, but the partnership was strained. 'She wanted to be on her own, and she wanted to be the boss,' says Wagoner. 'You can't be the boss when *I'm* writing out the cheques.' Parton documented the end of their business relationship in 'I Will Always Love You', revived by Whitney Houston to incredibly successful effect in the nineties. Massive solo hits confirmed the wisdom of their separation, with songs such as 'Jolene', 'Here You Come Again' and '9 To 5', which soundtracked a film of the same name in which she starred as a long-suffering but feisty secretary. Now in charge of a $100-million media empire and her own theme park, she's remained admirably level-headed and is still with Carl Dean whom she married in 1966.

5/ Hank Williams

Country points: 102

Hank Williams: 4 million US album sales
Hank Williams Jnr: 16.6 million US album sales
Recommended albums: Hank Williams: *The Original Singles Collection* (1992)
Hank Williams Jnr: *The Best Of* (1993)

Dubbed 'The Hillbilly Shakespeare', Williams learned the blues from an itinerant black street singer in Alabama in the forties, drifting through regular jobs while playing the honky tonk circuit. His rise to megastardom and sex symbol status came thanks to appearances at the Grand Ole Opry from 1949 onwards. On his first engagement, he was asked to perform an unprecedented six encores. The appeal was emotional simplicity, believes former bass player Hillous Butrum: 'Very seldom, if ever, did Hank Williams put a two-syllable word in a song.' He was eventually sacked by the Grand Old Opry in August 1952; they were appalled at his growing reputation for drunkenness. 'Hank was not a drunk', rebuffs Butrum, 'he was an alcoholic. He couldn't take a drink and stop, he would just go on and drink till he knocked himself out.' Williams died in the back of his Cadillac on New Year's Day 1953, aged 29. But his memory lived on: son Randall Hank Williams took the name Hank Williams Jnr and, under his mother's guidance, initially recorded copycat versions of his father's songs, notably 'Your Cheatin' Heart'. However, later songs such as 'Standing In The Shadows (Of A Very Famous Man)' amply explained Junior's growing disenchantment with the moulding of his career. In 1975 he inadvertently almost followed the family tradition of dying in unusual circumstances. Manager Merle Kilgore recalls his fall from a mountain in somewhat graphic detail: 'He fell 640 feet backwards, his head hit a boulder and his brains popped out, and his eye popped out. Luck was on his side, God was there, of course. These two doctors had just come back from Vietnam, and they were specialties [sic] in head trauma cases. So they operated on him immediately.' Two years of reconstructive surgery later, Hank Williams Jnr made a comeback.

> **Steel guitarist Don Helms:**
> 'When he would sing on the stage and talk, I think every individual in that audience thought he was singing to them alone.'

4/Reba McEntire

Country points: 150

Employs 15 songwriters ● 30 million US album sales
Recommended album: *Starting Over* (1995)

Though her profile outside America remains limited, she's sold 40 million records, more than Janet Jackson or Celine Dion. That figure makes McEntire the most successful female country artist of all time. She certainly boasts an immaculate country pedigree. Raised on an Oklahoma ranch, her father Clark was a three-time world champion rodeo steer-roper. Her first husband was a 'steer-wrestler' (don't ask). Her father booked her to sing at the National Rodeo finals in Oklahoma in 1974. A man called Red Steagall heard her sing the national anthem there and eleven months later she had a contract with Polygram Records.

Reba's success slowly unfolded through the seventies until, in 1983, she topped the country charts with 'Can't Even Get The Blues'. But it was with the dawning of the video age, and her carefully observed 'downhome' image, that her career ignited. In 1986 'Whoever's In New England' won a Grammy and became her first gold record. Her records continued to sell in successively larger numbers, until tragedy struck in March 1991. A plane carrying her backing band crashed into a mountain en route to Texas. Within a fortnight, she was saying an emotional goodbye on stage; Reba declares that she forgot the audience that night and sung instead to the seven band members, two pilots and the tour manager that she'd lost in the crash. She's certainly a determined lady, as attested to by several producers who mistakenly attempted to 'mould' her sound. That attitude's paid off big-time. Her Starstruck Entertainment company is currently the most successful in Nashville, and it can't be long before McEntire extends her reach beyond the US.

3/Willie Nelson
Country points: 157

Raised $14.5 million for Farm Aid ● 31.5 million US album sales
Recommended album: *Red Headed Stranger* (1975)

Nelson, who some say looks more like Albert Steptoe by the day, is one of country music's most uncompromising free spirits. He grew up on a farm in depression-era Texas, his parents separating when he was six. He started writing poems, putting melodies to them after he was bought his first guitar. By his teens he was working as an itinerant musician selling songs to put food on the table. Singer Marty Stuart says 'he was truly one of those guys who never got a break, he had to sell his songs, give them away for pennies, just to exist around here.'

Willie Nelson: 'I'm glad to see all those obstacles out there. What's a good soldier do without a war?'

Among those songs was 'Crazy', immortalized by Patsy Cline, although Nelson was so shy at the time that, having driven out to Cline's house, he refused to get out of the car to meet her, in case she didn't like his song. Fortunately, she did. Among the other unlikely songs written by Nelson during the period was 'Bring Me Sunshine', the song forever associated with Morecambe and Wise. The Nashville labels afforded him few chances to sing his own material, as his singing style didn't really fit in with what was going on in the rest of country music at the time. Eventually Nelson returned to Texas. In 1975 he recorded *Red Headed Stranger* and handed it to a bemused record company who, at first, didn't really know what to do with it. The album flew in the face of prevailing Nashville obsessions with presentation and gloss, but still topped the country charts. It also gave birth to the 'outlaw' country style, especially after Nelson teamed up with Waylon Jennings and started preaching the country gospel to hippies and student audiences. His 1978 collection of pop ballads covered in a country style, *Stardust*, stayed on the album charts for ten years. Inspired by Bob Geldof's Live Aid, Nelson organized Farm Aid in 1985 – an annual festival raising money for the rural poor, though he had his own fiscal problems to contend with at the time: the IRS hammered him with a $16-million tax bill. He recorded an album, *Who'll Buy My Memories*, to cover the debt, and remains one of country's great survivors.

2/Kenny Rogers

Country points: 250

Owns a chain of fast food restaurants: Kenny Rogers Roasters Wood Roasted Chicken
49.5 million US album sales ● Recommended album: *The Kenny Rogers Story* (1985)

Global gadabout Andy Kershaw reckons the only place he hasn't been offered Kenny
Rogers tapes for sale is North Korea. It can only be a matter of time. Before becoming
Nashville's favourite hirsute ladies man, Rogers started out playing in college rock bands.
He was the vocalist with First Edition, for whom Karen Carpenter once auditioned, when
they scored a US Top 5 hit in 1968 with the psychedelic rocker 'Just Dropped In (To See
What Condition My Condition Was In)'; Rogers claims Jimi Hendrix told him it was his
favourite song. The group was renamed Kenny Rogers and First Edition for the follow-up
hit 'Ruby, Don't Take Your Love To Town'. It was a song about a soldier returning from
Korea who'd lost his legs and was in mortal fear of losing his gal as a consequence.
Somehow it made sense in the context of the Vietnam war, then at its height. The group
split in 1974 and Rogers signed with United Artists. In June 1977 he topped the country
charts with 'Lucille', a farmer's plea to his wife not to dump him at harvest time. Rogers
admits being 'drawn to songs that tell stories. They're like mini-movies to me.' 'Coward
Of The County', released in 1990, marked the zenith of this tradition. A film was subsequently released, its plot built around the song's narrative of a humble young man having
to use his fists to make any sense of this ol' world. The silver fox then recorded a series
of slushy songs, such as 'Lady', targeted squarely at the female market, and performed
several duets with partners including Kim Carnes and Dolly Parton. But life on the road
took its toll in the form of four broken marriages. 'I'm not talking about the temptations
of the road, I'm talking about the separation. This concept of "absence makes the heart
grow fonder" is just not true,' he insists. Rogers is currently married to fifth wife Wanda
Miller and has become a celebrity photographer, working with Michael Jackson and
others. And why play the chicken-in-a-basket nostalgia circuit when you can simply buy
a franchise of chicken restaurants?

1/Garth Brooks

Country points: 445

1,711 albums sold while you read this ● 89 million US album sales
Recommended album: *The Chase* (1992)

A former javelin thrower, bouncer, and boot salesman, clean-living momma-loving,
Oklahoma native Garth Brooks is an untypical country superstar, though a uniquely
successful one. The youngest son of fifties country singer Colleen Carroll, he moved to
Nashville in 1987 and was spotted at the Bluebird Café by Len Scholds. 'Much Too
Young (To Feel This Damn Old)' hit number eight in the country charts in March 1989,
after which 'If Tomorrow Never Comes' and 'Friends In Low Places' reached the top. He
was soon generating unprecedented sales figures as his albums comfortably outsold
releases from Michael Jackson and Guns N'Roses. Brooks has now overtaken the
Beatles as the biggest-selling artist of all time. He believes the secret of his success lies

in the authenticity of his music. He pursues a classic story-telling country style, with a clean, cultured though some critics say, not particularly remarkable voice, employing a combination of bathos and uptempo bar-room rockers. Unlike the Hanks and Johnnys of the country world, Brooks has had few brushes with controversy. No drink binges, no drugs. The man even invites his momma on stage. Conversely for a country singer, his live performances are as extravagant as anything Bon Jovi or Aerosmith could muster, trashed guitars and flying harnesses notwithstanding. In short, he has made country accessible to a whole new audience a long ways from Hazzard County.

Honky Tonk Jukebox
some other great country recordings

Carter Family: 'Keep On The Sunny Side' (1906)
Jimmie Rodgers: 'Blue Yodel No.9' (1930)
Bob Wills: 'Panhandle Rag' (1949)
Lefty Frizzell: 'If You Got The Money, Honey, I Got The Time' (1950)
Jim Reeves: 'He'll Have To Go' (1960)
Patsy Cline: 'Crazy' (1961)
Townes Van Zandt: 'Waitin' Around To Die' (1968)
Merle Haggard: 'Okie From Muskogee' (1969)
Loretta Lynn: 'Coal Miner's Daughter' (1970)
Steve Earle: 'Fearless Heart' (1986)
Mary Chapin Carpenter: 'Come On Come On' (1992)

Holiday Songs

It's what our upstanding youth bring home from their summer jaunts, along with straw donkeys, timeshare contracts and a variety of nasty rashes. These are the songs they hummed in pursuance of skirt or trouser while skating on nightclub floors swimming in beer and vomit. Their sightseeing activities precluded to ogling fellow reptiles, these shining examples of humanity simultaneously attempt to convince Johnny Foreigner that the Middle Ages have returned while expanding their linguistic abilities to accommodate the name of the local beverage. The British abroad, with their lagered-up libidos, possess an in-built sense of national superiority that remains undiminished even while surrendering the contents of their stomachs to toilet bowls that will forever be England.

Our following selection, based on UK chart sales, offers the perfect accompaniment to that injudicious holiday romance, in all its squalid indifference to anything resembling dignity. It is rendered with our heartfelt apologies to any Spanish waiter who has ever had 'Miguel!' shouted at them by dull-witted inebriates in Union Jack boxer shorts. Ah, those summer nights. The scoring is based on weeks in the chart with bonus points for a top three hit and each week spent at number one.

10/Opus 'Live Is Life'   Sunshine points: 150

Chart position: No. 6 ◈ Weeks in chart: 15

The country that gave the world Mozart had done little to embrace popular music, Falco's 1986 hit 'Amadeus' aside. And even that was themed around the great composer. In between came this effort from Opus in 1985. Being Austria, it was no sun, sand and sea tune. Instead, its popularity grew in holiday chalets on the country's ski slopes. Alpine winter sports were suddenly all the rage with affluent Britons. 'Live Is Life', with its infectious 'na-na-na-na-na' chorus, had returning would-be Franz Klammers slaloming

their way to their nearest record shop. The song started out as a birthday present to the group's 'rabid' fanbase on the event of their eleventh birthday show at the Oberwart Stadium in September 1984. From there it became a staple of Austrian jukeboxes and cabaret bands. No-one in Britain really knew what the song meant, of course. The band claim it reflects their personal rationale to get up on stage and play live. 'On stage we have a great time, to give our power to the people, and get power back to the people,' states guitarist Ewald Pfleger. The group were naive to the machinations of marketing, however, and when asked to come up with an accompanying video, turned in a rather inadequate effort, with a plot so flimsy that any struggling actor would have thought twice about taking the audition. A gang of reprobates, played by the band, were wrecking their benign acoustic rendition of the song. They subsequently emerged from a dressing room belching dry ice and somersaulted across the stage, plugging into Marshall stacks en route. Our bothersome interlopers were dispelled by the boys' rockin' performance of 'Live Is Life', sung as if they'd transmogrified into a major rock band (in their infancy in 1973, Opus actually played Deep Purple cover versions). However, the video was banned by the BBC, because they didn't like the idea of the 'bad boy' Opus arriving at a gig tooled up with chains and knuckle-dusters. The group remain popular in Austria, and in 1998 they wrote the song for their country's World Cup football team. 'Live Is Life', meanwhile, has been covered by as many as thirty different artists around the world. It's fair to say they probably don't know what it's about either.

9/Sabrina 'Boys (Summertime Love)'   Sunshine points: 190

Chart position: No. 3 ● Weeks in chart: 14

Ah, Sabrina Salerno. Not the teenage witch of course, but the top-heavy Italian totty. Some argued that her records seemed to be a marketing excuse for close-ups of her ample bosom. 'I'm conscious that I sell a product,' she confesses. 'And in this product there is the music and Sabrina, and I think that the image in my career has been very, very important. I know it, and I use it.' Her early career was backed by none other than media magnate and future Italian prime minister Silvio Berensconi. 'Berensconi wanted to see me personally,' she glows. 'He told me, you'll be a star.' 'Boys (Summertime Love)' became a Top 5 UK hit in 1988 on the back of a predictably steamy video. It was filmed in about fifteen minutes, and Sabrina claims not to have realized that she 'popped out' while shooting the water scenes. Her subsequent appearance on *Top Of The Pops* received a stern rebuke from viewer Barbara Adamson of Bournemouth which was read out on the BBC. 'The song is great but her appearance on the show was appalling. She was jumping up and down, backwards and forwards, and all you could see was her chest moving in every direction possible.' Sabrina followed up with a Stock, Aitken and Waterman tune, 'All Of Me', which again saw her frolicking in the water. Miss Euro Wet T-shirt wanted to sign a contract with the UK production team, but was tied up with her Italian label. 'To be sexy-ful in the UK', she laments, in pidgin English, 'you must be produced by an English producer.' Her later work

Sabrina: 'I'm very attracted by Plato, Socrates, by all the biggest philosophers that I've studied.'

94

saw her record with the Smurfs. But she was outraged when an Italian gossip rag questioned the authenticity of that famous cleavage. 'So I had to go to this doctor and he certificated that I was like my mother and father had made me, that I'm real.' Sabrina won the court case and pressed on with a career that still thrives in European holiday resorts. She also claims she's not just a body and hopes to take up a university place one day, but for now, the lager louts of Lanzarote beckon.

8/Los Del Rio 'Macarena'   Sunshine points: 240

Chart position: No. 2 ● Weeks in chart: 19

This revered Spanish flamenco duo, comprising Antonio Romeo Monge and Rafael Ruiz, saw their 'Macarena' composition become a worldwide phenomenon long after they originally recorded it in 1993. The song was written in Venezuela, intended as a compliment to a dancer they'd seen named Diana. The song's original title was apparently changed because Antonio had a daughter called Esperanza Macarena, and thought it more prudent to honour her rather than the attractive dancing girl. The original flamenco version was a big hit in South America, before it was heard by two DJs from Miami, the Bayside Boys, who suggested having a girl rap over the Spanish lyrics. The remix sent the whole world mad, the record spending fourteen weeks on top of the Billboard charts. A whole new dance step was created to go with it. The video, too, caught the attention of international audiences. The song was subsequently performed at major league baseball stadiums, and even presidential pretender Al Gore performed a still-life parody of the dance at a Democrat rally. 'In one sense you cringe', says Paul Gambaccini, 'but then you think, this shows how deep into the culture it's gotten. Because it means he assumes that everyone knew what it was.' In Italy the tune was adopted by the far right – its lyrics amended to 'Comunismo? No, Grazie!' In the Philippines traffic control cops brightened up Manila's rush hour by directing traffic to the Macarena beat. There are rumours that Saddam Hussein was seen doing the dance, though anyone who got close enough to verify this was promptly executed. Probably. So, are they sex symbols now? 'Sex symbols? Us?' protests Ruiz. 'What you need is good health so you can drink plenty of Mosto and Manzanilla sherry.' We'll take that as a no, then.

7/Typically Tropical 'Barbados'   Sunshine points: 260

Chart position: No. 1 ● Weeks in chart: 11 ● Weeks at No. 1: 1

A number one hit in 1975, 'Barbados' was the genius idea of Geraint Hughes and Jeffrey Calvert, two previously unassuming north London studio engineers. 'I went to Barbados', recalls Calvert, 'and I came back and said to Geraint, "This is great, wonderful island. I want to write a song about Barbados."' Acknowledged by critics as throwing in every cliché in Caribbean Christendom, the song employed a reggae beat and what some thought was a deeply suspect impersonation of a Bajan airline captain, Tobias Wilcock. Hughes acknowledges that this story of a bus driver escaping Brixton to return to his

native Barbados might be considered a little non-PC these days. The lilting melody, strummed on an acoustic guitar with palm trees painted on it, was punctuated intermittently with incongruous 'whoop's. The duo's studio was located close to Trojan Records, and they'd often worked with visiting Jamaican musicians, affording them a basic grasp of reggae structure. It was only when the song reached number one that everyone realized it was two white guys, though Hughes couldn't believe his accent had fooled anyone for a moment. As dyed-in-the-wool backroom boys they were overawed at a beckoning *Top Of The Pops* appearance, so Calvert's dad gave Hughes a valium to calm his nerves. It only exacerbated his anxiety. He ran straight for the ladies and had to be supported by three female backing singers as he semi-collapsed and lost his BBC canteen lunch in the lavatory. Follow-up effort 'Rocket Man' flopped, so the duo returned to their mixing desks, working successfully with Judas Priest. Their writing credits include Sarah Brightman's 'I Lost My Heart To A Starship Trooper'. 'It would be great if Steps covered that, wouldn't it?' reckons Hughes. 'Barbados' enjoyed a new lease of life in 1999 when Dutch pop tunesters the Vengaboys turned it into an anthem for Ibiza club life. Those impish charmers wish Hughes and Calvert well, encouraging them to enjoy the benefits for their pension. Hughes currently composes relaxation music, some of it used on BA flights. Calvert is a qualified pilot and owns a jet with Coconut Airlines written on it. So Tobias Wilcock's spirit lives on.

6/Sylvia 'Y Viva Espana'   Sunshine points: 280

Chart position: No. 4 ● Weeks in chart: 28

Sweden's premier cabaret diva had to be persuaded to record this song, a big departure from her usual style. 'It's not for me, because I want to sing my jazz and swing and Brazilian stuff,' says Sylvia Viethammer. 'Then after a while, they came again and said, let's record it, listen to this song. And more and more I felt, yes, why not?' The song was 'Y Viva Espana', which became a Europe-wide hit and soundtracked the cheap foreign holiday boom of the seventies. With its opening 'Olé!', castanets, handclaps, flamenco rhythms and sing-along-chorus, it was a Spanish package tour repackaged. It could have been custom-made to instil a little Latin fervour in pasty-faced Brits abroad, before the overflowing water closet and building works next door snapped them back into indignant egg 'n' chips-demanding ignoramus mode. The song became so synonymous with the Costa Del Sol that departing jumbo jets, packed with expectant Brits awash with duty free booze, regularly reverberated to raucous communal versions of the song. On their return home, too, it became a post-bingo working-men's club staple. And nobody seemed to mind that this eulogy to the bargain bucket sun break was sung by a Swede. However, the song aroused controversy when it was alleged that it championed Franco's fascists. Sylvia found herself hounded by the Swedish press. 'I said, it's a summer song, it has nothing to do with what happens in Spain, political-wise.' Franco died in November of the following year, but Sylvia was determined to make her own political agenda clear. On a couple of appearances she changed the words to 'Non Viva Espana'. In Britain, where Euro politics were hardly a raging debate, the song reached number four in August 1974. This was another never-to-be-repeated

holiday hit, however, and afterwards Sylvia returned to cabaret and jazz. She also undertook her own stage show, featuring Gershwin standards and even an AC/DC song.

5/Tweets 'The Birdie Song (Birdie Dance)'

Sunshine points: 330

Chart position: No. 2 ● Weeks in chart: 28

It's a strange tale, how this bird whistle-inflected oompah and fairground organ-based pop extravaganza came into being. As label boss Henry Hadaway recalls, 'I was in my office. I had a phone call from one of my associates in Holland. They asked me if I'd heard the song they sent me. I said to everyone in my office, what do you think? Honestly, three directors of the company said they would resign.' They didn't want to be associated with 'a stupid novelty record', and frankly, some might say, who could blame them? Henry, however, was sure it would be a hit. Mickey Foote, who had previously produced the first Clash album, decided he didn't mind slumming it. 'It wasn't a question of did I want to do it or not. I'd done all kinds of music, and it makes no difference to me. In fact, it was a challenge.' It cost £75 to piece together, a figure that presumably included provision of bird seed and vet bills. A quartet of costumed bird characters (a canary, a chicken, a starling and a cuckoo, but I could be wrong here, I'm no ornithologist) appeared dancing on *Top Of The Pops* to promote the single, enjoying their brief moment in the sunbath. But they had no involvement with the song's creation, which apparently had something to do with someone in Belgium. It sold millions of copies in the UK and throughout Europe anyway. However, Henry couldn't get away from it. 'Since the Birdie Song, my name as a producer deteriorated. Everybody thought, Oh, my God, it's Henry Hadaway, the novelty producer.'

4/Black Lace 'Agadoo'

Sunshine points:360

Chart position: No. 2 ● Weeks in chart: 31

Unlike Kennedy's assassination, it's fair to say that absolutely nobody remembers where they were when they first heard 'Agadoo'. It's probable they must have been in an advanced state of inebriation ever to find themselves near a DJ playing it. The band members now attest to the fact that they can do the infernal dance associated with the song in their sleep. The references to pineapple gave the song a quasi-exotic edge, but the piece was actually written by two farmers in France. Manager John Wagstaff recalls the way it came about. 'Some friends of ours said there was a song being played in a nightclub in Derby called the Pink Coconut. We got there, and he said, "We'll show you what the dance is."' Those simple steps and hand movements ensured 'Agadoo''s place in the hierarchy of party tunes for ever. As the persistent portion of the duo, Colin Routh admits, 'without the dance, "Agadoo" means nothing. It's not a particularly good song. So we had to get this dance across. Once we could fill the dancefloor, people would see the potential and go out and buy the single and take it into the charts.' It became the soundtrack to every party you've ever been to,

particularly family occasions, when flatulent great aunties would seize terrified younger family members by the arm and insist that they had fun. Black Lace continued to ply the charts with similar holiday-themed tunes such as 'Do The Conga' and 'I Speaka Da Lingo'. The group split up when Alan Barton left to join Smokie (See Really Annoying Records chapter) and later died in a crash. Routh and Rob Hopcraft kept it going for another ten years. However, Rob says it's now 'Agadon't' for him. He's set up his own internet business, and got married. Colin is still at it with a new line-up featuring two female backing singers. They continue to appease audiences at caravan parks the length and breadth of Great Yarmouth.

3/Lou Bega 'Mambo No. 5'   Sunshine points: 440

Chart position: No. 1 ● Weeks in chart: 19 ● Weeks at No. 1: 2

'Mambo No. 5' was an insistent and joyful exposition of an ancient Perez Prado song, polished up for a 1999 audience. Basically a list of girls' names sung over the brassy mambo tune, with strong choreography in the accompanying video, it quickly crossed over into the charts, its appeal not confined merely to the young – a fact attested to by TV's *Royle Family*, the nation's best-loved dysfunctional couch potatoes, who were unable to do anything other than dance feverishly round the room to it. Even Jim Royle succumbed to one of the most insanely catchy songs of the year. It was never intended to be a summer song, however. Lou Bega, born and raised in Germany of mixed Sicilian and Ugandan parentage, just added words to the instrumental after his co-writer, Zippy, brought the record to him in the studio. 'I listened to it', says Bega, 'and the first thing that got to me was, man, you've got to move to this! Then I went home, wrote the lyrics to it. I laid my voice on the track, and it just felt like – pow!' The Democratic Party in America seem to have a bit of a thing about our holiday songs, and the Clinton administration adopted 'Mambo No. 5' as a theme tune. Ironically, one of the song's lines sang the praises of one Monica. Monica Lewinsky, of course, is believed to have had a little bit of Clinton in her life at one time. But Bega won't reveal who the real women who inspired the cast of characters used in the song are. 'I'm a gentleman,' he stonewalls. 'It should be your Monica, or your Sandra.' Tabloid journalist Rick Sky reckons it was a clever marketing ploy – every girl namechecked in the song was prone to buy a copy, and possibly even their boyfriends. 'Mambo No. 5' became the theme tune to Channel 4's Test match coverage – neatly tying in with a rare revival in English cricket fortunes. A feelgood record all round, then.

2/Whigfield 'Saturday Night'   Sunshine points: 630

Chart position: No. 1 ● Weeks in chart: 18 ● Weeks at No. 1: 4

The first number one in the UK for a Danish artist, Whigfield's 'Saturday Night' proved an irresistible dancefloor magnet that drew drunken holiday revellers under its spell. Sannie Charlotte Carlsson, together with her Italian producers Larry Pignagnoli and Davide Riva,

were behind the hit, naming the act Whigfield after Carlsson's fondly remembered music teacher. 'The interesting thing about "Saturday Night" is that it took no time to write,' says Riva. 'Within a couple of hours we had the main tune written down.' When they heard Carlsson for the first time, they decided her voice was perfect for the song. Carlsson herself protests that it wasn't her kind of music at all. 'I've always been more into folk, soul, or jazz.' The song's 'getting all made up ready to go out on the razz' video helped produce pan-European empathy and success. Asked what the appeal could possibly be, Whigfield says simplicity. Buoyed by reports of the song from Britons returning from holiday, 'Saturday Night' saw her become the first debut artist to go straight in at number one. It also finally nailed the seemingly endless run of Wet Wet Wet's 'Love Is All Around' at the top. Whigfield's press people claimed she'd come up with the banal dance steps that accompanied the song. It was those wacky Italian producers once again, who theorized the dance steps to death and suggested its charm lay in the fact that it was a seven-beat dance to an eight-beat tune, and hence, always on the off beat. Reggae act the Equals claimed 'Saturday Night' plagiarized their 1969 single 'Rub A Dub Dub'. Lindisfarne, conversely, reckoned it was a lift from 'Fog On The Tyne'. Both claims were thrown out of court. By the time of the follow-up single 'Another Day', however, it seemed punters were tired of Carlsson's efforts. It brought another litigation battle – this time Mungo Jerry's claim that it used part of their 'In The Summertime' melody was successful. Whigfield remains popular with European audiences, but Carlsson spends most of her time 'chilling' in Ghana.

1/Mungo Jerry 'In The Summertime'   Sunshine points: 950

Chart position: No. 1 ● Weeks in chart: 20 ● Weeks at No. 1: 7

A triumph of extraordinary vocal effects melded into a free-flowing jug band tune, 'In The Summertime' was the definitive seasonal anthem to easy living and girl chasing. Ironically, the perfect holiday song is the only one of our selection that was home-grown. It was created by Mungo Jerry, who took their name from a T.S. Eliot poem and were previously known as a hard-riffing blues band. Innocently libidinous rather than lascivious, its lyrics astutely captured the time of year when the sap rises. The song, which remains sunshine incarnate, has sold over 30 million copies. Gap-toothed and impossibly-sideburned guitarist and singer Ray Dorset reckons 'it's not bad for something I knocked up in ten minutes for a bit of a laugh.' It was released in May. 'We had a three or four week spell of weather which was really hot and summer-like,' recalls upright bassist Mike Cole. 'It seemed that things were conspiring with us.' The song certainly came as a breath of fresh air in the rock climate in which it was released. Dorset's playful guitar line was inspired by Robert Johnson's 'Crossroads'. Having been weaned on American teen movies, he thought of a lyric about guys cruising round in Chevvies picking up girls. They knew they'd chanced on something when they played the song at the Hollywood Festival in Newcastle. Playing bottom of the bill, they stole the show. No footage remains because, according to Cole, the Grateful Dead spiked the orange juice passed to BBC cameramen with LSD. 'Summertime' subsequently went 'even higher than the camera crew'. *Melody Maker* declared 'Mungo Mania', and the band were tipped to displace the Beatles. But,

according to Cole, 'We didn't take advantage of a number-one hit, we didn't follow it up for almost a year before we produced a second record.' 'Baby Jump', by which time Cole had left, also went to number one, yet few remember it. Cole went on to play double bass in a symphony orchestra and a Jewish jazz group. Ray kept Mungo Jerry on the road, and in 1980 penned Kelly Marie's 'Feels Like I'm In Love'. He claims he had Elvis in mind when he wrote it. 'In The Summertime' was revived by Shaggy in 1994 for a Top 5 UK hit. Mungo Jerry are still out there, though sometimes, Dorset notes, non-hardcore fans confuse them with TV series *Mary, Mungo and Midge*. Such is the legacy of the afterglow of true pop stars.

Some Other 'Going Away' Songs

A-Ha: 'Move To Memphis'
Biddu: 'Journey To The Moon'
Dead Kennedys: 'Holiday In Cambodia'
Eddie Cochran: 'Summertime Blues'
Human League: 'Holiday 80'
Jimmy Ray: 'Goin' To Vegas'
Madonna: 'Holiday'
MC Miker 'G' and DJ Deejay Sven: 'Holiday Rap'
Motors: 'Airport'
Ricky Nelson: 'Travellin' Man'

Duets

Two's company, three's a band, as they say in duet circles. This chapter celebrates those winning combinations who have, down the years, enchanted us with heartfelt declarations of lurve to their singing partner – whether the songs be a temporary association, a spin-off from separately successful careers or a permanent 'coupling'. Our only stipulations were that they must be male/female (though we point out here and now that we have no objection to boy/boy girl/girl action in this or any other theatre of love context) and that they were not one-hit wonders. The final placings are determined by UK album and UK and US singles sales.

10/Esther and Abi Ofarim

Points: 120

Sexual dynamism: Seven. Cinderella did, indeed, go to the ball.

Esther (Zaled) Ofarim is an established Israeli recording artist, with a career dating back to the late fifties, who works across a myriad of styles including Jewish traditional music, rock, pop and folk (some compare her work in the latter idiom to that of Judy Collins). Ofarim also represented Switzerland in the 1963 Eurovision Song Contest, billed as Ester Ofarim. She finished second with 'T'en Va Pas', the 100th song recorded in the contest, amid controversy over a 'revision' to the Norwegian panel's voting. Several of her records have been issued in English-language editions, but she became best-known in this country for her duet work with one-time husband Abi Ofarim (Abraham Reichstadt). Their first hit came with the novelty effort 'Cinderella Rockafella', written by Mason Williams, which reached number one in the British charts in 1968 after its preview on *The Eamonn Andrews Show*. The follow-up, 'One More Dance', stalled outside the Top 10. Their fleeting success was overseen by Scott Walker's manager Ady Semel, who encouraged Abi to sing 'Long About Now' on Walker's *'Til The Band Comes In* album of 1969. He also talked up the possibility of getting Scott and Abi to work together on a more permanent basis. In the seventies Esther, now divorced from Abi, continued to record widely both in Hebrew and English, including albums with Bob Dylan producer Bob Johnston, though she has yet to land another hit single outside Israel.

9/Peters & Lee

Points: 220

Sexual dynamism: Four. Far too proper for that sort of thing.

Lennie Peters was an amateur boxer before he was blinded at the age of fifteen, the result of a thrown brick. He turned to piano instead and sang at pubs around Islington before joining the Migils (but leaving before they scored a Top 10 hit with 'Mockin' Bird Hill' as the Migil Five in 1964). He then linked with Dianne Lee, formerly of dance group the Hayley Twins. As Peters and Lee they earned a reputation as a hot act on the tough northern club circuit before winning ITV's *Opportunity Knocks* talent show, in the days when to do so practically guaranteed a showbiz career. The winning song (registered on the arcane 'clapometer') was a version of Presley's 'Suspicious Minds'. As Lee remembers, Peters was afraid 'of going on there and being beaten by a group of children, or a singing dog or something'. Their popularity swelled and quickly transferred to the record-buying public, who sent their country-tinged single 'Welcome Home' to the top of the charts in 1973. The accompanying *We Can Make It* also topped the album list, producing simultaneous number ones for an act for the first time since the Beatles. This despite a fictitious tabloid story that Peters' blindness was 'faked'. On stage, Peters kept his bearings by stepping right to the edge so he knew he was facing the audience. 'That was fine for Lennie,' remembers Lee, 'but everybody else was having a heart attack. People sat on the front row would be ready to catch him.' While autograph hunters regularly mistook him for Roy Orbison, the assumption that the duo format also concealed a personal relationship was untrue, though the pair made few strenuous efforts to deny it. Further chart success ensued with 'Don't Stay Away Too Long', 'Rainbow' and 'Hey Mr Music Man', but thereafter the hits dried up and in 1980 the duo called it a day. 'It got to a point where we'd had our success,' says Lee, 'but we needed some time. We didn't have any private lives or anything. So that's when we decided to take a break.' Tom O'Connor introduced their final appearance on *London Night Out* and remembers that their professional divorce 'became a topic of conversation as big as the budget or the price of petrol'. They reformed again six years later and became a popular cabaret act. 'The second time around was even better,' says Lee. 'We didn't have the pressure, and I think we were singing better as well. But then Lennie started to get ill.' Peters was struck down by bone cancer in October 1992. Lee turned to acting work and in 1994 played the title role in Jim Davidson's 'adult' pantomime *Sinderella*. She's now back working as a duet act with Rick Price, formerly of Wizzard. Nostalgia for the duo's career was belatedly revived in the late nineties by the use of 'Welcome Home' in Gary Lineker's Walker's Crisps advertising campaign.

8/Marvin Gaye & Tammi Terrell

Points: 260

Sexual dynamism: Eight.
Who knows for sure, but, boy, did they look like they had it goin' on.

Though Motown legend Gaye was paired with several partners during his recording career, no collaborator worked as harmoniously with him as Philadelphia-born Thomasina

Montgomery, aka Tammi Terrell. By the time they began their partnership in 1967, Gaye was already an established star through hits such as 'How Sweet It Is (To Be Loved By You)', but his real triumphs still lay ahead of him. His previous duet work had been with Motown vocalist Kim Weston, producing hits such as 'What Good Am I Without You' and 'It Takes Two'. For her part Terrell, who had married boxer Ernier Terrell (brother of Jean Terrell of the Supremes) had worked with the James Brown Revue before signing with Motown as a solo artist. In July 1967 Gaye and Terrell cut 'Ain't No Mountain High Enough', the first of their joint ventures, which reached number 19 in the US charts. However, Terrell was diagnosed as suffering from a brain tumour, rumoured to have been inflicted on her by her boyfriend striking her with a hammer. She collapsed into Gaye's arms one night that summer, and thereafter her health faltered. An accompanying album, *United*, and a series of declamatory singles ensued from the pairing, including 'Your Precious Love', 'If I Could Build My Whole World Around You', 'Ain't Nothing Like The Real Thing', 'You're All I Need To Get By', 'Keep On Lovin' Me Honey' and 'You Ain't Livin' Till You're Lovin''. Their erotically charged performances fuelled rumours of a romantic relationship between the two, though that's denied by those that knew them best, including Gaye's brother. Their final two singles together were 'What You Gave Me' and 'The Onion Song', their biggest UK hit, though later it was revealed that producer Valerie Simpson substituted her vocals for Terrell's on this and several other recordings. After undergoing eight brain operations in eighteen months, Terrell died on 16 March 1970 in a Philadelphia hospital, aged twenty-four.

7/Ike & Tina Turner
Points: 298

Sexual dynamism: Nine. Eight for Tina, one for Ike.

One of the most famous, and troubled, relationships in popular musical history. Turner (Annie Mae Bullock) has emerged the dignified survivor, though her former husband Ike fares less well in the story. Ike (Izear Luster Turner) started out in pre-war R&B bands in his native Clarksdale, Mississippi. With a set of pick-up session men, his Kings Of Rhythm played at the sharp end of the southern US club scene. That group, under the name the Delta Cats, are widely acknowledged as authors of the first rock 'n' roll record, 1951's 'Rocket 88' – credited to saxophonist Jackie Brenston, who sang the vocal lead. Sam Phillips of Sun Records subsequently invited Ike to work on a number of the label's recordings, either as guitarist or pianist, before he met Annie Bullock for the first time in 1954. She and her sister, both of whom had been disowned by their mother, repeatedly asked if they could perform with the Kings Of Rhythm at their residency in St Louis. Ike eventually relented. Their first collaboration together was 'Boxtop', released in 1958 and credited to Ike, Carlson Oliver and Little Ann. In 1959 Turner had Brenston's child, but by the end of the decade she had moved with Ike to California to pursue a musical, then romantic, partnership. The first record credited to Ike And Tina Turner was 1960's 'A Fool In Love', a major R&B hit. The billing persevered for another fifteen years, though they weren't actually married until 1962. The Ike And Tina Turner Revue became one of the era's hottest R&B acts, touring coast to coast. Tina was put in charge of grooming female

backing singers the Ikettes, while Ike kept a tight grip on all other affairs, even fining singers for laddering their stockings. Although there was a large cast of contributing musicians, Tina's red-blooded R&B soul shakedown performances continually stole the show. Their hits included 1961's 'It's Gonna Work Out Fine' (co-written by Sylvia Robinson, the godmother of rap). At one point they released fifteen albums in three years, the Revue jobbing at various studios as they passed through town. In 1966 Ike allowed Phil Spector (who loved Tina's voice, but not Ike's production methods) to record Tina on 'River Deep Mountain High'. Credited to the duo, although Ike was not even in the studio when it was recorded, it stalled in the US but reached number three in the UK charts. In 1973 Tina's 'Nutbush City Limits', an endearing tale of smalltown restriction emboldened by a distinctive siren guitar sound, hit number four in the UK charts. But the friction between the two main protagonists was growing. For years Tina had been subjected to beatings at Ike's hands. In July 1976, after a particularly bloody exchange, she ran away from the Dallas Hilton with just thirty-five cents in her pocket. After the split Tina picked up some cabaret work in Las Vegas after initially living on food stamps, then managed to get back on her feet via two ex-members of the Human League (who got her to sing 'Ball Of Confusion' for their British Electronic Fund – BEF – project that explored various music using guest artists). Ian Craig Marsh and Martyn Ware also produced her comeback single, a version of Al Green's 'Let's Stay Together'. She went on to become one of the biggest stars of the eighties and nineties, the perfect antidote to the mainstream pop reserve of the time, while Ike cooled his heels in jail on drugs charges (he apparently got through $11 million's worth of cocaine in the sixties and seventies) and spoke bitterly of Tina's 'betrayal'.

6/Donny & Marie   Points: 330

Sexual dynamism: Zero.
Don't be silly. You can get arrested for that sort of thing. Even in Utah.

We've done the teeth jokes. By the time Marie joined the clean-living Mormon boy band the family were already pin-ups, and Donny was clear favourite with the girls. A duet career with any other female might just have ruined his teen appeal, but as Marie was his sister, and therefore didn't necessarily deserve to have her eyes scratched out, the combination was perfect. In fact, Donny deliberately teased his audience on the subject, announcing that he'd had dinner with a wonderful young girl after the show the previous night… only to reveal that it had been Marie. The pay-off line was met with roaring approval by lovestruck audience members. Marie made her solo debut in November 1973. She apparently admitted to dropping out of performing as a child because she'd 'got a little heavy' (in terms of weight rather than the Led Zeppelin sense of the word). Her first record was an instantly successful version of Anita Bryant's country ballad 'Paper Roses'. The duet idea apparently came about after Donny couldn't hit a top note in a recording session, and got Marie to help out. The record-buying public loved the duo, although some cynics couldn't help pointing out that there was possibly something a little 'Deep South' about a brother and sister singing love songs to each other while staring deep into each other's eyes. In 1976 *The*

Donny & Marie Show began its run in the US, the BBC carrying the show for UK transmission. After a further hit with a revival of Marvin Gaye and Tammi Terrell's 'Ain't Nothing Like The Real Thing', they recorded a Christmas special from the new Osmonds' studio in Utah alongside the Mormon Tabernacle Choir. But by 1978 their appeal was fading. The show was cancelled and 'On The Shelf', fatefully enough, became their final chart entry. Marie chanced her hand with a solo TV show and found acclaim for her country ballads, securing a country number one hit with 'Meet Me In Montana' with Dan Seals. By his own admission, Donny's solo career didn't really match up to that of his sister, although he scored a US number two with 'Soldier Of Love' in 1989. Instead he found redemption in a revival of Andrew Lloyd Webber's *Joseph and The Amazing Technicolor Dreamcoat*, after requiring professional help to overcome his 'social phobia'. In 1997 Donny and Marie reunited for another TV series, only to see it pulled.

5/Dollar

Points: 360

Sexual dynamism: Seven. They were made for each other.

It's possible even Paul Whitehouse's 'innit *great*' character in *The Fast Show* might have found it tricky to work up much enthusiasm over the efforts of Thereze Bazar and David Van Day. They were originally part of would-be Osmonds Guys And Dolls, who hit number two in the UK in 1975 with 'There's A Whole Lot Of Loving'. 'There were three boys and three girls, and they'd all paired off together, apart from us two,' recalls Van Day. 'So at hotels, instead of two doubles and two twins, they'd book three doubles. We'd end up in the same bed. That's how we got together.' Three years later they hatched a plan for Van Day to go solo; Bazar would keep him in spends by continuing with Guys And Dolls. When their bandmates got wind of the ruse, the pair were unceremoniously kicked out. In the classic girl-guy combination they got a flying start when 'Shooting Star' reached number 14 in the UK charts in 1978. 'David's ego was quite... sizeable,' Bazar reflects diplomatically, 'and he enjoyed the focus of attention on him. He automatically assumed he was the voice that would get most of the singing on the records and I'd be there doing frothy bits on the side.' Their next triumph was 'Love's Gotta Hold On Me', written by Van Day. When he couldn't get the singing right, Bazar took the vocal. 'Where's that put me now?' protests Van Day. 'I was meant to be doing the solo career, I've got her into a duo, and now she's doing the lead. There's hardly any of me on this track, and I wrote the bloody thing.' Cue Buggles' mainman Trevor Horn. Bazar convinced him to produce Dollar after a chance meeting on an aeroplane. 'Hand Held In Black And White' was the sumptuous result, a song that was well-received in some circles. The collaboration provided further success with 'Mirror Mirror (Mon Amour)', 'Give Me Back My Heart' and 'Videotheque'. But not everyone was convinced. As the *NME* once put it, 'everything about them – from their height to their sound to their fights – is on a very small scale.' Romance had long since left the picture, though the publicity machine never acknowledged the fact. The duo even went through the pretence of an engagement at the Savoy Hotel. Van Day remembers approaching one of the girl dancers about a dinner date. 'She said, "You're getting engaged, aren't you?" I said, "Yeah, I'll do that in a minute...."' The

bickering got worse, and Horn discovered he had some more pressing projects to work on. Van Day managed a token solo hit in 1983, but the inevitable reunion followed in 1986 as both components found themselves washed up on the shores of lake pop. Van Day ended up in court on charges of possession of cocaine, and worse, in the pages of the *Daily Mirror*, was pictured working in a mobile burger van. He has subsequently formed a cabaret band with Mike Nolan of Bucks Fizz ('it's a living') while Bazar has since raised a family in Sydney. However, the true test of eighties makeweights is, were they honoured by a tribute band? The Australian Dollar, formed in Liverpool by Joe Standerline and Dana O'Brien, say that Dollar provided a kind of magic but working out what kind it was, was possibly as challenging as trying to work out the lyrics of 'Hand Held in Black and White'.

David Van Day: 'I have as much fun selling burgers as I do records.'

4/Elton John & Kiki Dee

Points: 370

Sexual dynamism: Two. Minor compatibility problem.

Before he got to being the Queen Mother of British pop, Sir Elton John was a hitmaker with a mission, and his multi-pronged assault on the nation's charts included a duet with the slightly more chart-shy Kiki Dee. Not that Kiki (Pauline Edwards) was a passenger on their 1976 collaboration 'Don't Go Breaking My Heart', a stagey but enduring piece of pop. Everyone knows the story of the boy from Pinner with the big pianner and the penchant for Watford FC but Bradford lass Kiki was an established star in her own right at the time of the recording. Plucked from the northern club scene, she was invited to take part in the San Remo Song Festival before becoming the first white British act to be signed by Motown Records, releasing the album *Great Expectations*. 'I thought this is it,' recalls Dee, 'I'm going to do an album for Motown and become a big star. And I came back to England and it really didn't happen.' Undeterred she linked with Elton's Rocket Records via Elton's manager John Reid. The album Elton produced for her provided a Top 20 single in 'Amoureuse'. Subsequent successes included 'I Got The Music In Me' and 'How Glad Am I'. 'Meeting Elton and working at Rocket Records was so different from the Motown thing,' says Dee, 'from the experience of going to Detroit and feeling like an outsider. I felt like I'd come home.' Then came the US and UK-chart-topping duet 'Don't Go Breaking My Heart', though apparently Elton had to be persuaded to extend Dee's parts in the song. He cut his parts in America before the tapes were sent to London for Dee to add her vocal. Despite the odd circumstances of its origins, it shot to the top, aided by a video appearance in which some thought Elton looked awkward separated from his piano, and Dee wore shocking pink dungarees. Elton has put what Dee describes as a 'strange albatross' of a song to myriad uses. He's sung it to partners including Miss Piggy, the Spice Girls and Alan Partridge. Dee returned to her solo career thereafter, and also appeared in stage musicals such as *Blood Brothers*. It was a long while before Elton and Kiki got round to a follow-up, but 1993 saw them reunited as part of Elton's *Duets* album. 'I'd like to think the public can sense that Elton and I care about each other and it's not something you manufacture,' says

Dee. 'So when you do a duet together, you don't have to be madly in love with each other.' A revival of Bing Crosby and Grace Kelly's 1956 hit, this time 'True Love' reached number two in the charts. Which means they're probably due for another bash sometime in 2010, by my arithmetic.

3/John Travolta & Olivia Newton-John

Points: 400

Sexual dynamism: Nine. Electrifyin' (the power she was supplyin').

The year was 1978 and the soundtrack to the summer was *Grease*, a throwback fifties musical turned celluloid golden goose by the central performances of John Travolta and Olivia Newton-John. Born in Cambridge, but having grown up in Melbourne, Australia, Newton-John shacked up with one of Cliff Richard's Shadows before notching up her first UK hit with the Dylan cover 'If Not For You'. She also performed for the UK in 1974's Eurovision contest, losing out to Abba. Terry Wogan thought that would be 'the last we see of her'. Instead, she moved to America and almost immediately scored a number one album with the countrified *Have You Never Been Mellow*, leading to a series of TV specials. In 1977 she was approached to play the female lead, Sandy, in a film version of Broadway hit *Grease*. Predicated on fifties nostalgia with a regulation girl-meets-boy plot, it saw her star opposite Travolta, fresh from strutting the dancefloors of *Saturday Night Fever*. As director Randal Kleiser says, 'We always liked the idea of Olivia Newton-John, she was a singer, really good and very pretty. The one concern that she had was that she might look too old next to John.' Newton-John insisted on a screen test to ensure she looked 'nubile' enough. Bobbysox, ra-ra skirts and Americana abounded in the movie, despite the fact that Newton-John was an Aussie ex-pat pushing thirty. The public lapped it up, particularly in Britain, where the Leicester Square premiere sparked a near-riot. The buzz was inspired by the release of the duet 'You're The One That I Want', which topped the UK charts for the first of nine weeks in June 1978, becoming the third best-selling single in British chart history. It was written by Newton-John associate John Farrar as a last-minute 'out' song for the film, after Kleiser decided the projected version of 'All Shook Up' wasn't 'happening'. The initial reaction was hardly favourable. 'It was my first movie, my first musical, and I didn't know what a demo was,' recalls Kleiser. 'It just sounded horrible to me.' They used it anyway as the climatic finale to Sandy's makeover from demure girl-next-door to leather-clad mankiller. But was the on-stage frisson duplicated off-set? Newton-John admits to a mutual crush, although she points out that both were seeing other people at the time. As the film soundtrack topped the album charts, a further UK number one followed with 'Summer Nights', while Newton-John's solo effort 'Hopelessly Devoted To You' made number two. Afterwards she made hay as a mainstream pop star, while Scientology convert Travolta went back to 'straight' movies. Given the success they've enjoyed in their respective fields, it's hard to envisage any reunion, though *Grease* is still the word for many. A London stage musical version proved a smash hit, at one time featuring Shane Ritchie (who claims that more people have watched *Grease* than have read the Bible) in Travolta's role.

2/Captain & Tennille

Points: 640

Sexual dynamism: Three. Too homely by far.

This tree-hugging duo's roots lay in the 1972 rock musical *Mother Earth*. The ecologically themed show was co-written by Toni Tennille, the daughter of Frank, a musician who'd worked with Ben Pollack and Bing Crosby. Staged in Los Angeles, the house band featured keyboard player Daryl Dragon, the son of conductor Carmen Dragon (who'd won an Academy award for *Cover Girl* and scored the original *Invasion Of The Bodysnatchers* movie). The pair married during the show's run, before embarking on a close harmony partnership together. Their first engagement came as backing musicians to the Beach Boys, with whom Dragon had already worked extensively. His nickname came from his distinctive nautical headgear, which led to him being christened 'Captain Keyboard' by Mike Love. Their debut recording as Captain & Tennille was the self-financed 'The Way I Want To Touch You'. They were spotted by Elton John manager John Reid, who invited them to perform backing vocals on his charge's 'Don't Let The Sun Go Down On Me'. They also picked up a contract with A&M. In 1975 a version of Neil Sedaka's 'Love Will Keep Us Together' brought them their first hit and, later, a Grammy award. Further Stateside success followed with 'Lonely Night (Angel Face)' and a cover of 'Muskrat Love', which they subsequently performed before President Ford and assorted guests during the bicentennial festivities at the White House in 1976. 'When we started singing "Muskrat Love",' remembers Tennille, '[Henry] Kissinger was right in front of me, I could have touched him. He just wanted to get out of there, that's all he wanted to do. And Queen Elizabeth, they had run her around, she literally was asleep. She was dozing. I don't blame her.' Prince Philip apparently loved the song. Maybe it reminded him of small furry animals back home; the sort he shoots on a regular basis. At the height of their popularity in the late seventies they also had their own TV show. 'They tried to squeeze us into the Sonny & Cher formula', reflects Tennille, 'and we really didn't fit.' A label switch from A&M to Casablanca Records produced their biggest hit when Tennille's composition 'Do That To Me One More Time' topped the US charts. Tennille wrote it about the first time the lurve captain had planted a smacker on her lips: 'My first thought was, mmm, I wish he'd do that again.' The duo's career declined in the eighties, Tennille later going on to record several solo albums of jazz and big band material as well as appearing in musicals. The Captain? 'I had a mental breakdown and was in a hospital for fourteen years,' he reminisces, before being chided by his wife for telling whoppers. Him indoors rejoined her in 2000 for a Captain & Tennille 25th anniversary tour, but otherwise they live a 'good, natural, normal kind of a life' in Reno, Texas. Despite two platinum albums and one platinum single, the impression remains for many that they were the Carpenters without the problems.

1/Sonny & Cher

Points: 760

Sexual dynamism: Five.
Cher got to be sexy in her forties. Sonny never made it at all.

Sonny and Cher were the sixties' chosen ones, the beautiful people of the hippy era. Well, maybe not Sonny. Cherilyn Sarkasian La Pier was born in 1945, after her mother abandoned a planned abortion. It's fair to say Cher was a bit forward – aged fifteen she bluffed her way onto a film set apparently with the singular intention of meeting Warren Beatty. When she travelled to Los Angeles to take acting lessons she met Phil Spector's errand boy Salvatore Bono, aka 'Sonny'. Bono had already recorded under various guises before getting a job with Spector. Influenced by Spector's 'gilded cage' treatment of wife Veronica ('Ronnie') Bennett, and embarrassed by his own clumsy vocals, he attempted to emulate his mentor by moulding Cher, who was immensely impressionable, into his protégé. He managed to sneak her into a Crystals recording session, where she made her debut singing back-up on 'Da Doo Ron Ron'. Cher's vocals also adorned hits by Darlene Love and most of the Ronettes' output. Her first solo single for Spector, 'Ringo I Love You', was a novelty record inspired by Beatlemania, credited to Bonnie Jo Mason. Eventually Sonny tired of being turned down by Spector and pushed the concept of the two of them as a singing duo to anyone who'd listen. His first idea was to cash in on the success of the Taylor-Burton film *Cleopatra* by having photos taken of the pair in Egyptian garb. Needless to say the single, credited to Caesar and Cleo, flopped. Their first single as Sonny & Cher was 'Baby Don't Go'. Thereafter they secured support gigs with Ike and Tina Turner, before Sonny convinced Ahmet Ertegun of Atlantic Records to finance the recording of his latest composition, 'I Got You Babe'. Released in August 1965 it topped the charts on both sides of the Atlantic. Their reputation grew, bolstered by an extravagant dress code – nobody wore bell-bottoms as well as Cher (although her choice of trousers was actually informed by a lack of confidence in the way her legs looked). Hogging the limelight for all they were worth (critics acknowledge that any perceived deficiencies in talent was made up for by naked ambition), they turned up on *The Man From U.N.C.L.E.* and cut a series of solo as well as duet efforts. They were advised to produce a film by Presley manager Colonel Tom Parker, and came up with *Good Times*, a lightweight but essentially entertaining romp. After the purchase of a huge mansion and multiple motorbikes and cars, the acid rock of Jimi Hendrix arrived to wipe out their complacency. Suddenly they were thought of as 'squares' by some, an impression exacerbated by Sonny's decision to make a government anti-drug film. Another film flopped, though its title, *Chastity*, was the name Cher gave their first daughter. With record sales declining, Sonny put together a cabaret show. CBS took a gamble and televised the format. Colourful but cheesy, it immediately became a huge hit, not least because of Bob Mackie's dress designs for Cher. It helped her gain her first substantial solo hit with 'Gypsies, Tramps And Thieves'. Thereafter their relationship cooled, and Sonny had to beg Cher to complete a final TV series in 1973. They were divorced a year later, as Cher went on to a phenomenally successful solo and acting career. Some felt reactionary old Sonny revealed what a hippy turncoat he was by becoming Republican mayor of Palm Springs (speaking out against same-sex marriages, despite daughter

Chastity being a lesbian activist). He died in January 1998 after a skiing accident. Cher gave the eulogy at his funeral.

Some Other Top Pop Duets

George Michael & Mary J. Blige: 'As' (1999)
Luther Vandross and Mariah Carey: 'Endless Love' (1994)
Peter Gabriel and Kate Bush: 'Don't Give Up' (1986)
Nancy Sinatra and Frank Sinatra: 'Somethin' Stupid' (1967)
Joe Cocker and Jennifer Warnes: 'Up Where We Belong' (1983)
Cliff Richard and Sarah Brightman: 'All I Ask Of You' (1986)
Kenny Rogers and Dolly Parton: 'Islands In The Stream' (1983)
Lulu and Bobby Womack: 'I'm Back For More' (1993)
Diana Ross and Michael Jackson: 'Ease On Down The Road' (1978)
Deborah Harry and Iggy Pop: 'Well, Did You Evah!' (1991)

Caribbean

White sands, skimpy bikinis, rum and reefers. Pass the coochie, or, if it's before the watershed, the Bounties and Lilts. The Caribbean comprises over 1,000 islands stretching from Cuba to Trinidad and Tobago. Many are beach paradises. Sixteenth-century Europeans loved the Caribbean so much, they nicked it. In post-colonial days, the sunshine sounds celebrated here have become one of the fundamental planks of the Caribbean economy, exporting reggae, salsa, soca and calypso to the world.

Caribbean music first influenced the broader culture via the fifties calypso of Harry Belafonte. Jamaica then took the lead. In 1962 ska achieved indigenous supremacy, powered by the wonderful Prince Buster and producer Coxsone Dodd. Ska then switched tempo to the more sedate rocksteady, mutating finally into reggae – also an umbrella term for all Jamaican music. This more soulful, R&B-influenced derivative was politicized by Rastafarianism into cultural or roots reggae, crossing many international borders. Its dominance of the seventies was then superseded by the rough-and-ready hybrid of ragga or dancehall music, a controversial and lurid style employing new digital equipment.

Yet there's more to Caribbean music than reggae – witness the sultry romanticism of Cuba, the island that gave the world the rumba and the mambo, the sizzling salsa of Puerto Rico, Haiti's voodoo (or spirit) musicians and the calypso and soca of Trinidad. The following ten Caribbean-born artists are not necessarily the best examples of their art, nor do they represent all of those traditions, but they are the ones who have had the biggest impact on British record buyers.

10/Jimmy Cliff

Points: 103

33 weeks in chart ● 2 Top 10 hits

Jimmy Cliff brought Jamaican music to a world audience and forged the commercial path followed by Bob Marley and every subsequent reggae artist. A recording star from the age of fourteen, Cliff was mentored by ska veteran Derrick Morgan, who remembers him as a quiet non-drinker and non-smoker. After being signed by Chris Blackwell of Island Records

and relocating to London, he was groomed as reggae's first crossover star. However, some of the compromises that entailed – including what some felt was an ill-advised cover of 'A Whiter Shade Of Pale' – tested Cliff's patience at least as much as that of his core audience. At one point in 1969, stranded in Kent without money and forced to subsist on fish and chips, he wrote the lyrics to 'Many Rivers To Cross', probably the only reggae song to reference the 'White Cliffs of Dover'. 'He just wrote a song based on that experience,' explains friend Delroy Washington. 'He was wondering how much more he had to do to gain total acceptance.' Cliff then wrote and sang the soundtrack to 1972 film *The Harder They Come*, in which he starred as an aspiring singer being short-changed by the industry. Carl Bradshaw appeared in the film and remembers it opening in Kingston. 'It was like a sea of people. And to get inside the cinema, people were walking on people's heads.' The film's theme predicted Cliff's own problems with Island. When he departed, Blackwell immediately recruited Bob Marley in his stead, but this time let the artist work, unhindered, within his own idiom. Cliff maintained his popularity in Jamaica, as well as the South American and African markets, where his stature rivals that of Marley. He has recently written extensively for Hollywood films including *The Lion King* and *Cool Runnings*.

9/Ricky Martin   Points: 203

63 weeks in chart ● 4 Top 40 singles

Sending them 'Loco' down the youth club disco, Ricky Martin is largely responsible for sending the globe Latin music crazy at the turn of millennium. Having sung professionally since childhood in San Juan, he joined Puerto Rican institution Menudo in 1984 at the age of twelve. Menudo traditionally dropped members on the day they turned sixteen. 'At night time we would escape, go out and get drunk and have a good time,' remembers Robi Rosa, fellow Menudo member and solo collaborator. 'Later on, you realize how evil the whole thing was.' Martin outgrew Menudo in 1989, and completed his high school studies before launching himself as a solo artist in 1991. In 1994 he took the role of Miguel Morez in soap opera *General Hospital*, subsequently appearing on Broadway. His first English-language pop album, 1998's *Ricky Martin*, made him an international superstar. 'La Copa De La Vida' was the official song of the France 98 World Cup finals. He then scored a worldwide number one with the rump-shaking 'Livin' La Vida Loca'. Wayne Isham was the video director. 'You've got this beautiful lady laying with Ricky – "Do you want her to pour candle wax on you?" The record company's going, "No! You can't do that!" Ricky's going, "Yeah! Come on!".' As his success spiralled, some queried his authenticity, though he challenges his critics to come up with a better description than 'Latin' for the music he makes. Others questioned his sexuality. Boy George was accused of 'outing' Martin by an English newspaper, although he denied the charge, broadening his argument to point out that there was no need for anyone to stay in the closet any more, and that George Michael could have had a whole lot more fun if he'd declared his true sexuality twenty years ago. In contrast to his sex symbol image, Ricky's someone who has talked about having a brood of children in the future. A case of living the quiet life instead of the 'vida loca'.

▲ **Eighties Romantics: Duran Duran**

▼ **Caribbean: Bob Marley**

◗ **Comedy Records: the Goons' 'Ying Tang Song'**

▲ *Teen Idols: Donny Osmond*

▼ *Disco: Bee Gees*

▲ *Progressive Rock: Pink Floyd*

 **Holiday Songs: Mungo Jerry's 'In the Summertime'**

Eurovision: Ireland – Dana

Stadium Rock: Aerosmith

▲ **Punk: Sex Pistols**

 **Christmas Songs:
Bing Crosby's
'White Christmas'**

▲ **Glam Rock: Slade**

8/Shabba Ranks

Points: 217

77 weeks in chart ● 8 Top 40 hits

When reggae switched from 'cultural' to 'slack' or sexually explicit themes in the eighties, no-one got down and dirty with more gusto than Rexton Fernando Gordon, aka Shabba Ranks. Shabba pioneered the stripped down, mercilessly rhythmic distillation of conventional reggae riddims that denoted ragga, which displaced roots reggae in Kingston's dancehalls. Traditionalists decried the new hybrid for its violent imagery and denigration of women. Shabba was having none of it. 'It's music. And music is a power and a universal language that communicate with people even more than the telephone.' After becoming the dominant force in reggae in 1989, Shabba signed to Epic for a telephone number fee. He was the first reggae artist to win a Grammy for *Raw As Ever*, then repeated the feat with follow-up album *X-tra Naked*. 'Mr Loverman', which was released in 1993 and eventually hit number three on its re-release in the British charts, underlined Shabba's carnal fixations. 'Why is it that you can't deal with sex with your gal,' is his incredulous retort. 'If someone sing about it, it offends you?' Eddy Grant believes implicit racism lay behind the attacks. More controversially, in December 1992 Shabba, live on *The Word*, observed that gays deserved crucifixion. Boy George, an unlikely ragga fan, was saddened, as he admired Shabba's voice; he comments that it appears as soon as Shabba realized the detrimental effect his comment had had on his career, he retracted it. However, Shabba denies being even a little bit apologetic. 'I'm not apologizing for nothin'. I done nothin' wrong.' Shunned by an outraged media, Shabba's career nosedived, and he currently lives in semi-retirement in New York.

Singer Marcia Griffiths: 'I'm totally against those lyrics, because I'm a woman, and a lot of these lyrics disrespect women.'

Shabba Ranks: 'Look at how much millions of dollars Playboy makes. It's sex. It sells. Without sex, we are not here.'

7/Desmond Dekker

Points: 265

75 weeks in chart ● 6 Top 20 hits

In the mid-sixties, as ska became a worldwide contagion, its rude boy adherents giving it those crazy dance steps, no-one was a more effective missionary than Desmond Dekker. It had taken him two years to convince Derrick Morgan at Beverley's Records to give him a chance. Frustration, in the end, proved to be his salvation. After telling Morgan that he didn't care if he listened to his song or not, Morgan finally gave in. The song was 'Honour Your Mother And Father', which was to become an instant hit in Kingston. Dekker then enjoyed an international breakthrough in 1967. '(007) Shanty Town' mixed imagery from James Bond films with echoes of the Kingston riots. The engineer on the session was Graeme Goodhall. 'He had this beautiful voice that was just so easy to get down, it was just incredible.' Invited to Britain to record, some genius had the bright idea of getting him to drive a double decker bus – Dekker remembers having no clue where he was going. His biggest hit was inspired by a more contemplative moment. He was sat in a London park

when he overheard an argument about maintenance payments. He started humming the lines to what became 'The Israelites', the first UK reggae chart-topper. By the time he followed up with 'You Can Get It If You Really Want', his label realized that Dekker could use some serious dental help. His molars had become so rotten, his face was contorting. Goodhall remembers that there was so much work to do, Dekker required a general anaesthetic. 'When he came out of the anaesthetic, there must have been a reaction. He kicked the nurse into the next room – unconscious.' When Morgan came to London to check out his one-time prodigy, he claims Dekker didn't want to know him. Dekker has continued to perform, prospering from his reputation as a reggae innovator and the author of one of the great songs of the sixties.

6/Shaggy
Points: 293

73 weeks in chart ● 6 Top 20 singles

If Shabba Ranks brought dancehall reggae to the UK, it was Shaggy that broke America. Elastic-limbed Orville Burrell was nicknamed Shaggy after Scooby Doo's sidekick, but he never liked the moniker. 'I actually hated it,' he confesses. 'Then I went to England and found out that "shag" meant… something else.' He learned his craft on the tough, hyper-competitive Kingston sound circuit. 'I could diss you, and have the crowd laughing at you, but you could not be mad at me, because I was doing it in such a way that it was fun.' He moved to New York aged eighteen and found work selling ice cream. There he met friend and co-singer Rayvon. 'We was in a Caribbean neighbourhood when we met, Flatbush, Brooklyn. We stay in New York, but we still have a Caribbean background and influence.' Then, rather impetuously perhaps, Burrell joined up. 'The Marines had the best-looking uniform, that's the one I went with. I didn't know what it was about. I thought it was a little summer camp thing.' That summer camp thing turned out to be the Gulf War. 'I wasn't the gung-ho type of kid running round trying to shoot people. I just gave a lot of trouble. I had a big mouth.' While still in the Marines, he enjoyed domestic hits with the likes of 'Big Up', but his international breakthrough came in 1992, three months after his discharge, with a show-stopping version of the Folks Brothers' classic 'Oh, Carolina'. It topped the UK charts in early 1993. It was widely thought that Shaggy was merely a one-hit wonder. However, in 1995 his version of Mungo Jerry's 'In The Summertime' re-established a chart presence. Then came Shaggy's finest hour. The dynamic 'Boombastic', reminiscent of Shabba's 'Mr Loverman', shot straight to the top of the US and UK charts, buoyed by its appearance on a Levi's advertisement.

5/Fugees
Points: 350

130 weeks in chart ● 4 Top 10 hits

Haiti, officially the poorest country in the West, is the unlikely home of one of the world's most successful groups, one that co-exists happily within a pop, R&B or hip-hop framework. They qualify for inclusion because Wyclef Jean and Pras Michel (Prakazrel Michel)

were both Haitian refugees – a fact alluded to in their choice of band name. Wyclef recalls arriving in New York as a nine-year-old. 'I remember looking out the window and seeing all those big skyscrapers. I said, "Wow, $100 bills is going to fly from the ceiling, and I'm going to be grabbing it from out of the sky." Then reality struck, and I was in a project.' There he met cousin and fellow musician Pras. He was already working with fifteen-year-old Lauryn Hill, who completed the trio. *The Score*, released in 1994, became an international best-seller following two massive hits. The first was a revival of the Roberta Flack standard 'Killing Me Softly', the second, 'Ready Or Not', was based on Wyclef sampling Enya, of all people. The lyric? 'Lauryn came in the room and just started singing,' he remembers. Both songs topped the UK charts. The group were feted on their 1997 homecoming to Haiti as guests of President Aristide, the latter subsequently declaring Wyclef to be a star who represented the dignity of Haiti among the world's artists. The Fugees also began an annual benefit concert for the country's impoverished citizens. Jamaican producer Maxine Walters believes 'they're very moved by the plight of Haiti'. On a subsequent trip to Jamaica in 1996, the Fugees met and worked with Bob Marley's extended family, Lauryn having a daughter by Bob's son Rohan. Thereafter the Fugees splintered, though a permanent split was initially denied. Wyclef Jean hit first as a solo star with 'Gone Till November', followed by Pras with 'Ghetto Superstar (That Is What You Are)'. Both were eclipsed by the success of Lauryn Hill's debut solo album, which won an unprecedented five Grammys. It seems unlikely they'll work together again, though. Pras: 'I left on good terms. But Clef and Lauryn....' Over to Wyclef: 'Nobody be returning my calls. Lauryn, if you're listening....'

4/Eddy Grant

Points: 650

220 weeks in chart ● 7 Top 10 hits

Never a favourite among reggae purists, Guyana native Eddy Grant has nevertheless constructed an enviable track record after four decades in the business. He started out in the sixties as producer and songwriter of the Equals, one of the first successful multi-racial bands. As well as the 1968 number one 'Baby Come Back', they enjoyed a week-long stint on the classic BBC children's TV programme *Playschool*. But the pace of the pop lifestyle got to him. On new year's morning 1971 he had a heart attack, aged just twenty-one, an incident that should have, if nothing else, warned him to ease up on things. Grant responded by setting up his own record label, studio, pressing plant and publishing company. Jamaican writer Dermot Hussey reckons he's 'never met an artist out of the Caribbean experience that is so knowledgeable about music and the business of music.' Grant started manufacturing records for companies including CBS and Motown. In 1984 he used the profits to buy all his own catalogue back. A musical as well as business perfectionist, he plays all his own instruments, which confused *Top Of The Pops* during his successful early eighties run. He was therefore forced to recruit imaginary band members for hits such as 'Living On The Front Line', 'Do You Feel My Love?' and his only number one, 'I Don't Want To Dance'. While aficionados dismissed him as a lightweight, Grant insists that there's protest in every one of his songs, and that it remains a key part of his

art. The most explicit example is 1988's 'Gimme Hope Jo'anna', attacking South African apartheid. These days Grant's pioneering a hybrid of reggae and calypso he calls 'ring-bang'. Now happily settled in Barbados, he's bought up the rights to thousands of calypso songs to prevent them passing into the hands of multinational record companies.

3/Billy Ocean
Points: 745

295 weeks in chart ● 10 Top 10 hits

Leslie Charles was born in Trinidad. Shortly after his father left for England in 1958, he followed. He took a job at Ford's Dagenham car plant while nursing ambitions of getting his singing career off the ground. The success of 'Love Really Hurts Without You' in February 1976 saw him leave the production line for a spot on *Top Of The Pops*. His first global success came with 1984's 'Caribbean Queen (No More Love On The Run)' – the video filmed in glamorous Charing Cross Road. Now an established star, the bumper sticker-slogan-turned-song, 'When The Going Gets Tough, The Tough Get Going', hit number one in 1986. However, a video featuring *The Jewel Of The Nile* cast Danny De Vito, Kathleen Turner and Michael Douglas on backing vocals was banned because they weren't members of the Musician's Union. Ocean's next Top 10 hit, 'Get Outta My Dreams, Get Into My Car' also

Billy Ocean: 'Imagine leaving the Caribbean, with all the sunshine and everything else. I came here in just a short-sleeved shirt, and short grey trousers. And I froze my b*******s off.'

found trouble – incredibly, it was thought that it might encourage kerbcrawling. Nowadays, Ocean keeps a low profile, playing incognito in West London's Ebony Steel Band. In 1991 the police interrupted a rehearsal and charged Ocean and other members with supplying cannabis. When he told the detectives who he was, Ocean says, 'even the temperature of the room changed.' The charges were dropped. 'It wasn't a very nice experience. I often wonder, had I not been who I was, what would have happened.' A born-again dreadlocked Rasta, these days he is happy to idle away his time away from the entertainment industry, tending his Surrey garden. 'You're closer to God in the garden than anywhere else on the Earth,' he concludes.

2/Gloria Estefan
Points: 1189

449 weeks in chart ● 28 Top 40 hits

Born Gloria Fajardo in Havana a year before Fidel Castro came to power, Estefan's family sensibly fled to Miami when she was two – her father had been a bodyguard for the deposed Batista regime. But Gloria kept in touch with her roots through following the traditions that her family maintained after they left. Her childhood was spent nursing a father crippled by the chemical Agent Orange in the Vietnam war. Music gave her some release from her chores. Her singing career developed in tandem with ever-present husband Emilio Estefan – legendarily, the only man she's ever kissed. Together they

formed Miami Sound Machine, best known for 1984's 'Dr Beat'. They had strong hopes for follow-up 'Conga' and the track was set to become another British hit until its success was stymied by some likely lads from Yorkshire: Black Lace stole Estefan's thunder with 'Do The Conga'. Estefan then went solo, becoming the most successful Latin act in pop history, with over thirty hit singles and three US number ones. In 1990 she broke several vertebrae in her back when she was involved in a tour bus collision. Fearing she'd be confined to a wheelchair like her father, she underwent extensive surgery after being temporarily paralysed. A complex rearrangement of her skeleton was required. However, she reveals with a smile that she doesn't set off security alarms at airports as she comes reinforced with titanium. As well as pursuing her musical career, now almost exclusively in her native Spanish tongue, she has become a prominent anti-Castro campaigner. She and Emilio doubt if she'll ever return to mainstream pop music, however.

1/Bob Marley

Points: 1264

634 weeks in chart ● 8 Top 10 hits

The man who made reggae a global pulse and gave the disenfranchised a sincere and eloquent voice, Bob Marley remains as loved today as he was in his prime. Born in Jamaica in 1945, the son of a white captain in the British Army, his early years were informed by experiences in the ghettos of Kingston. He became the leader of vocal trio the Wailers, additionally featuring Peter Tosh and Bunny Wailer, in 1963. After local success with Lee Perry and their own label Tuff Gong, the Wailers were signed by Chris Blackwell to Island and sent to London to record 1973's *Catch A Fire*. As friend Delroy Washington notes, it was the beginning of their journey 'from Kingston, Jamaica, to Kingston, Surrey.' The Wailers soon splintered. In 1974, Marley asked keyboard player Earl 'Wire' Lindo why he was smoking so much ganja. Washington remembers 'Bunny coming down the stairs and saying to Bob that he should leave Wire alone. Bob spoke to Bunny in no uncertain terms and told him what he'd do to him.' Bunny and Tosh left the picture, leaving Bob to recruit backing vocalists the I-Threes – Marcia Griffiths, Judy Mowatt and wife Rita. 'We used to take care of Bob,' says Griffiths, 'make sure his hair is washed and greased.' Bob, however, had a wandering eye. His most famous liaison was with Cindy Breakspeare, who won Miss World for Jamaica in 1976. 'I epitomized everything that Bob should not have been looking for in a woman,' Breakspeare admits. 'I was someone who went on stage in a bikini and exposed my entire body and said, here, judge me on my flesh.' Nevertheless, they had a son together, one of at least fourteen Marley fathered. But it was his transparent integrity and ability to write uplifting music of unparalleled emotional reach that was his true legacy, a reflection of the fact that Marley had the common touch and never lost his ability to communicate with the people on the street. Jamaican politicians courted him, which made him vulnerable to Jamaica's warring political factions. Two days before a concert at Kingston's National Heroes Park, Marley was the victim of an attempted assassination. Despite a bullet lodging in his elbow, he performed anyway. It took his lifelong love of football to fell him. A toe injury diagnosed in 1977 developed into cancer. Three years later, he collapsed in Central Park. Breakspeare was at his bedside during his final hours in a

Miami hospital. 'He was down to 90lbs, it was just tubes and needles. Not the way you want to see anyone you loved.' Marley was dead, aged just thirty-six. His loss was felt far beyond Jamaica's shores.

White Boys Can't Skank
Ten White Acts Who Cashed In On Caribbean Music

Andy Fairweather-Low: 'Reggae Tune' (1974)
Typically Tropical: 'Barbados' (1975)
Paul Nicholas: 'Reggae Like It Used To Be' (1976)
10cc: 'Dreadlock Holiday' (1978)
Goombay Dance Band: 'Sun Of Jamaica' (1982)
Enya: 'Caribbean Blue' (1991)
Zig And Zag: 'Them Girls Them Girls' (1994)
Sid 'Ricky!' Owen: 'Good Thing Going' (2000)
The Police: Everything
UB40: Everything, only more often

Eurovision

$\boldsymbol{\mathcal{S}}$ince 1956 the Eurovision Song Contest, 'a triumph of bad taste and bad music' according to long-suffering (but hard-laughing) observer Terry Wogan, has grimly ritualized cheap sentiment, cheesy songwriting and bad dress sense. The idea came from Frenchman Marcel Baison, who had noted the success of the San Remo song Festival, which began four years previously. The contest became an anachronism as soon as the Beatles redrafted the possibilities of pop. But somehow, nobody could be bothered to put it out of its misery and show this well-flogged horse the way to the knacker's yard. Over four decades the competition has retained notoriety as a feast of kitsch and a smorgasbord of schmaltz. Originally intended to foster peace and goodwill amongst nations, that spirit has been eroded as the voting system is systematically reduced to a xenophobic network of shameless alliances and enmities. Yet a Europe-wide audience of 600 million suggests some nations haven't cottoned on to the joke yet.

Those who missed the Top Ten include Germany (put your handkerchief away, sir), Italy (who twice didn't enter because they cheekily decided it was rubbish) and Norway, bless them. The Scandinavian country synonymous with the expression 'nul points' has plumbed depths unimagined by their neighbours. Floored by a record-breaking third pointless finish courtesy of Finn Kalvik in 1981, they eventually broke their duck when Bobbysocks scored in 1985 and again with Secret Garden a decade later. So there's hope for everyone. Unless you're Greece.

This list of the crème de la crud is based on appearances, finishing positions and win bonuses. Can you hear me, Copenhagen? These are the results of our international jury...

10/Switzerland
Points: 65

43 Appearances ● 2 Wins

Switzerland won the first Eurovision contest in 1956 with Lys Assia's 'Refrain'. 'I had the best vocals, the best song and lyrics, of course,' she says, with typical Swiss assurance. Her follow-up efforts in 1957 and 1958 got nowhere, however. Peter Reber, a five-time loser, is Switzerland's patron saint of Eurovision. Four times he was a member of singing group Peter, Paul and Marc, first coming twelfth in 1971 with 'Les Illusions De Nos Vingt Ans'. They tried again in 1976 (coming a respectable fourth with 'Djambo Djambo'), 1979 and 1981. 'I realized it was a great chance to play in front of an audience of 500 million people without paying the cost of the marketing campaign,' Reber says, in an attempt at self-justification. Reber also wrote the 1977 entry for the Pepe Lienhard Band. 'Swiss Lady' was the first pop record to employ the Alpine horn. 'Some people who are purists, they say you can't do that with Swiss folk music. But I think music is fun, everything is allowed.' Not to be deterred, Reber clung to his Eurovision ambitions by augmenting core trio Peter,

Terry Wogan: 'The Celine Dion we know and love is a handsome woman. That's not the way I remember her from Eurovision.'

Paul and Marc with Pfuri, Gorps and Kniri for the 1979 Jerusalem finals. The additional trio were famed in Switzerland for employing bottle openers, hoses and refuse bags to produce 'trash' music. 'When we arrived in Israel,' recalls Reber, 'the security people wouldn't believe these were musical instruments. People didn't like it too much, because they were thinking we were making fun of the Eurovision Song Contest. Maybe we did.' Switzerland had to wait another nine years before lifting the trophy again, and they required the assistance of a French Canadian girl of some notoriety. Wearing a see-through chandelier of a mini-skirt and modelling a memorable hairstyle, Celine Dion took 'Ne Partez Pas Sans Moi' to the top in 1988.

9/Spain

Points: 66

39 Appearances ● 2 Wins

Massiel pursued her dream to win the Eurovision Song Contest in 1968 with 'La La La'. She got her chance only because a recalcitrant Catalonian had refused to sing the lyric, such as it was, in Spanish. Franco was not impressed, and the Catalonian got the bullet. Not literally, we hope. In winning, Massiel managed to beat off the thrusting challenge of our very own Cliff Richard and his 'Congratulations'. 'He's a very good person,' says the generous Massiel, 'and a very good performer'. The contest was hosted in Madrid the following year, and Salome's 'Vivo Cantado' was hot favourite to retain the title for Spain. No-one could have predicted the final result: a four-way tie on 18 points between Spain, the UK, Holland and France. At the turn of the seventies a very youthful Julio Iglesias, bedecked in turquoise flares, offered the world 'Gwendolyne'. However, he was outgunned by Ireland's Dana, finishing fourth. 'As a Eurovision entry I simply don't remember him,' admits Terry Wogan. Mocedades' 'Eres Tu' finished a creditable second in 1973, relegating poor old Cliff Richard (again) to third place. The nineties have been less fertile, Eurovision-wise, for Spain, though Azucar Moreno's 1990 effort 'Bandido' did amuse. The backing tapes malfunctioned and the performers, unsure of their cue, started in too early and were forced to leave the stage and come back on again.

Terry Wogan on Julio Iglesias: 'I had the privilege of interviewing him a couple of times. Without doubt, he's one of the greatest eejits I've ever talked to in my life.'

8/Malta
Points: 75

12 Appearances ● 0 Wins

Joe Grech became the first proud son of Malta to take part in the contest in 1971 with 'Marija L-Maltija'. He came last. Popular duo Helen and Joseph then upped the ante with 'L-Imhabba' in 1972, their performance styled on hippy lovers Sonny and Cher (although some noted a passing resemblance to Tarby and Olive from *On The Buses*). They too finished bottom of the heap. Helen's younger brother Renato then took up the mantle. He was the first Maltese entrant to sing in English, though the lyrics were classic Eurovision. Renato claims he came back a hero, simply by dint of not finishing last. The Maltese thought they'd finally struck gold in 1998 when the amply proportioned Chiara sang 'The One That I Love'. 'A lot of people say, "oh, she's a fat girl,"' says Renato. ' It's irrelevant. It's the voice they're listening to after all. It's a nice voice. It's a song contest, not a beauty contest.' 'I did have faith in the song and I did know I could do it', reckons Chiara, 'so I gave it my best.' Israel and Malta were neck and neck on the final count until Macedonia gave their twelve points to Croatia, tipping the balance in favour of Israel. 'I coped very well,' insists Chiara. 'I was very relaxed. I was going to my dressing room, and this man from the BBC told me, "You were the real diva of the night." That was it, I spent two hours in my dressing room crying.' Trust Auntie to rain on her parade. When she flew back to Valetta, however, she was greeted as a conquering heroine, 6,000 fans clamouring for a bit of Chiara.

7/Netherlands
Points: 79

42 Appearances ● 4 Wins

Homeland of the Smurfs and bereft of any worthwhile musical pedigree, the Dutch nation got off to a flying Eurovision start when Corry Brocken won the second competition in 1957. The next year she entered again, but was awarded only a single point. The Dutch triumphed in 1959, however, when the funkily named Teddy Scholten charmed the punters with 'Een Beetje'. A decade later, Lennie Kuhr restored Dutch pride, winning with 'De Troubadour'. Sandra & Andres then performed a vibrant 1971 duet ('infectious, gay and bouncy', according to a smitten commentator, whose view sadly did not coincide with that of the judges). Sandra Reemer also made a solo attempt in 1979, but only managed twelfth. In 1974, as Abba took the title in Brighton, Mouth & MacNeal's surreal duet 'I See A Star' came in a creditable third. The following year, a Dutch act collected the trophy. Getty Friel was the lead singer with Teach-In, Holland's final winners, who entertained us all with the erudite 'Ding Dinge Dong'. 'In that time it was very trendy,' claims Friel, mysteriously. The song had a message, though, beneath the somewhat impenetrable title. If your lover leaves you, it suggests, simply sing 'Ding Dinge Dong' and you'll feel better. Go on, try it.

6/Luxembourg

Points: 85

38 Appearances ● 4 Wins

Luxembourg is the Chelsea of Eurovision, a hugely cosmopolitan state preferring to import aspirants rather than nurture domestic talent. As Eurovision rules do not preclude the use of foreigners, with a population of less than half a million, perhaps they can be forgiven for employing the odd ringer. Nana Mouskouri (Greece), Baccara (Spain), Plastic Bertrand (Belgium), Geraldine (Ireland), Vicky Leandros (Greece again) and Anne-Marie David (France) have all flown Luxembourg's flag of convenience. And that's all the more understandable when you consider domestic efforts such as Sophie & Magaly's 1980 abomination, 'Le Papa Pinguoin', performed in full-size penguin regalia. Luxembourg first appealed for outside help in 1963 in the sexy but speccy shape of Nana Mouskouri, currently hounding the British government for the return of the Elgin Marbles. She finished eighth and headed for the hills. Two wins in the sixties (Jean-Claude Pascal and France Gall) were followed by consecutive winners in 1972 (Vicky Leandros) and 1973, when Anne-Marie David successfully defended the title in Luxembourg. The show was interrupted by threats from international terrorists Black September. Terry Wogan was faced with machine-gun nests, tracker dogs and razor wire on his way to the auditorium. 'I'll never forget the floor manager saying to the audience: "Please do not stand up to applaud, or you may be shot by security."' Anne-Marie's sterling efforts received a sitting ovation, naturally. For their next success, Luxembourg's talent scouts looked to Spain where they recruited Baccara, a group who'd enjoyed UK chart success with 'Yes Sir, I Can Boogie'. They rewrote that successful formula for their 1978 entry, 'Parlez Vous Français?' Luxembourg won again in 1983 with Corinne Hermes, but haven't bothered to enter for the last six years.

> **Baccara singer:** 'We were Spanish, with a record company in America, with a contract in Germany, representing Luxembourg and singing in French. So it was a mix-up.'

5/Sweden

Points: 93

39 Appearances ● 4 Wins

Our Swedish friends were late bloomers in Eurovision terms. Enter Abba, or Björn, Benny, Agnetha and Anni-Frid as they were then called. The group submitted 'Ring, Ring' to domestic judges in 1973, but failed to get past the qualifying heats. Perhaps that mishap could be attributed to the group's tortuous moniker, thought Björn Ulvaeus. 'We had a competition in a Swedish evening paper. "What should they be called?" Something like 80% said Abba. There is a fish cannery in Sweden called Abba, the biggest one, really. All the herrings we get are from there. We had to ask them. "Yes," they said. "As long as you don't dabble in fish."' A year later the rechristened band sang of their 'Waterloo', in so doing unveiling the definitive Eurovision song (though due to IRA bomb threats, the historic win almost never happened). Ulvaeus insists he was taken aback by the reception. 'I didn't dare think that this could win. There were many contenders, difficult ones.'

Mistress of Ceremonies Katie Boyle also remembers the occasion well, though perhaps not for the obvious reasons. 'I chose a satin dress, salmon pink. The dresser was sweet. She said, "Hate to tell you, the bra shows, the pants show, everything shows. We'll whip those off." So I solemnly went on stage, knowing I was going to be in front of 600 million, with not a stitch on underneath.' Abba went on to unprecedented international success (temporarily overtaking

Björn Ulvaeus: 'Benny said it was the most exciting thing in his life, watching those twelve points coming in, realizing with three or four countries left, we already had enough.'

Volvo as Sweden's highest foreign currency earners), but the country had to wait a decade for another Eurovision winner. The Herreys did the trick with the altogether awful 'Diggy-Loo Diggi-Ley' in 1984. 'It may not be the worst song', reflects Terry Wogan, 'it may just be the golden boots they wore on the night. That was shocking in its own right.' The group never enjoyed Abba's post-Eurovision longevity, however. As Richard Herrey admits: 'Time moves on. We were basically a boy band. We're not boys any more.' Sweden struck again in 1991 with Carola. She pipped France's Amina after they tied on 146 points and the jury had to award the trophy on the basis of who had the most maximum twelve-point verdicts. Some could be forgiven for thinking Amina hasn't quite gotten over it. 'For me, it was rubbish, anyway,' she opines. Carola gets in the last word. 'It's always something to remember, and to talk to your grandchildren about. So, I'm very happy.' The Swedes won again in 1999 with Charlotte Nilsson's 'Take Me To Your Heaven', even if that old upstager Dana International forgot to present her with the trophy.

4/France

Points: 101

42 Appearances ● 5 Wins

The French, being effortlessly superior and all, have tried vainly to infuse Eurovision with a touch of Gallic sophistication. They won in 1958 with the Nat King Cole-like André Claveau and again in 1960. Jacqueline Bower's 'Tom Pillibi' inspired generations of future divas, including 1971 winner Severine (who won it for Monaco, who competed separately between 1959 and 1979). She recalls it as a wonderfully 'romantic' moment. Marie Myriam, who represented France in 1977, found the experience more gruelling. 'Everybody said, you must win, because you are representing France. At this time in 1977, Eurovision was very important in France.' Throughout her performance her hands shook uncontrollably. The delight at her victory was tempered by a few logistical problems. A cameraman attempted a tracking shot of Myriam moving from the backstage area to accept the award but tripped over and smacked himself in the face with his lens. 'I stopped crying, and said, "Give me some ice, give me some ice!" And everybody was waiting for me.' As the auditorium collectively stared at its shoes, Angela Rippon attempted to fill. 'I can imagine the scene backstage now, someone rushing to find the winning artist,' she bluffed, desperately trying to keep the ship steady. Suddenly her voice rose an octave: 'Where is she?' As if to atone for their tardy timekeeping, it was the last time France won. Ann-Marie David, having scooped the contest for Luxembourg previously, attempted to bring le bacon home in 1979, but fell short. She now keeps sheep on a hill farm, which is probably a more honourable profession than that of Eurovision chanteuse.

3/Israel   Points: 119

22 Appearances ● 3 Wins

Terry Wogan confesses that he likes it 'when a warm country wins'. No, Israel is not in Europe, but since blagging their way onto Eurovision they've bagged several trophies. The road was not always smooth. Temptresses Chocolate Menta Mastik came sixth in 1976 after they met doing national service in the Israeli army. Their 'Emor Shalom' could have smoked out snipers on the Gaza Strip. Israel finally struck gold in 1978 with Izhar Cohen and Alphabeta. 'A-Ba-Ni-Bi' was classic Eurovision, though it had most observers convinced he was singing 'I Want To Be A Polar Bear'. Cohen brushes aside such jibes. 'Israel is a very small country concerning the international scene. I was the first one that opened the village doors. And that's something that I'm very proud of.' Arab stations screened adverts throughout his appearance as a spoiler tactic, then went off the air when it looked like an Israeli win was imminent. Milk & Honey featuring Gali Atari successfully defended the title a year later on home turf with 'Hallelujah', a song that Atari describes as a simple, optimistic song that grows in the heart. Thereafter Israel spent twenty years in the wilderness before once again becoming the chosen people of Eurovision. Terry Wogan has mixed feelings about transsexual champ Dana International, who sensationally won in 1998 with 'Diva', but Eurovision's huge gay following finally had their own icon – a man-turned-woman who'd adapted her stage name from a previous Eurovision winner. You couldn't have scripted it. Izhar Cohen saw Dana International's success as a symbol of freedom, but not everyone agreed. Israel's religious right were outraged, prompting death threats. 'In Jerusalem in 1999 it was her job to hand over the trophy to the winner,' remembers Wogan. 'And she was so busy fooling around, she fell over. As soon as she fell over, Mossad, or Israeli security, thought she'd been shot. So everybody swarmed around her, flung themselves upon her in case she'd be shot again. And the poor winner, the Swedish girl [Charlotte Nilsson], never actually got the award at all!' Get her, as they say in the circles Dana International moves in.

> **Terry Wogan, on Dana International:** 'She left me standing like an eejit on the stage, along with Ulrika and everyone else, while she changed into another frock.'

2/United Kingdom   Points: 127

42 Appearances ● 5 Wins

The Brits are not ones to readily engage with the idea of a united Europe, and we certainly don't like losing to Johnny Foreigners, be they German football teams or Israeli transsexuals. The fact that we've been Eurovision runners-up a record fifteen times has only piqued our competitive resentment. It's possible that it irked Sir Cliff Richard on two occasions, the first in 1968, and he's nearly a saint. His 'Congratulations' was pipped at the post; slightly more generous voting from Ireland or Yugoslavia would have swung it for him. Presenter Katie Boyle tried to affect impartiality. 'I wanted Cliff to win so much, and I was trying not to show it. Inevitably, I did.' Cliff tried again in 1973 with 'Power To All Our Friends', but only managed third. His old muckers The Shadows also managed a second place finish in 1975. But we've also had our successes. The UK's first win came in 1967 when a barefooted Sandie Shaw declared she was just like a 'Puppet On A String'. Brotherhood Of Man triumphed in 1976 with 'Save Your Kisses For Me', the most successful Eurovision song of all time. Its continued popularity has provided a solid-gold pension scheme, reckons singer Sandra Stevens. 'We work for Butlin's, we open bingo halls, we have a ball.' Bucks Fizz, whose Cheryl Baker previously appeared on Co-Co's lamentable 1978 effort 'Bad Old Days', were the UK's next winners. In 1981 they hit on the noble gimmick of disrobing the female members of their skirts (to reveal respectable-size pants, we hasten to add) at the climax of their performance. So many schoolchildren attempted to recreate this theatrical tour de force, shops sold out of Velcro. Bucks Fizz subsequently amassed a string of UK hits. However, the early nineties were a bleak time (actress Samantha Janus's attempts to sound 'foxy' notwithstanding) for the UK's Eurovision entrants, until the venerable Katrina And The Waves finally won it back for us in 1997, with 'Love Shine A Light'. And so what if Katrina was from Kansas, it's not as if we haven't used the odd Aussie (Gina G and Olivia Newton-John) when it suited in the past. Maybe Nana Mouskouri would consider performing on our behalf if we handed over her marbles...

> **Terry Wogan, on the eye-catching highlight of Bucks Fizz's act:** 'The Irish maintained that one of the girls wasn't wearing any knickers. Which is very Irish.'

1/Ireland

Points: 154

34 Appearances ● 7 Wins

Only in Ireland could a former Eurovision Song Contest winner, Dana, run for president, or end up an MP. Cheryl Baker for parliament, anyone? Tezza Wogan believes Ireland pick up votes because they've never had a decent war with anyone else. But it's taken a rich cast of characters to propel Ireland to the top of the Eurovision dung heap. Boxer Barry McGuigan's old fella had a swing at it in 1968. He was leading at the halfway stage with 1968's 'Chance Of A Lifetime' before fading in the final rounds. The fact was, in the sixties Ireland couldn't get arrested in Eurovision terms. Indeed, when poor old Dana left Ulster to sing at the 1970 contest, the only people to wave her goodbye at the airport were, allegedly, a couple of cleaning ladies – oh, and one of them had her daughter with her, so that made three. She made sure her homecoming was better attended when she dazzled the audience with the Carpenters-like whimsy of 'All Kinds Of Everything'. Dana herself had been dazzled at the contest by a prime piece of Spanish hombre in the shape of Julio Iglesias. It was some time before Ireland capitalized on Dana's trailblazing performance. The Swarbriggs tried twice with 'That's What Friends Are For' in 1975, and, with the addition of a couple of handsome lasses, 'It's Nice To Be In Love Again' two

> **Terry Wogan on Dana's win at the 1970 Eurovision Song Contest:** 'That was the beginning of the Irish economic revival. Ireland pulled itself together having won the Eurovision, and went on to greatness. And it owes it all to Dana.'

years later. They were leading in 1977 until the votes came in from those nations Ireland was currently engaged in a fishery war with. In 1980 Johnny Logan, Mr Eurovision himself, arrived on the scene and quickly laid waste to the spectre of Ireland's under-achievement. His slushy ballad 'What's Another Year' somersaulted to victory. Logan became the competition's first dual victor in 1987 with 'Hold Me Now', then wrote Linda Martin's 1992 winner 'Why Me?' in 1992. Ireland cleaned up for the next two years too. Niamh Kavanagh and Paul Harrington & Charlie McGettigan benefited from the after-glow of 'The Riverdance', the 1994 interval extravaganza that sent everyone Gaelic-giddy. After a year's gap, Eimear Quinn's 'The Voice' restored the trophy to smiling Irish eyes, though those belonging to organizers were filling up at the prospect of staging the damned thing yet again. A veritable dynasty of winners then, and they don't seem even slightly embarrassed by their success.

Ten Completely Terrible Eurovision Entries

Luci Kapurso & Hamo Hajdarhodzic: 'Jedan Dan' (Yugoslavia 1968)
Henri Des: 'Retour' (Austria 1970)
Nicole & Hugo: 'Baby Baby' (Belgium 1973)
Poogy: 'Natati La Khaiai' (Israel 1973)
Fredi & Friends: 'Pump-Pump' (Finland 1976)
Lynsey De Paul and Mike Moran: 'Rock Bottom' (UK 1977)
Jahn Teigen: 'Mil Etter Mil' (Norway 1978)
Dschingis Khan: 'Dschingis Khan' (Germany 1979)
Sheeba: 'Horrorscopes' (Ireland 1981)
Riki Sorsa: 'Reggae OK' (Finland 1981)

Seventies Soul

Unlike its earlier incarnation, seventies soul was brasher, more confident and stylistically varied. Where the records had once shimmered, now they strutted. Adam White of *Billboard* compares the isolated 'sparks' of the sixties with a seventies 'power grid'; running parallel to the mainstream music business but maintaining its own identity. Soul II Soul's Jazzie B remembers the outlook having changed, and that artists were now 'superproud' to be black. This surge in confidence produced a new breed of musical risk-takers, as artists expanded the possibilities of their sound and lyrics – experiments that had a lasting impact on the course of popular music.

This Top Ten celebrates the achievements of the genre's giants. It is based on record sales, cult status, the average width of flares multiplied by the square root of the number of times they've been sampled. And just plain coolness.

10/Curtis Mayfield

Soul points: 450

3 R&B No.1s ● Legend Grammy Award ● *Superfly* Soundtrack
Recommended album: *Curtis Mayfield And The Impressions: The Anthology 1961–1977* (1992)

A literate and thoughtful soul man, Mayfield grew up in the impoverished Chicago projects. He learned to play guitar soon after he could walk, and composed his first song at the age of twelve. Mayfield wrote songs for the Impressions that reflected the civil rights struggle, notably 1968's 'We're A Winner'. Jerry Butler was the Impressions' original leader and recalls Mayfield talking to him about personal aspirations that mirrored the hopes and dreams of black people worldwide. In 1970 Mayfield turned solo under the guidance of manager Marv Heiman, though he personally recruited Leroy Hutson as his replacement and continued to guide the Impressions' career. A film score gave Mayfield his breakthrough. He was on tour in New York in 1970 when two men turned up back-stage, carrying a script, and asked whether he would be interested in reading it and providing a soundtrack; the film was called *Superfly* and the soundtrack Curtis wrote eventually

sold two million copies. As Jerry Butler notes, some other writers had their music used in major movies – Mayfield had great music that the movies were about. Extracted from the soundtrack, 'Freddie's Dead' (a song about a junkie street casualty) and the title track were million sellers. However, by the mid-seventies Mayfield's commercial profile had dwindled, though he continued to record and produced Aretha Franklin. He was also feted by British 'soul boys' such as Paul Weller (the Jam covered 'Move On Up') and the Blow Monkeys. Tragically, in 1990 Curtis was paralyzed when scaffolding fell on him at an outdoor show in New York. The news was greeted with disbelief by fans and friends alike. Curtis was presented with a Grammy Legends award in 1994 and shortly afterwards he expressed the hope that his music would live on after his own death. Curtis Mayfield died on Boxing Day, 1999, but there is little doubt that his legacy will indeed endure.

Jazzie B: 'Curtis Mayfield, for me, is an encyclopedia. Every time I listen to his songs they never seem to age, and they always seem appropriate for whatever else is going on in society.'

9/The Isley Brothers
Soul points: 500

5 R&B No.1s ● 5 platinum albums ● Gave Jimi Hendrix a job
Recommended album: *The Isley Brothers Story, Vol.1: Rockin' Soul* (1991)

Brothers Ronald, Rudolph and O'Kelly Isley were dynamos of seventies soul, recklessly energetic performers in a manner that recalled Sam And Dave's shows of a decade earlier. Despite big hits such as the original 1959 version of 'Shout' and 1969's 'It's Your Thing', they were primarily a road band. They had to play live to earn their keep, picking up a host of musicians along the way. Among those they employed in the mid-sixties was a penniless guitarist of no fixed abode called James Marshall Hendrix, aka Jimi. The Isley Brothers tracked him down and bought his guitar back from the pawn shop where he'd left it so that he could join them. After Hendrix departed, younger brothers Ernie and Marvin joined the ranks, along with cousin Chris Jasper. The band took on a momentum of its own, and early plans to finish their education and study to become lawyers soon went up in smoke. The expanded group was rejuvenated by the new arrivals. Hits like 'Live It Up', 'Fight The Power' and 'Harvest For The World' melded Ronnie's authentic, emotive soul voice, still one of the most resonant in black music, with deft rock guitar and instrumentation. The combination may not have pleased purists, but the group achieved five platinum albums during the seventies. However, there were some tough times ahead. In 1984 the younger and elder brothers experienced an acrimonious split; two years later, eldest brother O'Kelly died of a heart attack. Marvin contracted diabetes and had both legs amputated below the knee. As for the rest, Rudolph became a minister, while Jasper went solo, then into real estate. That just leaves Ronnie and Ernie, but as far as the latter is concerned, when the two of them stand on stage the rest of the Isley Brothers are there too.

8/Isaac Hayes

Soul points: 550

1 US No.1 ● Oscar for *Shaft* ● Lives on through Chef
Recommended album: *Hot Buttered Soul* (1969)

Hayes was orphaned at the age of one and brought up by his sharecropping grandparents. Hired by Stax Records, he got a start by co-writing hits with Dave Porter for label colleagues Sam And Dave as part of Stax's 'big six' house band and writing team. (At the time Stax were seeking to create a self-sufficient creative team to rival Motown.) Stax musician Steve Cropper remembers Hayes as a 'wizard', who could always come up with a winning new idea. Sam Moore (of Sam And Dave) also marvelled at his genius ability to shape a song although he couldn't actually read music. Hayes the singer made his breakthrough with *Hot Buttered Soul*, a succulent blend of mellow grooves with spoken dialogue and dramatic brass. With his muscular build, shaved head and extravagant dress sense, Hayes was a striking figure. He shot to megastardom with the theme to 1971's *Shaft*, the definitive blaxploitation film. As well as delivering a million-selling single and platinum album, *Shaft* saw him become the first Afro-American to win an Oscar for music. Though he continued to record, Hayes's hulking persona was now so admired that offers began rolling in for acting work. *Truck Turner* in 1974 was trailed thus: 'Hide your mommas, big brother is comin'. And he's comin' on strong. Isaac Hayes, the big brother of soul, is making a new type of music. And it's *mean* jive.' Yikes. In the seventies, Hayes practically defined black cool, though during the eighties he was more visible on film than on record. Roles in *Escape From New York*, *It Could Happen To You* and *Robin Hood, Men In Tights* ensued, alongside DJ work and the advocacy of scientology. Most famously, he has become the voice of Chef, *South Park*'s oversexed, overweight soul food overlord.

Dave Porter: 'He was able to take someone's song, who had a hit with it, and interpret it in a fashion that made it take on another life.'

7/George Clinton

Soul points: 575

4 R&B No.1s ● Landed a spaceship on stage ● Funky hair-raiser
Recommended album: *Mothership Connection* (1975)

His act built around the concept of total eccentricity, George Clinton was a technicolour fashion grenade whose records happened to be underpinned by heart-stoppingly good funk musicianship. A former hairdresser, Clinton simultaneously led two of the seventies' most distinctive and life-affirming acts. Parliament and Funkadelic – collectively known as P-Funk – were essentially the same band. Clinton's first group, regulation doo wop act, the Parliaments, were formed in the fifties. But when the flower power movement arrived, Clinton became black music's keenest convert. DJ Greg Edwards recalls that the group clearly had their own concept – one that you might not understand, but that made you want a piece of the action. Their dress sense was as bracing as the pure funk of their music, while Parliament's elaborate stage shows became ever more complex, soon encompassing

full-size replica spacecraft. Hip hop pioneer Afrika Bambaataa was knocked out by their show remembering that when Clinton stepped out of the flying saucer, people would start throwing the funk sign (index and little finger aloft) as if welcoming a god. Trombonist Fred Wesley compared their show to 'James Brown on acid'. Bambaataa was one of the first to use P-Funk samples, on 1984's 'Renegades Of Funk', and readily acknowledged the musical impetus that Bootsy and George gave to the hip hop community. Looking back over his career, Clinton remembers that it was all funny – the fact that they got away with it being the most comical of all.

6/Sly and The Family Stone

Soul points: 700

3 R&B No.1s ● 4 US No.1s ● First mixed-race, mixed-sex band
Recommended album: *There's A Riot Goin' On* (1971)

A stew of rock, jazz and funk influences, Sly Stone neatly integrated all three elements into wickedly effusive performances, breaking down barriers between black and white audiences. Sly's vision for the band was that it embrace a number of traditions, his appetite for musical deviance stirred by former careers as a DJ and producer. Moreover, he was an inspirational band leader: trumpet player Cynthia Robinson remembers that he had a real knack for turning defeat into victory, the negative into the positive. The group, propelled by Larry Graham's fluent bass lines, was deliberately mixed in race and sex, and unafraid of tackling sensitive issues – as on their 1969 hit 'Don't Call Me Nigger, Whitey'. However, just as the group's commercial ascent was confirmed by the quixotic 'Thank You (Falettinme Be Mice Elf Agin)' topping the US charts, Sly began his descent into drug addiction.

Jim Irvin, writer, on Sly Stone:
'[He was] the true representative of the dream of the crossover between rock and soul and funk and psychedelia – all those things that people talked about, but only Sly could bring it off.'

He bought a Bel Air mansion from John Phillips of the Mamas And The Papas, but failed to keep up the mortgage payments. It was soon overrun by pushers and hangers-on, though Sly was also 'fond' of animals – the mansion housed a baboon and a pit bull called Gun, trained to attack anyone wearing a hat. The trauma of his personal life bled into Sly's records. *There's A Riot Goin' On* remains one of the darkest artefacts in the soul canon, an album informed by Stone's increasing drug dependency and instability. These days saxophonist Jerry Martini, and Robinson play with Graham Central Station, formed by Larry Graham in 1972. Sly himself, after spells in prison, rehab and sheltered accommodation, is contemplating a return to recording.

Bobby Womack on Sly Stone's menagerie: 'He had this big fence for the monkey to play in. He'd put the pit bull in there to play with him. The monkey would run down, slap the pit bull, and run up on the gate. The pit bull would look like: "If I could just catch his tail..." One day, Sly put some Vaseline on the fence. The monkey came down to the pit bull and looked at him. The pit bull took off at him, he hit the fence and his feet slid, and he fell down. That's where he died. The monkey tore a big hole out of his chest, turned him over and screwed him.'

5/Al Green

Soul points: 775

6 R&B No.1s ● 1 US No.1 ● Lives on with *Ally McBeal*
Recommended album: *Greatest Hits* (1975)

Green was thrown out of his family gospel quartet when his father caught him listening to Jackie Wilson on the radio. He met bandleader and producer Willie Mitchell while struggling on the southern blues circuit. Mitchell was immediately impressed by Green's emotive voice, promised Green he could 'make him' and invited him to Memphis. Green asked how long it would take for Mitchell to make him a superstar. When Mitchell told him that it would probably take eighteen months, Green replied that he couldn't wait that long – a cheeky response, given his career trajectory at the time. In the end Green relented and flew to Tennessee to cut 'Tired Of Being Alone' in 1971. His voice made an instant impression on all who heard it. Mitchell claims to have mellowed Green's original style into the soft, clear delivery with which he is now synonymous, encouraging the singer to slow down and 'float on top of everything'. Green's next engagement was in London, where he cut 'Let's Stay Together'. It took 140 hours to get his voice right, but Mitchell's perfectionism was rewarded when the record went gold within three days of release. Green became a big hit with the ladies, and was one of the first soul stars to court mainstream white audiences. Yet his new lifestyle led him into conflict with his 'more elevated' beliefs, a contradiction exemplified when ex-girlfriend Mary Woodson burst in while he was taking a shower in October 1974 and threw boiling grits over him. Woodson shot herself with his gun afterwards and Green was hospitalized with burns. Since the mid-seventies Green has led services at his own church in Memphis, recorded predominantly in the gospel idiom and turned up, looking inordinately youthful, in the occasional *Ally McBeal* episode.

DJ Greg Edwards: 'It was, to me, as if Sam Cooke and Otis Redding had been reincarnated together in one person.'

4/O'Jays

Soul points: 900

8 R&B No.1s ● 1 US No.1 ● Seventies' fashion at its best
Recommended album: *Love Train: The Best Of The O'Jays* (1994)

Philly soul at its finest, the O'Jays featured three beautifully matched voices belonging to Eddie Levert, Walter Williams and William Powell. Formed in 1961, their career was going nowhere until crack songwriting team Kenny Gamble and Leon Huff signed them to Philadelphia Records in 1972 (having released one O'Jays single on their previous label, Neptune). The group became the conduits for Gamble and Huff's civil rights-themed messages. Williams notes that they were songs very much of their time, with substance, and food for thought for the people. Huff's admiration for the group's vocal abilities made him unwilling to provide them with anything but the very best material; he asked them to record the didactic 'Backstabbers', as their debut single for the label. Levert was initially reluctant to follow this new direction. He felt they were better off playing for a market of screaming young girls. Williams's sheet music fell on the floor at the first session, leading to the still prevalent urban myth that he 'threw it away in disgust'. Aided

by suits costing anything up to $2,000 each, the combination of culturally aware statements and strong songwriting left an indelible mark on the seventies. When Powell was diagnosed with cancer in 1976 he was replaced by Sammy Strain, and the group slowly edged into obscurity. Philadelphia Records is still going strong now, led by Gamble and Huff's sons. The O'Jays, too, remain part of soul music's furniture and, at fifty-six, Walter Williams has no thoughts of retirement.

3/Marvin Gaye

Soul points: 1,400

10 R&B No.1s • 1 UK No.1 • *What's Going On*, an all-time classic
Recommended album: *What's Going On* (1971)

In 1968 'I Heard It Through The Grapevine' became the biggest hit in Motown's history and cemented the reputation of soul's most troubled but prodigiously talented star. A fixture in the R&B charts since 1962, Gaye was never going to be just another cog on the Motown production line. When singing partner Tammi Terrell (with whom he'd dueted on 'Ain't No Mountain High Enough' and other hits) died in March 1970, having collapsed in his arms three years previously, he was devastated. Terrell's death brought to a head Gaye's conflicts with Berry Gordy and Motown, which, the singer felt, were restricting his artistic freedom. Gaye was also hugely affected by the stories of Vietnam that his soldier brother Frankie brought home with him. Those experiences were distilled into the landmark album *What's Going On*, which Smokey Robinson still rates as his favourite record, remembering Gaye telling him while he was working on it that he was merely an instrument: God was writing the album. *What's Going On* bemused Motown's hierarchy. Berry was given an ultimatum: if he wouldn't release it, Motown would never have another Marvin Gaye album. Much to Berry's consternation, the album was a huge commercial hit. *Let's Get It On* followed, a collection of explicit ballads exploiting the sexual charisma that Gaye always had in buckets. Yet behind the musical brinkmanship lay a trail of personal problems. His sixteen-year marriage to Berry Gordy's sister Anna collapsed, debts escalated, and his drug addiction worsened. In the eighties he moved to Belgium and recorded 'Sexual Healing', his final international hit. Friend Dave Simmons describes the completion of the accompanying tour as 'a miracle'. By the end of it, Gaye was totally incoherent through cocaine use. He returned home to the house he'd bought his parents in Los Angeles, having sold his own mansion to pay tax bills. On 1 April 1984, following a weekend-long argument, his father shot Gaye dead.

2/Stevie Wonder

Soul points: 1,700

12 R&B No.1s • 5 US No.1 • First to use a synthesizer
Recommended album: *Song Review: A Greatest Hits Collection* (1997)

A child prodigy, Steveland Judkins was blinded at birth when too much oxygen was administered while he lay in an incubator. He signed to Motown at the age of ten and in

1963, aged thirteen, topped the US singles chart with 'Fingertips – Pt. 2'. Former manager Keith Harris is not alone in believing Wonder possesses unique musical abilities. Such was his creative impetus that by the end of the sixties, Wonder was keen to be let off the Motown leash. Aged twenty-one, he renegotiated his contract to wrest complete artistic control from his paymasters. Thereafter his main collaborators were producers Malcolm Cecil and Robert Margouleff. Cecil still speaks warmly of Wonder's prodigious workrate, recalling that instruments would be laid out in a big circle in the studio, and Wonder would effortlessly play one after another: 'He has no sense of day or night, being unsighted,

Robert Margouleff on 'Songs In The Key Of Life': 'This was one place where everyone was working together; black, white, every religion, every colour, every race. And the music spoke to everybody.'

so all of a sudden we'd get a call at four in the morning: "Time to go to the studio!"' Wonder was particularly excited by synthesizer technology, then in its infancy, and was the first to use the synthesizer as 'the nucleus of the record', according to Keith Harris. It allowed Wonder complete autonomy and powered three seminal albums, *Music Of My Mind*, *Talking Book* and *Innervisions*, between 1972 and 1973. Each was infused with a powerful sense of social justice, and 1976's *Songs In The Key Of Life* is considered by many commentators to be the greatest album ever recorded. Wonder hasn't been short of hits since, but his seventies output can truly be said to have been touched by genius.

1/James Brown
Soul points: 1,750

16 R&B No.1s ● Godfather of Soul, of Dance, of… everything
Recommended album: *Live At The Apollo* (1963)

An institution of stern constitution, James Brown's sobriquet of 'Hardest Working Man In Showbiz' is a justifiable accolade. Recordings such as 'Papa's Got A Brand New Bag' (1965), 'It's A Man's, Man's, Man's World' (1966) and 'Say It Loud – I'm Black And I'm Proud' (1968) established him as soul's most energetic, emotive performer. He was also a skilled bandleader and the orchestrator of a sound so all-consuming, that it rumoured said even dead people could dance to it. Trombonist Fred Wesley remembers that many times Brown would ask him to do things that he initially regarded as musically impossible, only to find they were possible after all. Brown is credited with the creation of funk, the soul music derivation with the accent on primal rhythm and he

James Brown, speaking in 1968, on his ambition as a child: 'My ambition was to eat. We were very hungry.'

remains its finest exponent. He was also disciplined and vigilant: musicians would be fined for trespasses, the severity of the rebuke hand-signalled to (former) manager Charles Bobbit by Brown. Band members were also reprimanded for improper clothing, timekeeping and sundry misdemeanours. However, Brown wasn't mean-minded; Bobbit remembers that the fines

Saxophone player Pee Wee Ellis: 'James has more funk in his little finger than most people have in their life.'

would be returned to the musicians in the form of Christmas savings. Bass player Bootsy Collins recalls the first time he played with Brown, an explosive dancer with lightning

footwork. It wasn't just his feet that moved quickly. Signature song 'Sex Machine' was written on the back of a paper bag in the tour coach. Brown has remained a concert draw for fifty years now, despite spells in the slammer along the way. But the influence of his music – sampled by every hip hop act on the block – has been astronomic. As Wesley surmises, Brown and his band blazed trails that others still follow today.

Ten More Great Soul Records Of The Seventies

Stylistics: 'Stone In Love With You' (1972)
Chi-Lites: 'Have You Seen Her?' (1972)
Tina Turner: 'Nutbush City Limits' (1973)
Drifters: 'Kissin' In The Back Row Of The Movies' (1974)
Commodores: 'Slippery When Wet' (1975)
Labelle: 'Lady Marmalade' (1975)
Rufus: 'Once You Get Started' (1975)
KC & The Sunshine Band: 'That's The Way (I Like It)' (1975)
Earth Wind & Fire: 'Fantasy' (1978)
Quincy Jones: 'Stuff Like That' (1978)

Teen Idols

An adjunct to the chapter on boy bands, teen idols is our pigeonhole for those solo singers who fought for space on the walls of teenage girlhood. Artists so beloved by their worshipful devotees, we had to hand-inspect them for evidence of blu-tac stains on their behinds. Like first boyfriends for the nubile sisterhood, they provided non-reciprocal relationships that didn't end up in tears in the schoolyard. Boys, meanwhile, suffered the indignity of being frustrated by girls who were 'saving themselves for Donny'. The history of teen idols can be traced back to Frank Sinatra in the forties and his army of Bobbysoxers. Then came Elvis and the Beatles. Anthropologist Desmond Morris tells us that when the Beatles played, menstrual cycles synchronized because of the 'massive physiological jolt' the girls' hormoned-to-Hades bodies received at the concert. Between them, these artists have generated enough screaming to power the national grid, and caused more young women to lose consciousness than third-form biology lessons.

The following list is based on chart positions here and in America, augmented by a bodycount of fainting fans and the all-important high-pitched screaming index.

10/Chesney Hawkes   Points: 40

Biggest hit: 'The One And Only' (1991, No. 1)

The son of Chip Hawkes, lead singer of the Tremeloes, young Chesney had a musical upbringing. 'Dad did encourage all of us when we started to play, so there wasn't anything I ever wanted to do apart from music.' He got his break after auditions for the part of Roger Daltrey's son in *Buddy's Song*. Critics mauled the film, though Nik Kershaw's soundtrack was more successful. Hawkes hit the big time when he was offered a spot singing the song 'The One And Only', taken from the film, on *The Little And Large Show*. Blond and leather jacketed with his prominent facial mole catching the light just so, Chesney 'knocked them dead', his guitar slung behind his back like an upstart Bruce Springsteen. After the show the song 'skyrocketed', according to Hawkes. 'Being a nine-teen-year-old kid, you release your first single and it goes to number one – it's going to

be great. It's going to be like this for ever.' It wasn't. Five weeks at number one, then nothing. Second single 'I'm A Man Not A Boy' pushed all the wrong buttons. Soon radio stations were running competitions in which a brown marker pen could be won in order to paint on your very own Chesney mole. He topped a series of worst act polls, and humiliatingly came second to spiders in a teeny mag's list of The Most Very Horrible Thing. Hawkes returned to acting, including an appearance as a drug-taking reprobate in *The Bill*. 'You filthy slag, you're going down!' was quite probably shouted at him. 'That's the pop game, isn't it?' he sighs. 'It's a fickle world and I'm not bitter about anything that happened. It's made me the person I am today.' Nowadays he's trying to relaunch his career – and hoping for that second hit. Finally.

Nik Kershaw, writer of 'The One And Only': 'I've got this affliction, which is writing those type of songs. I just have to write them and get them out of the way. I don't know why people like them.'

9/Leif Garrett

Points: 40

Biggest hit: 'I Was Made For Dancin'' (1979, No. 4)

Californian whizzkid Leif Garrett came on like a boyish Suzie Quatro – without the songs. 'If ever there was a casualty of teen idoldom,' reckons Magenta Devine, 'it's Leif Garrett. You see him now – the man is raddled. The man looks a wreck. And what a pretty boy he was.' Garrett scored in 1979 with 'I Was Made For Dancin'', a song that, it was rumoured, even he thought was 'hokey'. Like it or not, it turned him into a teen dream superstar. For a while, he had to arrive at concerts in an armoured car. Leif had grown up in public, with a string of film and TV credits by the time he was a teenager. After he appeared in the film *Skateboard* record producers the Scotti Brothers asked if he could sing. 'I Was Made For Dancin'' attempted to cash in on the disco boom, but as Katy Puckrik notes, 'deep down, he was good old-fashioned pubescent love pump'. Follow-up hit 'Feel The Need' just scraped into the Top 40. Still, Leif was having fun. 'There's nothing better,' he confesses.

Leif Garrett: 'The worst part was people wanting to take something from me. People grabbing at clothing, hair. That was the stuff that freaked me out more than anything.'

'Imagine a young man in his most libido-crazed years of his life, having women throw themselves at him.' At the height of the madness, he got one very disturbed letter addressed to 'Dear beautiful boy' that turned out to be from an adoring LA detective. Others asked whether his prominently displayed crotch was padded. We may never know the truth. At the height of his success, he was sucked into the drug scene. Friend Roland Winkler accompanied him in the downward spiral. They came a cropper when they shared a Quaalude, washed down with alcohol, and got into Garrett's car to embark on a search for more drugs. Winkler was paralysed from the waist down after Garrett's car spun down an embankment. Garrett faced a lawsuit for $25 million, which only added to his problems. The two finally patched it up twenty years later with a reunion on an American TV special.

8/Nick Heyward

Points: 80

Biggest hit: 'Love Plus One' (1982, No. 3)

The former lead singer with mid-eighties pop sensations Haircut 100, Heyward was obsessed with children's TV and the minutae of English life. 'He is very off the wall', admits Haircut 100 percussionist Mark Fox, 'and the ideas he had were all thrown together in a stream of consciousness.' Haircut 100's job was to make sense of it all. Founded in Kent, they played a timid but infectious Anglicized funk pop, with melodies so bright they were a stake through the heart of the emergent Goth scene. Paul Morley went out on a limb at the *NME*, recording one hundred ways in which the band were 'wonderful'. 'Nick Heyward satisfied the *NME* brigade,' says broadcaster Muriel Grey, 'satisfied the lusts of young pubescent women, and he seemed very cheery about the whole affair.' Heyward reckons they were just 'gits from Beckenham who couldn't get girlfriends. But we were interesting.' Their dress sense, meanwhile, reinvented knitwear as pop fashion. Heyward even convinced his colleagues to dress as fishermen for 'Favourite Shirts (Boy Meets Girl)'. Their debut song, it was a nouveau pop funk homage to young men dressing up in

> **Muriel Grey:** 'They seemed to be attacking pop with a sense of irony and understanding, of deconstruction.'

their best togs. 'The shirt is obviously the fabulous appendage which is going to secure you a date for the evening,' says Fox, sceptically. Yet the clean-cut image belied the bizarre lyrics of efforts such as 'Fantastic Day', accompanied by a video in which Heyward yodelled at exotic plants and swung, semi-naked, from a vine. Unlikely as it seems in retrospect, at the start of 1982 teen mania surrounded the band. Artists of the calibre of Paul McCartney and Elvis Costello were ringing up offering to work with Heyward. Being a bit shy, not to mention eccentric, the pressure freaked him out a bit. Heyward's remedy was a solo career. 'The problem was, I don't think we'd got to the best bit yet,' reckons Fox. 'That was the upset for us all.' Typically, Heyward comes up with a cartoon-inspired metaphor for his state of mind. 'I was Captain Pugwash, but I didn't want to be on the ship I'd set sail in.' Despite a handful of hits, he admits he wasn't actually equipped for a solo career. Repeated comebacks, including an album for Creation, have yet to restore former glories.

7/David Soul

Points: 160

Biggest hit: 'Don't Give Up On Us' (1976, No. 1)

David Soul, instantly recognizable to audiences through his crime-busting role in *Starsky and Hutch*, didn't trade on his hard man image when he launched his musical career. Instead he sang, really rather sweetly, a series of watery ballads. But few could deny that the show's popularity undoubtedly helped. 'It was a buddy show,' says co-star Paul Michael Glaser. 'There hadn't been one of those with two men playing cops, but also showing their sensitive side. That perhaps made us more available to young girls.' But Soul (aka Hutch) had been secretly strumming away for years, and he wanted his shot at

the charts. A producer named Tony Macauley played him some tunes, one of which was 'Don't Give Up On Us'. Soul immediately recognized its potential. Macauley, for his part, thought that Soul combined good looks with the ability to express vulnerability, recalling Glaser's summary of the *Starsky and Hutch* success formula. Whatever he had, it certainly garnered him substantial chart success. Soul only realized the extent of his burgeoning British popularity when he was mobbed at Heathrow airport. Among the screaming masses was Jackie Bridger. 'It was amazing,' she recalls. 'I can still hear everyone screaming and shouting, crying, waving their scarves around. Screaming "David!" It was the blond hair and blue eyes. I wanted to marry him.' However, David's own soul was troubled. He admits he was never comfortable with fame, and didn't handle it very well. He attacked a couple of photographers and got a reputation as a barfly. After two further hits with 'Going In With My Eyes Open' and 'Silver Lady', Soul's record company crashed and took his singing career with it. He switched career to host a chat show with Sally James. He still lives in Britain, is a keen Arsenal supporter (though reports of him singing 'Don't Give Up On Us Bergkamp' from the terraces during the latter's contract negotiations were later revealed to be a hoax), does the odd stroke of acting work and remains admirably philosophical about the transitory nature of fame.

6/Peter Andre
Points: 180

Biggest hit: 'I Feel You' (1997, No. 1)

Born Peter Andrea, the youngest of six children, Peter moved with his family from London to Australia when he was only six. 'I was a skinny little rake,' he admits. 'I had this shy approach to go up to girls. I never felt that I was liked at all. So I started training.' All muscled up, he attempted to get a spot on Australia's *New Faces* show, pestering the producers for over a year. When he finally made it, he was offered a recording contract on air. 'I came back to England aged twenty-two or twenty-three', he reflects, 'and I'm very thankful for that. Otherwise now I'd have my house and picket fence, beer, barbecue. That does still sound good, actually.' As compensation he became the teen sensation of 1996, starting out on the hit trail with 'Mysterious Girl' in June. There was much baring of torso in the accompanying video. Six-pack nirvana was all very well for the girls, but his flab-free chest made Phillip Schofield, for one, feel inadequate. 'We all lived in fear of someone saying, now, let's have a look at yours.' The follow-up was 'Flava', a foray into tropical hip hop. Presenter Andi Peters reckons he was a good sport, 'but I don't think he realized we were all taking the mickey out of him'. Andre was soon the subject of widespread derision, especially after Swedish girlfriend Sharleen spilled the beans on their sexual encounters to the tabloids. His lovemaking 'moves you to tears' she announced. His follow-up singles were having the same effect on critics, but that didn't stop 'I Feel You' from becoming his second chart-topper. Some of the tabloid stories turned out to be kiss-and-tell-on-yourself affairs. 'There was a story perpetuated by Peter Andre', remembers Katie Puckrik, 'that in those intimate moments with a lady person, that he employed the use of an Alka Seltzer tablet in some orifice or other. But he was careful to add the tip that you had to employ ice, or the lady would burn.' At the height of his success he switched to a high energy banana-

based diet. It led to him being hospitalized after his potassium levels shot through the roof. 'He affectionately earned himself the nickname Monkey Boy from then on,' says *Smash Hits* editor Kate Thornton. And watch out, public, he's on the comeback trail.

5/Paul Young
Points: 220

Biggest hit: 'Wherever I Lay My Hat (That's My Home)' (1983, No. 1)

Born and raised in sun-drenched Luton, Young enjoyed his first hit when Streetband's eulogy to the hardened crust, 'Toast', became a novelty hit in 1978. Young reckons his subsequent *Top Of The Pops* appearance was 'probably one of the worst debuts you could ever have as to giving the wrong impression of what you want to be and where you want to be going'. He went on to front the Q Tips, a multi-instrument ensemble that reprised Motown classics to a fervent fanbase but never really scored a hit. Trumpet player Tony Hughes says that even at that stage Young was 'a very gifted singer. His voice is one of the all-time greats as far as I'm concerned.' Q Tips never quite found their chart feet. 'We'd given it two or three years,' reckons Young, 'the label had dropped us. The manager came to me and said I can't get a deal for the band, but they're very interested in you.' Young abandoned his former cohorts and struck gold immediately when his version of Marvin Gaye's 'Wherever I Lay My Hat (That's My Home)' reached number one in 1983. Debut album *No Parlez* sold 7 million copies and suddenly Young's back-combed hair was a fixture of the teen rags. 'It started quite small, my haircut, on *No Parlez*,' argues Young. 'It got bigger as that new romantic thing went on.' Not everyone was a fan. 'He didn't walk right, he didn't handle himself right,' says journalist Paul Morley. 'No matter how hard he tried to convince us, it wasn't going to happen, because of the way he filled time and space.' 'Every Time You Go Away' proved he at least had staying power when it became an American chart-topper. The press was full of rumours of nodule and larynx problems, which were exacerbated by Young's untutored singing style. His doctor told him to go on holiday. The hits dried up in the mid-eighties, and his only other Top 10 single was 1991's 'Senza Una Donna (Without A Woman)', with Italian singer Zucchero. Then his personal life fell into turmoil when pregnant girlfriend Stacey ran off with motorbike stuntman Eddie Kidd. These days he's happily playing his old hits and his new love, country music, to a hardcore of fans that never deserted him.

> **Paul Young:** 'I still say I'm innocent of having a mullet.'

4/David Essex
Points: 240

Biggest hit: 'Gonna Make You A Star' (1974, No. 1)

Directly descended from gypsy stock, Romany romeo David Essex started out as a drummer in a pub band before landing the lead in *Godspell*. Producer (Lord) David Puttnam remembers his 'easy charm'. 'My impression was that he was exactly what I was looking for to play the lead in *That'll Be The Day*. The camera fell in love with David, he

has an extraordinary charisma.' Essex did a solid job of playing aspiring rock 'n' roll star Jim Maclaine in Puttnam's film, before teaming up with producer Jeff Lynne to embark on his singing career proper. 'Rock On' was an affecting but unusual pop single with mannered, abstract vocals. It sold 5 million copies worldwide. Essex still remembers the freaky moment when the porter came up to him at the Midland hotel and told him he was number one in America. Essex returned to films with *Stardust*, a libidinous account of Maclaine's post-success career. '*Stardust* was a very lucky film to make', admits Puttnam, 'because we were making it right at the top of David's adulation, and we were able to get a lot of topspin from that. The scene shot at Manchester Belle Vue is real. The girls rushing up on stage is not something we faked.' Essex took the film's lessons to heart, describing it as a textbook on how to survive the rock lifestyle. Instead his career went from strength to strength, Essex retaining his sanity when all around him were losing theirs. Hits such as 'Gonna Make You A Star' sagely followed the film's theme, but the serious artist inside was struggling to punch his way out. After playing Che Guevara in *Evita*, he began his 'mature' phase with 'A Winter's Tale'. 'It was Cliff Richard territory,' bemoans broadcaster Muriel Grey. 'Hearing it come out of David Essex's mouth was quite sad. It was almost like goodbye youth.' Essex has been awarded an MBE and is also honorary patron of the Gypsy Council Of Great Britain. More importantly, he's kept his fanbase from the seventies, a body of middle-aged women who will never forget the moment they first encountered those twinkling eyes.

3/Jason Donovan

Points: 280

Biggest hit: 'Too Many Broken Hearts' (1989, No. 1)

The Oz soap *Neighbours* gave us a girl with pop staying power, Kylie Minogue, and it also gave us Jason Donovan. The all-Australian guy's on-screen relationship with Kylie's character Charlene had viewers glued to their TV sets. Scott Robinson and Charlene Ramsey were the Montagues and Capulets (had Juliet been an apprentice mechanic) of daytime TV. Inevitably, they launched musical careers. Donovan remembers Kylie getting a phone call at six in the morning informing her 'I Should Be So Lucky' was number one in Britain, making him instantly rather jealous. Donovan hooked up with her UK production factory Stock, Aitken and Waterman, who couldn't believe their luck at getting a blond-haired, blue-eyed surfer boy who was already an established TV star to work with. A duet with Kylie ensued, though the public were unaware that 'Especially For You' was powered by a real-life passionette. The duo left Ramsey Street behind but then Kylie ran off with a rock star, Michael Hutchence, leaving Donovan in the lurch. At least he had the love of a million teenagers to console him as he racked up number ones with 'Too Many Broken Hearts' and 'Sealed With A Kiss'. He took a part in Andrew Lloyd Webber's *Joseph & The Amazing Technicolour Dreamcoat* while rumours about his sexuality persisted. After *The Face* published faked photos of him implying he was gay, Donovan sued them, and won. However, a good sport, Donovan returned the £200,000 damages he won to stop the magazine folding. He then had a few personal problems, although the birth of his child ensured he was soon back on the rails.

2/David Cassidy

Points: 320

Biggest hit: 'Daydreamer'/'The Puppy Song' (1973, No. 1)

If you were a teenage girl in the seventies, loving David Cassidy was part of your job description. 'My mum and dad split up when I was three or four,' Cassidy recalls. 'My father was a struggling actor. He married my step-mom, who became a very famous Academy award-winning actress. When I was seven my father was very self-involved. That's the thing that became the biggest obstacle in my life, trying to understand why he didn't want to be with me.' On *The Partridge Family* Cassidy found himself working alongside step-mother Shirley Jones. Oddly enough, it was the first mainstream series to address single parenthood. After major success as a featured vocalist on *The Partridge Family Album,* 'Could It Be Forever' became Cassidy's debut solo hit in April 1972. He then reached number one with September's 'How Can I Be Sure'. When he flew into Heathrow for his debut British tour, it was mayhem. 'For me those were my college years, nineteen to twenty-four. And any red-blooded American boy who was seriously into rock 'n' roll who had women chucking themselves at them... I found it to be irresistible.' He earned himself a reputation as a bit of a ladies man, although apparently locked in a hotel room for most of the day, and faced with a steady stream of nubile women clamouring for his lithe Yankee flesh, it's hardly surprising. The adulation and hysteria culminated in tragedy at a gig at London's White City stadium in 1974. 'It was insane,' says Cassidy. 'There were hundreds of people being hauled out, people screaming and crying because they were being crushed. I kept saying "Push back". It was beyond my control.' More than 1,000 teenage girls received medical assistance; fourteen-year-old Bernadette Whelan died of a heart attack. After fading from the limelight Cassidy made a brief comeback in the eighties, recording 'The Last Kiss' with George Michael. Cassidy is currently a big draw on the Las Vegas nostalgia circuit.

1/Donny Osmond

Points: 640

Biggest hit: 'Puppy Love' (1972, No. 1)

Donny was the handsomest and best loved of the Osmonds, a family of singing Mormons with teeth so pearly white some of their minions may have complained of snowblindness. But he wasn't an original member, and looked on forlornly as his brothers recorded their first *Andy Williams Show* slots. His siblings recall Donny being scared to death of his first appearance, aged five, but the man himself only recalls the thunderous ovation he received after his first song. After the Osmonds set out on their own, Donny was quickly established as the band's focal point, garnering the majority of press coverage (and allegedly angering some of his brothers in the process). MGM decided to market him as a solo act, and in 1971 'Sweet And Innocent' reached number seven in the US charts, the first record by the family to sell a million copies – Donny's solo records would outsell the Osmonds' collective efforts until the arrival of lil bro' Jimmy. Donny's success finally transferred to the UK market via 'Puppy Love', a song that emphasized his own cuddly innocence. The

fans were voracious, however, and he nearly lost his eye to the pen of a hyperventilating autograph hunter. By 1974 he was singing in tandem with sister Marie on a series of duets and a joint TV show, but his teen appeal was waning. After the Osmonds split in 1980 he appeared in the Broadway revival of *Little Johnny Jones*. 'Soldier Of Love', released in 1988, became the pop comeback of the decade when it reached number two in the US charts. Jimmy Osmond fondly remembers his brother going through a period of trying to be something he wasn't – a hard-living rock'n'roller. By the nineties Donny was complaining of social phobia, but he was soon back before a live audience as the star of *Joseph And The Amazing Technicolour Dreamcoat*, a role that Donny feels has given his career some legitimacy and put his teenybopper past in some kind of context.

Ten Teeny Idols

Kriss Kross: 'Jump' (1992)
Hanson: 'Mmmbop' (1997)
Aled Jones: 'Walking In The Air' (1985)
Little Jimmy Osmond: 'Long Haired Lover From Liverpool' (1972)
Charlotte Church: 'Just Wave Hello' (1999)
Cleopatra: 'Cleopatra's Theme' (1998)
Jackson 5: 'I Want You Back' (1970)
Chicken Shed Theatre: 'I Am In Love With The World' (1997)
Our Kid: 'You Just Might See Me Cry' (1976)
New Edition: 'Girlfriend' (1986)

Disco

When disco (abstracted from the French word *discotheque*) arrived in the mid-seventies, America was reeling from Vietnam, the country was running out of petrol and President Nixon stood revealed as a pathological liar. What the kids wanted, then, was some escapism. Disco emerged as a flashier New York-based variant of R&B, accentuated by the 'pea soup' hi-hat sound and a driving, 4/4 beat. It was a music that celebrated and empowered the act of dancing, whereas much rock music militated against movement or joy. Manhattan's Studio 54 and New York label Salsoul set the agenda, and soon disco had the world dancing to its party tunes – relying on black pop and R&B styles, as well as early seventies funk grooves peppered with punchier rhythms. The beat was the thing, sometimes at the expense of both singer and song.

The 1977 film *Saturday Night Fever* was the vehicle that exported the disco craze to a global audience (ironically, the movement was creatively a dead duck at that point), powered by John Travolta's characterization of a New Yorker whose miserable weekday existence saw release at the weekend when he competed for the crown of disco king. The Bee Gees' soundtrack, meanwhile, confirmed the fact that any singer who performed in anything less than eye-watering falsetto had no place in disco. So git up, git up, and git back down again – catching your reflection in that spinning mirror ball as you do so – as we trip the light fantastic with the disco divas, dollies and Daves who shook the traffic light colour schemes of seventies dancefloors everywhere. These are the acts that sold the most singles (specifically disco records) in Britain from 1975 to 1981.

10/KC & The Sunshine Band
Disco points: 70

Definitive song: 'Get Down Tonight' ● 1 UK Top 10 hit

Harry Wayne Casey (aka KC) reckons the summer feel of his group's disco-lite sound can be attributed to its regional origins in Miami. Casey (along with co-writer Rick Finch) had been working successfully as a member of the TK Records house band, writing for artists such as George McCrae. He'd always wanted his own band, and when McCrae's 'Rock

Your Baby' topped both the British and American charts, he put the Sunshine Band on a permanent footing. 'After "Rock Your Baby" hit the charts, I went to the guys and said, something is really happening here. Why don't we just become the group?" I thought, this is going to become the rage. This is going to happen all over the world.' A run of singles, featuring deliberately simple light funk riffs with strong pop hooks, brought KC international success. 'Queen Of Clubs' (1974) was followed by two major hits in 1975, 'Get Down Tonight' and 'That's The Way (I Like It)'. Further hits included a ballad that didn't stray too far from the formula, 'Please Don't Go' (1979). After TK Records collapsed, Casey moved the operation to Epic, but he was involved in a head-on car crash in January 1982 that temporarily paralysed him.

Harry Wayne Casey: 'Twenty-five years later, I'm just glad to be still here. We're having the time of our lives and I don't plan stopping any time soon.'

The trauma had long-term repercussions, leading to extensive drug and alcohol use. 'I just went ballistic.' he admits. 'I don't know if it was because I was such a goody-two-shoes during the whole period. It was stupid.' After a few health frights he cleaned up, and in the nineties 'Get Down Tonight' was revived in a Budweiser advert, persuading him to put the band back together. 'I'm just happy to be alive,' he says today.

9/Gloria Gaynor

Disco points: 100

Definitive song: 'I Will Survive' ● 1 UK Top 10 hit

Emboldened as a youngster when a neighbour heard her singing under the stairs and presumed it was the radio, Newark, New Jersey-born Gaynor recorded extensively in the sixties before the disco era swept in and transformed dance music. Cabaret clubs were changing to discos overnight; DJs were bringing in their turntables and tables were cleared away to make dancefloors. 'Never Can Say Goodbye' became her first hit in the genre in 1974. She struggled to capitalize on the breakthrough after a stage fall saw her undergo spinal surgery. Four years passed without a major hit until the president of record company Carrere had a UK hit with 'Substitute', sung by South African female vocal group Clout. He asked Gaynor to record a version for America, a task she and her producers agreed to, providing they could write the B-side themselves. The lyrics were penned on a brown paper bag and passed to her; Gaynor and her husband scanned them and realized that they were looking at the lyrics of a hit, not a B-side. The Gaynors were proved correct when 'I Will Survive' became the definitive disco diva anthem. Gaynor recorded it wearing a back brace, a legacy from her stage fall; the song was given extra emotional urgency by the fact that Gaynor couldn't help thinking about her mother's death, some years before, as she sang about survival. It was a massive hit with disco's core gay following as well as women, and remains the only karaoke favourite to threaten 'Stand By Your Man' in terms of popularity. It's also thought to be Prince Charles's favourite song. After a lapse into substance abuse, Gaynor became a born-again Christian and has sung predominantly gospel-based material since her disco heyday, though she still occasionally rocks the pulpit with 'I Will Survive'.

8/Kool & The Gang

Disco points: 140

Definitive song: 'Celebration' ● 3 UK Top 10 hits

The premier exponents of seventies deep-fried boogie riffs, Kool & The Gang were raw and intense (particularly on 'Jungle Boogie', later reprised in *Pulp Fiction*) where other disco acts had many of their rough edges smoothed out. They were founded in 1964 in New Jersey by Ronald Bell, the leader of the band in all but name, after he hooked up with bass-playing brother Robert 'Kool' Bell to form a jazz band to jam out with. They had some success in the seventies, but in 1979 James 'JT' Taylor became their first established lead singer as they dived head first into disco's deep end. They played astonished British DJ Chris Hill demos of 'Ladies Night' and 'Too Hot'. 'It was such a change of style,' he notes. 'It was like, what?!' In 1979 'Ladies Night' firmly established them in the new idiom – Ronald Bell had twigged that 'ladies' nights' were happening all over the country and realized that he could come up with the perfect theme tune for them. The song's closing refrain also inspired their next hit: 'Celebration' captured the mood of optimism and escapism that disco revelled in and coincided with the release of fifty-two American hostages in Iran. The song has endured not just as a disco staple but as a lucrative standby to soundtrack any happy event. Follow-ups such as 'Get Down On It' stuck fast to the party-themed formula. In the eighties their music attempted a widescreen post-disco soul sound, and Ronald Bell moved increasingly into production – giving the world Colour Me Badd and, more successfully, the Fugees. Meanwhile, the rest of the band have continued playing their funked-up hits to nostalgic audiences.

7/Village People

Disco points: 190

Definitive song: 'Y.M.C.A.' ● 2 UK Top 10 hits

Village People were an idea that sprung from a walk in Greenwich Village by French production duo Henri Belolo and Jacques Morali. 'We heard the sound of bells behind us,' recalls Belolo. 'We turned round and saw an Indian walking in the street. We discovered he was a bartender, dancing on the bar. I saw a cowboy standing smoking a cigarette, watching the Indian dancer. Jacques and I looked at each other and said, Hey!' The Indian was Felipe Rose, but the original cowboy didn't cut it. Instead they recruited Broadway singer Victor Willis. They decided to expand the line-up and placed an advert in a casting newspaper asking for 'macho types'. That brought in the other Village Persons, each representing a macho male stereotype (soldier, biker, builder). The new line-up scored an initial hit in 1978 with 'Macho Man', but the act still didn't quite gel. Frontman Willis needed his own **Victor Willis:** 'Village People are about partying, a twinkle in the eye, and a bump in the groin.' 'image' and decided to dress up as a policeman. His rationale? 'I don't like cops, no offence to y'all, I'm just not a policeman-lover, OK?' At the end of 1978, Morali came up with an idea for a song inspired by his local refuge for homeless men. A demo of

'Y.M.C.A.' brought tears to Willis's eyes. 'It was a hell of a message in that song,' reckons Willis. Its nuanced invitation to 'hang out with the boys' passed largely unde-tected among record buyers, who bought the song in sufficient numbers to push it to number one in the UK. 'In The Navy' followed, and an equally unsuspecting US Navy invited them to film a video clip aboard one of its ships. However, the ill-fated film venture *Can't Stop The Music* in 1980 capsized the group. The public was informed that Willis had quit, though he insists he was pushed out. His former bandmates made a disas-trous attempt to reinvent themselves as a new romantic band. Thereafter, no-one wanted to know, especially after awful efforts such as 1985's 'Sex Over The Phone'. Morali walked out after contracting Aids. 'He became completely bitter about life,' says Belolo. 'He flew back to Paris and died in Paris, completely alone and enraged against all the world.' The nineties saw a revival in Village People's fortunes, no thanks to their bizarre appearance on the 1994 German World Cup Song. The band, which has endured several line-up as well as costume changes, is still controlled by Belolo. Willis is a little embit-tered but insists he regrets rien.

6/Earth,Wind & Fire

Disco points: 230

Definitive song: 'Boogie Wonderland' ● 3 UK Top 10 hits

Though they achieved considerable success with disco-themed singles, only a fraction of Earth, Wind & Fire's output belongs within that genre. Indeed, they are considered by many experts (including Chic's Nile Rodgers) to be the best R&B act of all time. The group was the brainchild of Chicago's Maurice White. After establishing a permanent line-up in the seventies, the hits began to roll in. Singer Philip Bailey was one of the contributors that White hand-picked to articulate his obses-sions with spirituality, fantasy and ancient Egypt. 'Those were things that he was checking out,' says Bailey, 'things that got people thinking, and gave the band a certain mystique.' Despite double album *Gratitude* topping the US charts, White decided that the lucrative disco boom should-n't pass them by altogether. Some soul purists were upset, though Bailey defends the decision to cosy up to disco. 'You have to sell records and be abreast of what's going on,' he reasons. They proved just how abreast they were in 1979 with 'Boogie Wonderland', a typically lush effort that, along with the same year's 'Star', placed them at the heart of the disco revolution. Unlike many of the anonymous artists in the genre, Earth, Wind & Fire could also cut it on stage. They maintained an elaborate stage show influenced by Broadway and Las Vegas production values and featuring a full-scale rocket ship. The group's sales declined in the eighties as the disco fad faded, though Bailey embarked on a successful solo career (despite a lamentable collaboration with Phil Collins). Maurice White still steers the band, who have continued to record, from the wings.

Writer Nelson George: 'They were one of the biggest groups in the world, but they felt obligated to address the dancefloor very directly.'

5/Odyssey

Disco points: 235

Definitive song: 'Going Back To My Roots' ● 3 UK Top 10 hits

Odyssey began as a female trio comprising Lopez sisters Lillian, Louise and Carmen. When the latter left, male vocalist Tony Reynolds stepped in. Their breakthrough came in 1977 with the dreamy 'Native New Yorker'. Though the sisters were actually born in Connecticut, they had spent enough time in New York to consider it home. After its release Reynolds was replaced by Billy McEachern, who sung on subsequent UK hits 'Use It Up And Wear It Out', 'If You're Lookin' For A Way Out' and 'Going Back To My Roots'. None garnered the same level of sales in America, however. After a final Top 10 hit with 'Inside Out' in 1982, their profile declined even in Britain. When McEachern left, Lillian's husband Al Jackson was persuaded to come out of management and join the trio – mainly because booking agents were insistent on the two-girl-one-boy line-up. In 1989 'Going Back To My Roots' was reclaimed as a club anthem, but Lillian was far from impressed by the FPI Project's version, contrasting house music's repetitive beats to the variety of rhythms prevalent in disco. These days Lillian and Jackson perform as a duo, lighting up the lives of the Basildon nightclub cognoscenti. Louise has long since left the fold to pursue a career as an art dealer.

DJ Frankie Crocker on 'Native New Yorker':
'The record was an anthem for any New Yorker. Like Frank Sinatra's "New York, New York", it reinforced the cockiness that we New Yorkers have.'

4/Chic

Disco points: 240

Definitive song: 'Good Times' ● 5 UK Top 10 hits

Bernard Edwards and Nile Rodgers, the brains behind the most musically gifted of all the disco acts, took their inspiration from seeing Roxy Music play live. In tribute, they settled on a formation featuring female singers, Alfa Anderson and Luci Martin. Chic had already established a unique musical footprint, the chiming southern R&B guitar style of Rodgers intertwining with the supple, elastic bass lines of Edwards – a musical sophisticate devoid of arrogance. Rodgers remembers an interview for *Guitar Player* where his partner was asked what strings he used by an awed journalist. 'He said "What strings come on a Music Man?" He hadn't changed the strings since he bought it.' Songs like 'La Freak' and 'Good Times' encapsulated the disco era, always expanding rather than conforming to its musical agenda. Those songs served as the perfect soundtrack to the great seventies party. The Sugarhill Gang's 'Rapper's Delight', the first hip hop record proper, borrowed the tune from 'Good Times', predicting the era of sampling (though in this case it was actually a studio recreation of the original). Queen used the bass line to underpin 'Another One Bites The Dust' too. Unlike less enlightened old school musicians, Rodgers is

Nile Rodgers: 'When we got the concept of Chic, we realized there was a form of music that was happening called disco, and even though we didn't have to be a disco group, we could conform to the beat, the style and the lyrical concept.'

'proud' of any producer sampling Chic's wares. The duo enjoyed spectacular success as producers in their own right with Sister Sledge. In the eighties they went their separate ways, Rodgers proving especially in-demand, working with David Bowie, Madonna, Aretha Franklin, Mick Jagger and others. Chic reunited in 1992. At a

Nile Rodgers: 'That's what Chic and that whole hedonistic late seventies/early eighties thing was about – it was about the money, the drugs, the cars, the women, the fast life.'

special Tokyo performance four years later, Edwards refused to cancel Chic's set despite suffering from pneumonia. Rodgers called him later that night to check on his condition. 'In a very distorted, gravelly voice, he said to me, "It's all right. I just need to sleep." Those were the last words he ever uttered to me.'

3/Jacksons

Disco points: 290

Definitive song: 'Blame It On The Boogie' ● 5 UK Top 10 hits

By the advent of disco, Indiana's Jackson 5 had established themselves as the amiable bubblegum pop band critics as well as grandmothers adored. Mind you, they'd worked at it from a young age, and were far from an overnight success. In the process of moving from Motown Records to Epic, the truncated Jacksons (in name as well as personnel, Jermaine having married into the Berry Gordy family, stayed at Motown and been replaced by youngest sibling Randy) decided they needed an outlet to escape their previous niche in R&B and attract and retain a new mainstream audience. Epic brought in legendary soul writing team Gamble and Huff to pen material and were immediately rewarded when 'Show You The Way To Go' topped the UK charts. Afterwards the Jacksons began to write their own material, much of it in a disco vein. However, their first such-styled hit, 1978's 'Blame It On The Boogie', was actually composed by Mancunian singer Mick Jackson (nope, no relation). They followed it with further winning examples of the disco formula in 'Shake Your Body (Down To The Ground)' and 'Can You Feel It'. Thereafter the group members embarked on solo careers, of which Michael's was by some margin (ie world domination) the most successful. There have been several Jackson family reunions since, though Michael's far too busy being 'The King Of Pop' to consider anything more permanent.

2/Donna Summer

Disco points: 310

Definitive song: 'I Feel Love' ● 4 UK Top 10 hits

LaDonna Andrea-Gaines was broke and living in Germany in 1973 when she met producer Giorgio Moroder. Together they recorded some minor European hits, until Moroder came up with the idea of doing 'something sexy', inspired by Serge Gainsbourg and Jane Birkin's 'Je T'aime… Moi Non Plus'. 'One day Donna came in the studio and said she had an idea for a song,' recalls Moroder. She was playing about with the words that became 'Love To Love You, Baby'. Summer herself thought she was simply laying

down a guide track for someone else to record. The resultant single was a minor European hit, but it won over the boss of American label Casablanca Records, who licensed it and had it remixed to seventeen minutes in length. Due to Summer's incessant sexually provocative moaning over the track it was banned from radio, but it still reached number two in the US charts. Moroder remembers Summer being embarrassed by the song's content, and being unwilling to record it until the lights were dimmed and all the technicians were pushed out of the studio. For her part, Summer recalls that she had to imagine how Marilyn Monroe would have performed the song, and thereby effectively adopt another personality, to produce such a sexually charged vocal. Moroder was a fan of Krautrock pioneers Kraftwerk and applied their mechanical, minimalist production values to 'I Feel Love', a UK number one in 1977. Further disco smashes included 'Hot Stuff', before Summer left Moroder to work with Michael Jackson's producer Quincy Jones and Britain's Stock, Aitken and Waterman team. However, her religious views and an alleged remark that Aids was a 'punishment from God' alienated her large gay fanbase. Pursuing a parallel career as a neo-primitivist painter, Summer teamed up with Moroder again in 1998 for the Grammy award-winning single 'Carry On'.

1/Bee Gees

Disco points: 390

Definitive song: 'Stayin' Alive' ● 7 UK Top 10 hits

Whether they like it or not the Bee Gees (Maurice, Robin and Barry Gibb) will forever be associated with disco. But there are various other misdemeanours in their past to take into consideration. Barry Gibb had been given two years probation, aged eleven, for stealing a car when Manchester police persuaded his family it might be wise to emigrate. They were marketed as the Australian Osmonds when they first recorded Down Under. On their return to England they turned to the guidance of manager Robert Stigwood. Despite ongoing success and celebrity marriages (Maurice made an honest woman of Lulu), the group splintered in 1969. They regrouped with a more soulful approach, notably on 1971's US number one, 'How Can You Mend A Broken Heart', later covered by Al Green. Barry Gibb began to assume the position of lead vocalist and his falsetto became a group trademark. The new Bee Gees formula was perfectly attuned to the emergent disco wave, a fact confirmed by mid-seventies singles 'Jive Talkin'' and 'You Should Be Dancing'. Stigwood invited them to provide music for a film project, *Saturday Night Fever*. He explained the plot to the band. Maurice thought the idea might pull in a few Oscars. Both the aforementioned singles were reprised for the soundtrack, along with new compositions 'Stayin' Alive', 'How Deep Is Your Love', 'Night Fever', 'More Than A Woman' and 'If I Can't Have You' (recorded by Yvonne Elliman). Stigwood hoped to sell a million copies of the soundtrack album – about the group's average – but it clocked up more than that in a single week. The group's feet barely touched the ground for the next four years as they rode the crest of the disco wave and became its accidental ambassadors. The Brothers Gibb wrote for Barbra Streisand, Diana Ross and others, and became the only act to score number ones in four separate decades. By the year 2000 they were one of the five biggest-selling acts in history. Still, for a

generation who grew up in the seventies they remain synonymous with the disco years, and John Travolta – a woman's man, with little time for talking, evidently – strutting down a New York sidewalk gobbling pizza.

Blame It On The Boogie
ten disco acts who nearly made it (and their big disco hit)

Amii Stewart ('Knock On Wood', 1979)
Anita Ward ('Ring My Bell', 1979)
Chaka Khan ('I'm Every Woman', 1978)
Dan Hartman ('Instant Replay', 1978)
Heatwave ('Boogie Nights', 1977)
Joe Tex ('Ain't Gonna Bump No More [With No Big Fat Woman]', 1977)
LaBelle 'Lady Marmalade (Voulez-Vous Couchez Avec Moi Ce Soir?)', 1975)
McFadden & Whitehead: ('Ain't No Stoppin' Us Now', 1979)
Rose Royce ('Car Wash', 1976)
Tavares ('Don't Take Away The Music', 1976)

Christmas Songs

As well as the birthday of old JC, 25 December is a magnet to music's biggest egos. You ain't nothing till you've had that Christmas number one, and a properly 'festive' chart-topper is the icing on the Yuletide log. Many of the greats recorded whole albums of this dreck – Presley, the Beach Boys, Stevie Wonder, Chas And Dave. And seemingly everyone's put out a Christmas-themed single – from the saucy (Eartha Kitt inviting Santa to come down her chimney on 1953's 'Santa Baby') to the rather less suggestive offerings from Sir Cliff Richard.

Each December, amid re-runs of *James Bond* and *The Great Escape* and the best family rows of the year, the music industry packs the shelves with a soundtrack conceived in hell, executed by morons and played at deafening volume by store managers so misguided that they honestly believe hearing trite sentiments about the season of goodwill will keep the tills-a-ring-ring-ringing and get them their sales bonus. Everyone with half a mind hates Christmas records, but someone is buying them. Just don't let us catch the culprit.

So behold our Christmas turkeys. And this Crimbo, do Rudolph a favour and buy him some ear muffs. They're not just for keeping the cold out, you know.

10/'I Wish It Could Be Christmas Everyday'

Mince pie points: 32

Chart position: No. 4, December 1974

The full accreditation for one of the most enduring Christmas records reads 'Wizzard featuring vocal backing by the Suedettes plus the Stockland Green Bilateral School First Year Choir with additional noises by Miss Snob and Class 3C'. The song was released when Wizzard were at the height of their commercial powers – two previous 1973 singles had topped the charts. Roy Wood, whose dress sense was eccentric at best,

decided that after years of dross it was about time for a proper rock 'n' roll Christmas record. The song reached number four in December 1974 – but that was only the start of the fun. A school choir was invited to the recording to emboss the record's festive acoustics. However, the poor wee mites were banned from appearing on *Top Of The Pops* because of union laws. Replacements were summoned from a nearby stage school and given cardboard instruments. During filming, Wood was instructed to hoist tiny Lisa Moss aloft at the song's climax in an act of shameless chutzpah. She was told she had to gratefully kiss the technicolour grizzly – hardly fair on any kid at Christmas – and was rewarded with a mouthful of glitter, which she spat out as soon as the cameras stopped rolling. The song is now a confirmed Christmas staple.

> **Roy Wood:** 'We tend to be nice at Christmas. It would be nice to be like that all year.'

> **Roy Wood:** 'I was walking round Asda with my trolley, as you do. And Santa came up and said – "I hope you don't mind me saying this, you've always been my hero."'

9/'Walking In The Air'

Mince pie points: 38

Chart position: No. 5, December 1985

Aled Jones had already enjoyed a minor hit with his version of 'Memory' from the musical *Cats*, when he was recruited to sing soprano on Howard Blake's 'Walking In The Air'. The theme to hit animation movie *The Snowman*, the original vocalist was unavailable for the single. Aled performed the composition on *Top Of the Pops* with good grace, though he was worried about how the audience would dance to the song, and, indeed, what they would make of him; in the end, a record company stylist dispensed with the chorister look for something 'smart but casual'. But there was to be a nightmare reckoning back at school in Wales. Schoolyard bullies not only sang 'Walking In The Air' back at him *ad infinitum*, but made up a cruel rhyme – 'My name is Aled Jones, I like to pick my nose, I like to pick my bum, especially with my thumb'. Thus chastened, he hasn't sung 'Walking In The Air' since he was fifteen. His voice fully broken, he embarked on a new solo career with 'Tell Me Why' in 1999. But as Noddy Holder points out, he remains the boy whose Christmas baubles will never truly drop.

> **Aled Jones:** 'Coming from Wales, you're forced to sing almost from the day you're born.'

> **DJ Dave Lee Travis:** 'It's only when you see Aled Jones on *Top Of The Pops*, singing that song with his hands in his pockets that you actually begin to realize why his voice was so high.'

8/'Fairytale Of New York'

Mince pie points: 42

Chart position: No. 2, December 1987

Do all Christmas records have to be shite? 'Fairytale Of New York', one of the most moving songs ever written, suggests otherwise. And perhaps Christmas isn't as glum as some people make out, if you're a member of the Pogues' drinking circle. As the late Kirsty MacColl noted, it's the one day of the year when drinking Bailey's for breakfast is not frowned on. Shane MacGowan, the anti-Cliff Richard, was born on Christmas Day, and came up with arguably his finest song to mark the occasion. Far from the 'frolicking in the snow' variety of the other entries, its subject matter was unique: an Irish couple go to New York to become Broadway stars, but she ends up a junkie and he ends up an alcoholic loser. Kirsty

Pogues banjo player Jem Finer: 'There was an idea around that we should write a Christmas song, and us being in the band we were in, there was no way we were going to write a soppy, syrupy song.'

MacColl believed the song's appeal lies in the fact that, 'Christmas is a time when a lot of people have arguments. That's what's good about the song. Two people love each other, but hate each other at the same time. I think that's a more realistic relationship.' Matt Dillon appeared as a policeman in the video, shot in a real precinct, though much to MacColl's disappointment, she didn't get to meet him ('They protected him from me'). The song was held off the number one spot by the Pet Shop Boys' version of Presley's classic, 'Always On My Mind', which MacGowan saw as little more than karaoke fare. 'Fairytale Of New York' remains a remarkable effort.

Shane MacGowan: 'It's a great song, it really is. I wish I could remember it.'

7/'I Believe In Father Christmas'

Mince pie points: 57

Chart position: No. 2, December 1975

In the early seventies Greg Lake was best known for playing bass and singing in monolithic prog rock supergroup Emerson, Lake And Palmer. Lake launched his solo career, alongside co-writer Pete Sinfield, with 'I Believe In Father Christmas' – a song not quite as naff as its title suggests. Lake had come up with a simple guitar melody and played it to Sinfield, who immediately saw it as a Christmas tune. The finished piece employed a refrain taken from Prokofiev, and was intended as a more melancholy contemplation on the festive season; Lake felt that there was a sadness about Christmas time that should be acknowledged. The song's sombre pay-off line was 'The Christmas we get, we deserve'. Sessions were arranged at Abbey Road recording studios and to get people into the 'spirit' of things, Lake invited a stripper to attend. When she sat on the lap of the first violinist she caused a stampede in the orchestra, resulting in the demolition of a double bass – which Lake had to pay for. The video was shot in the Sinai desert in Israel, with Lake surrounded by Bedouin tribesmen with whom he struck up cordial relations. Whereas others would be red-faced after securing a hit with a Christmas-themed single, Lake positively glows today at his achievement, reckoning it makes him part of the festivities. The song was resuscitated by Toyah in the eighties.

6/'Mary's Boy Child'

Mince pie points: 60

Chart position: No. 1, December 1978

German producer Frank Farian built Boney M as a vehicle for his treacly pop compositions in 1976, populating the group with crazy boy Bobby Farrell, Marcia Barrett, Liz Mitchell and Maisie Williams. After initial success in mainland Europe, they secured a run of UK Top 10 hits. Farian reasoned that the group's fans would relish a Christmas offering, citing festive releases by Frank Sinatra and Elvis Presley as precedents. Farian's modest choice of comparisons aside, he struck on the perfect cover version – an update of Harry Belafonte's 1958 number one, 'Mary's Boy Child'. The single shot to number one in 1978, and Boney M were invited to play an unprecedented ten-date tour of Russia. Thereafter the group hit problems. Having originally been thrown together as a dance group there were conflicts over the authorship of the songs. Farian himself was responsible for dubbing Bobby's vocals. The relationship soured further during the group's post-fame years and Farian underwent protracted court proceedings to secure rights to the name Boney M. That doesn't stop Bobby from heisting it from time to time – as Farian admits, he can't follow the errant performer all around the world with a lawyer. Liz Mitchell, who knows which side her bread is buttered, continues to perform as the *legal* Boney M.

Frank Farian: 'Bobby made a lot of problems. It was like… I saw red in front of my ears.'

Liz Mitchell: 'The producer asked me to hum the first part for him, to hear how my voice would sit. When I did, he said, "Oh, my God, I'm getting goosebumps. We're going into the studio tomorrow."'

Frank Farian: '[Bobby] used to say, "My legs, your voice, we're great!"'

5/'When A Child Is Born'

Mince pie points: 74

Chart position: No. 1, December 1975

A song never envisioned as a Christmas record, Johnny Mathis nevertheless scaled December's charts with 'When A Child Is Born' in 1975. Pressed in interview, however, he can't actually remember the name of the song's authors. The king of MOR, Mathis had already had a major Christmas hit in 1958 with 'Winter Wonderland', a song recently corrupted on the terraces of Highbury (via Alan Shearer and Blackburn) to celebrate Dennis Bergkamp's footballing talent. Whatever your opinion of Mathis – Shane MacGowan considers him 'a great interpreter of shitty songs' – the consensus is that he's recorded far too much mush. 'When A Child Is Born', with its stark religious sentiments, can be seen as a career departure. Mathis himself acknowledges that his success has been built on sentimental fare, but admits that he is no longer as touchy on that subject as he once was. Nor need he be. Mathis has played for five presidents over the years, and countless first ladies. Moreover, despite working on some very moderate material, only Presley and Sinatra can take credit for more hit albums as male US singers, and they're not around to compete any more.

Johnny Mathis: 'My people in Britain called me and told me I had a number one hit at Christmas time. I said – "Wow! Christmas!" Then I thought yes, it does celebrate Christmas.'

4/'Mistletoe And Wine'

Mince pie points: 77

Chart position: No. 1, December 1988

What can you say about Sir Cliff Richard that doesn't involve superlatives? For many, 'Mistletoe And Wine' kick-started the national pastime of praying to whatever deity you thought may listen that Cliff wouldn't reach number one. 'Bachelor Boy' (coupled with 'The Next Time') had given him a number one single at Christmas in 1962, but the sentiments in that song were hardly conducive to cuddling up around a fireplace and divvying up the Chocolate Orange. However, having tasted success with 'Mistletoe And Wine', Cliff brought us 'Saviour's Day' in 1990, and 'Millennium Prayer' (widely derided as sanctimonious tosh and controversially not played on Radio 1) in 1999. Despite his legendary work ethic, he does insist on taking Christmas Day off. Some critics have suggested that, if he could only extend his holidays by another 364 days, that truly would be a millennium gift to the nation.

> **Cliff Richard:** 'We all release records at Christmas, and I have to compete with the biggest and the best of them. I've won a couple of times but lost a load of others.'

3/'Merry Xmas Everybody'

Mince pie points: 81

Chart position: No. 1, December 1973

By the time of this single's release, Slade were established as leaders of the glam rock pack, but for this stab at a festive chart berth they elected to return to the first song Noddy Holder had ever written. His Slade co-writer Jim Lea remembered the song, written in 1967, and suggested its use as a Christmas single. However, the original psychedelic lyric was hardly chestnuts-by-the-fire material. Noddy sat up one night drinking whisky and came up with more seasonal lyrics. Creating a festive air on the track was no mean feat, given that it was recorded in a hot New York studio in September. It remains a Crimbo classic, however, public affection for it barely diminishing with the passing decades and it's as familiar as mince pies. But while it's a festive classic for us, it's a pension plan for Noddy who has never got fed up with it and admits to being pleased as punch every time he hears it on the radio. Most people would acknowledge a little corner of their heart that is forever Slade when they hear Noddy's immortal pay-off line, 'It's CHRRRIIIISST-MAS!' (you try spelling it phonetically).

2/'Happy Xmas (War Is Over)'

Mince pie points: 89

Chart positions: No. 4, December 1972, No. 48, January 1975, No. 2, December 1980, No. 28, December 1981, No. 56, December 1982

Like turkey after Boxing Day, for a while it looked as if John Lennon and Yoko Ono's Crimbo gift to the world, which reappeared in the charts four times over the next decade, was never going to be finished. It was written in bed, a place the happy couple were

proving inordinately fond of being photographed in during the early seventies. John orig-inally told Yoko that he wanted to write a Christmas song that would be bigger than 'White Christmas'. They wrote the song, one of those typically aspirational Lennon pleas for small things like world peace, over breakfast. The producer was Phil Spector, a veteran of Christmas records. It never overtook 'White Christmas' in the public's affection, but as Yoko notes, many people of their generation definitely relate to their festive offering more closely than the Irving Berlin classic. Its creation wasn't all flowers and hippy romance, though. Having written the song, John and Yoko had a falling out and promptly forgot about it. Nearer Christmas, John remembered it again and suggested putting it out, but by then the festive season was nearly upon them. Denied proper publicity, the song didn't make its mark first time out in America. It did better in the UK, however, reaching number four in 1972. Yoko came up with the slogan, 'War is over. If you want it. Happy Christmas from John and Yoko,' which John plastered on hoardings nationwide as a festive greeting from the two of them. Whenever she talks about Christmas, Yoko cannot help but be reminded of John's death in 1980, and her subsequent discovery of the presents John had already bought for herself and Sean before he was shot.

1/'White Christmas'

Mince pie points: 102

Chart position: It was released in the forties, before the first UK chart appeared (in 1952). It was never an official British hit until 1977 (then again in 1985 and 1998).

There is only one true Christmas anthem, and as its singer, Bing Crosby, admitted on a UK chat show, it has had more influence than anything else he was ever involved in. Crosby's second wife Kathryn, who grew up in Texas where it's far too hot to have snow, has her own idea about what made this Irving Berlin song special: she suggests that the listener substitutes anything that is precious to him or her for the word 'white'. Several dozen unworthies have attempted it, but the key to the song is Bing's warmth and charm. After the world first heard the song, in the 1942 film *Holiday Inn*, Crosby's name became synonymous with Christmas. The entire family appeared in seasonal specials, several filmed in England. It was there that Bing was joined by David Bowie in another Christmas standard, 'The Little Drummer Boy'. Though his children were treated like showbiz professionals by their father, none of them followed his career path. The boys busied themselves with golf and management consultancy while daughter Mary Francis joined the cast of *Dallas*. Bing's serene, effortless rendition of 'White Christmas' remains as intrinsic to the season of goodwill as mince pies.

Ken Barnes, Bing Crosby's producer: 'There was only one voice that was right for the winter months. It was like warm brandy on a cold night.'

Ken Barnes: 'Over the years, no artist has been more Christmas than Crosby.'

Some Other Wacky Christmas Songs

Dickie Valentine: 'Christmas Alphabet'
Nat King Cole: 'The Christmas Song'
Elvis Presley: 'Santa Bring My Baby Back To Me'
Elton John: 'Ho, Ho, Who'd Be A Turkey At Christmas Time'
Blues Magoos: 'Santa Claus Is Coming To Town'
Stefan Bednarczyk: 'When Santa Kissed The Fairy On The Christmas Tree'
John Cale: 'A Child's Christmas In Wales'
Four Seasons: 'I Saw Mommy Kissing Santa Claus'
Waitresses: 'Christmas Wrapping'
Run D.M.C.: 'Christmas In Hollis'
Wombles: 'Wombling Merry Christmas'
Gonads: 'Bollocks To Christmas'
Elmo And Patsy: 'Grandma Got Run Down By A Reindeer'
Damned: 'There Ain't No Sanity Clause'
Mud: 'Lonely This Christmas'

And one wonderful Christmas fact

Michael Hutchence's first recording was a version of
'Jingle Bells' used in a talking doll.

Eighties Romantics

It was the early eighties and Margaret Thatcher was in office. The new romantics (which the key participants never liked being called) responded by dressing up like pantomime dames lost in an Alice In Wonderland theme park. This new breed of urban gadfly and clothes horse was determined to inject a little sparkle into dreary lives. The new romantics were a hybrid of glam (definitely Marc Bolan and David Bowie rather than Slade) punk and disco, its musical soundtrack liberated by emergent synthesizer technology.

It all began at the hugely pretentious Blitz club in London's Covent Garden, where art students, punks and transvestites queued to get in past doorboy Steve Strange. Regulars at the club were Boy George (the coat check boy), Spandau Ballet's Kemp brothers, Rusty Egan and Stevo – all to play a major part in the movement. Also gathered were artists, designers and film directors. The entire rationale at Blitz was that you were no-one unless someone was pointing a Nikon at you. This was the most conceited, arrogant and self-satisfied musical movement ever, more concerned with its own posterior than posterity. Still, it did produce one or two good records.

10/Visage

Points: 73

Definitive single: 'Fade To Grey' (1980) ● 4 Top 20 singles ● 2 Top 20 albums

Visage came about because Rusty Egan – a man with an eye for the main, the secondary and the tertiary chance – DJ'd at the Blitz club. Steve Strange (aka Steve Harrington), who was a doorman there, describes him as a South London wide boy. Attempting to convince his friends he had a band, Egan dragged in session musicians Midge Ure (with whom he'd played in the Rich Kids) and Billy Currie. Strange confesses that he and Rusty only had a handful of records. Keen to create music that people could dance to, Egan started touting the band, titled Visage, to interested parties. He didn't have to go far. Above the Blitz club were the offices of Radar Records, run by Jake Riviera and producer Martin Rushent. Rusty simply kept hassling Rushent until he gave in. The result was debut single 'Tar', an ode to the joys of smoking, released shortly before Radar went under. The group moved to Polydor for 'Fade To Grey' which became a Top 10 hit in 1980. Thereafter this ever-fractious band destabilized further. Egan and Strange balked when contracts were produced that gave them no share in songwriting royalties. Egan insisted on an equal split, while Strange protested that it was his idea for the French vocals on 'Fade To Grey'. Currie and Ure subsequently joined Ultravox. Visage released some further, increasingly weak material – 'Mind Of A Toy', 'Visage', 'Damned Don't Cry' and 'Night Train'. Thereafter management and drug problems (Strange became a heroin addict) beset the band. According to Egan, Strange became impossible to manage. Visage, in many ways the quintessential new romantic band, disappeared as quickly as they'd arrived.

9/Japan
Points: 80

Definitive single: 'Ghosts' (1982) ● 3 Top 20 singles ● 2 Top 20 albums

When Alan Partridge calls you effeminate futurists from the eighties, you know you've been rumbled. Japan was formed around singer David Sylvian, his drumming brother Steve Jansen, Rob Dean on guitar, Richard Barbieri on keyboards and Mick Karn on saxophone. Manager Simon Napier-Bell had formerly steered the Yardbirds, but had since spent several years abroad. Initially excited at the prospect of working with what he took to be eighteen-year-old hipsters, Napier-Bell soon discovered that the band were quite out of step with contemporary youth culture. That impression was confirmed when a succession of albums for Ariola-Hansa failed to make any impact. Frustrated, Napier-Bell told them to record a cover version. The band selected Smokey Robinson's 'I Second That Emotion', which gave them their second Top 10 hit. After winning a new contract with Virgin, Barbieri started to dabble with synthesizers, which became the dominant musical strain within Japan. However, he maintains that the band were ultimately purveyors of artistic pop. Recorded after the departure of Dean, *Tin Drum* was easily the group's most effective statement, matching oriental influences to increasing musical sophistication. Extracted from the album, 'Ghosts' became a Top 5 hit in 1982 and saw the band embraced by journalists who'd previously scoffed at their labours. After a series of solo projects and collaborations, the group simply walked away from it all in November 1982. Speculating on the reasons for this, Karn thinks that it was an inevitable result of suddenly being able to do whatever they liked – there was no fight left any more. Feeling that there was still potential there, they reunited fleetingly as Rain Tree Crow in 1991. The reclusive Sylvian now works solo while Jansen, Barbieri and Karn perform as JBK.

8/ABC

Points: 146

Definitive single: 'The Look Of Love' (1982) ● 6 Top 20 singles ● 3 Top 20 albums

Formed by keyboard player Steve Singleton, guitarist Mark White and singer Martin Fry, Sheffield's ABC were the conceptualists of the new romantic movement. According to Singleton they wanted to distance themselves from the preoccupations with industrial decay that informed many Sheffield acts and drew on a broad spectrum of influences from Noël Coward to Sammy Cahn who wrote lyrics for Sinatra. Their 1981 debut, 'Tears Are Not Enough', was inspired by an argument Singleton had with his girlfriend on a late night bus ride. Later he contacted producer Trevor Horn after being impressed by his work with Dollar. 'Poison Arrow' was their first collaboration, followed by 'The Look Of Love'. The band had the latter pretty much worked out by the time they got into the studio. All that was missing was a middle section of eight bars. Fry inserted a little spoken aside which included a line about finding true love. 'That speech has haunted me to this day,' grimaces Fry. 'I still get people coming up to me in the street saying, "Have you found true love?"' Attendant album *Lexicon Of Love*, considered by many to be the best record to emerge from the new romantic era, became a global success. However, the resultant 150-date tour placed intolerable pressures on the group. At one stage, Fry vainly attempted to flush his trademark gold lamé suit down the toilet. After contracting Hodgkin's disease, which put the group on hold, Fry hit back in 1987 with 'When Smokey Sings', ABC's last Top 20 hit. In 1999 they embarked on a nostalgia package tour alongside Culture Club and the Human League. A fitting fate for a man who once sang about looking for a girl who could meet supply with demand.

> **Martin Fry:** 'We would go to clubs and listen to Chic, Sister Sledge and Earth, Wind & Fire, and we'd come home and listen to the Clash and Elvis Costello. We wanted a band that glued it all together.'

7/Soft Cell

Points: 228

Definitive single: 'Tainted Love' (1981) ● 6 Top 20 singles ● 4 Top 20 albums

Left-field Leeds duo Soft Cell added a dark twist to the early eighties, a time that 'was all champagne, cocaine and model girls', reckons singer Marc Almond. 'We were singing about cheap gin, barbiturates and prostitutes.' Almond met collaborator Dave Ball at Leeds Polytechnic, and got a record deal via teenage prodigy Stevo, who teamed them with producer Mike Thorne. After initially releasing 'Memorabilia' for Stevo's Some Bizzare label, a cover of Gloria Jones' 'Tainted Love' went straight to number one. Almond, a long-standing fan of northern soul, loved the song's twisted undercurrent, and applied a theatrical, effeminate vocal over Ball's striking electro pop arrangement. It topped charts in seventeen countries. 'Bed Sitter' and 'Say Hello Wave Goodbye' followed, the latter representing Ball's attempt to write Marc something in the vein of Scott Walker. Thorne argues that the duo worked so well together because Ball's sober musical approach found a perfect complement in Almond's vocal and verbal excesses.

However, it wasn't long before the duo began to go off the rails; Stevo puts it all down to their discovery of ecstasy in New York. The appropriately named Cindy Ecstasy dueted with Almond on number two hit 'Torch' – and when she wasn't singing, doubled as the band's dealer. Soft Cell lost any appetite they may have had for mainstream success with *The Art Of Falling Apart*. One further album, *This Last Night In Sodom*, concluded their career, which was only three and a half years old. Almond pursued a successful solo path, topping the charts with Gene Pitney, while Ball found success with the Grid.

6/Ultravox

Points: 263

Definitive single: 'Vienna' (1981) ● 10 Top 20 singles ● 6 Top 20 albums

After three underachieving albums for Island, Ultravox lost their record label and their singer, John Foxx, who opted to pursue a solo career. Those setbacks, plus the fact that the media were fond of renaming the group Ultrahype or Ultracrap, would have done for lesser mortals. Instead, keyboard player Billy Currie's old friend Rusty Egan convinced him to get Midge Ure on board, a sideburned graduate of teenyboppers Slik and post-punk act the Rich Kids. 'Vienna', arguably the most enduring of all new romantic songs, was instigated by Currie, who decided the time was ripe for a ballad. A deeply atmospheric and moody piece written by all four members of the band, it was played on tour in America to spellbound audiences. However, Ultravox themselves were unsure about whether such a languid song would work as a single. Chris Wright at Chrysalis Records gave them a shove, convinced of the haunting track's commercial potential. Despite the record's huge sales, Joe Dolce's novelty 'Shaddap You Face' held it from the top spot, an ignoble state of affairs that clearly disturbed members of the band. More swirly-synthesizer-led hits such as 'All Stood Still' and 'The Thin Wall' followed, with Ure embarking on a parallel solo career with 1982's 'No Regrets'. Currie felt Ure was being opportunistic and sowing seeds of discontent within the band. However, the partnership remained intact long enough for Currie to write 1984's 'Dancing With Tears In My Eyes', which saw a return to the charts after a three-year gap. The same year Ure teamed up with Bob Geldof to write 'Do They Know It's Christmas?', with Ultravox appearing at the subsequent Live Aid jamboree. But by 1985 the group was finished. Today, Currie writes film scores and occasionally reconstitutes the band, while Ure has appeared to be doing his best to distance himself from the eighties in general and the new romantic scene in particular.

5/Human League

Points: 316

Definitive single: 'Don't You Want Me' (1981) ● 11 Top 20 singles ● 5 Top 20 albums

We covered the Human League story back in our electro-pop chapter. But hell, it's a good one, so let's make like we're accommodating a masochistic hedgehog and run over it one more time. Phil Oakey, Susanne Sulley and Joanne Catherall were the handsome but bickering trio with a good line in synth pop melodramas and perverse hair statements.

Having evolved from an arty post-punk trio (Oakey with Ian Craig Marsh and Martin Ware) who wrote songs about scoring hit singles in deep space, Oakey recruited his two chirpy colleagues from a Sheffield disco and found success on planet Earth. When 'Sound Of The Crowd' became an unexpected hit in May 1981, Sulley's mum appeared at school to whisk the girls out to prepare for their *Top Of The Pops* debut. The song was their first collaboration with Martin Rushent, who understood the band's sonic temperament and could handle their highly strung characters with tact and diplomacy. Sulley believes that the triumphant *Dare* wouldn't have got off the ground if not for Rushent's vision. The album sold five million copies and hosted one of the biggest hits of the eighties. Virgin MD Simon Draper wanted to put 'Don't You Want Me' out as a single, but the band were terrified it would end their careers. The lyric was lifted by Oakey from a trashy 'true story' magazine, with co-writing credits for Callis and visuals director Adrian Wright. A persuasive rags-to-riches melodrama, it topped the UK charts for five weeks. However, just as in the song, success seemed to go straight to their heads. Rushent became depressed by the bickering and walked out in 1983. The last song he worked on was '(Keep Feeling) Fascination', but after that, nothing from second album *Hysteria* reached the Top 10. In desperation, the League teamed up with US R&B producers Jimmy Jam and Terry Lewis. The liaison produced a US number one, 'Human'. They have kept bouncing back throughout the nineties. According to Oakey, the Human League demonstrated that the music business was no longer exclusively for men, and that men and women were capable of having success by working together on equal terms. And, as Martin Rushent states, even those who hate 'Don't You Want Me' can probably sing every line of the song.

4/Culture Club
Points: 339

Definitive single: 'Karma Chameleon' (1983) ● 8 Top 20 singles ● 5 Top 20 albums

Brought up in a family where the main cultural activity was boxing, the redoubtable George O'Dowd was always more pantomime dame than pugilist. After marking out his territory at the Blitz nightclub, the extravagantly attired George was introduced to drummer Jon Moss. Moss fell in love with this larger-than-life apparition, in both a musical and romantic sense. 'Do You Really Want To Hurt Me' was hastily written for a Peter Powell radio session and ended up being the most successful record in America since the Beatles. Boy George was all over the nation's telly screens looking butter-wouldn't-melt coy under his techni-colour plaits. It was a look quickly copied by Susan Tully on Grange Hill and Bobbie Mitchell in Prisoner Cell Block H, as well as thousands of schoolgirls. 'The whole thing was a total-ity, I don't think you can separate the music from the clothes or the sexual politics,' George says today. A second number one followed in 1983 with 'Karma Chameleon', though when George first sang it to the band, they laughed at him. Its success masked the conflict at the heart of the group, according to guitarist Roy Hay and bass player Mikey Craig who remember the tension caused by the covert relationship between George and Jon. 'The War Song', not as strong as their

Boy George: 'I'd like the band to be remembered as a good band, not as a funny old drag queen in a hat with some silly pop songs.'

previous output, became the group's last Top 5 hit. Moss started a family while George self-destructed. 'I think we're all masters of our own destiny. I think I created myself and I destroyed myself,' he argues today. After a conviction for heroin possession, George got into Buddhism, became an acclaimed DJ and sang the theme to the film *The Crying Game*. Eventually he put the band back together for a US tour, and unveiled plans to stage a musical about his new romantic days.

3/Spandau Ballet
Points: 367

Definitive single: 'True' (1983) ● 15 Top 20 singles ● 6 Top 20 albums

New romanticists *in extremis*, from their berets and kilts to their jaunty little synth pop ditties, Spandau Ballet were in reality a bunch of East End geezers, to borrow a phrase from journalist Robert Elms. Gary Kemp (guitar), Martin Kemp (bass), Tony Hadley (vocals), John Keeble (drums) and Steve Norman (guitar and saxophone) were initially indebted to the innovative management of Steve Dagger. Celebratory gigs performed at locations such as HMS Sheffield won the band a lucrative recording contract, and their stylish debut single 'To Cut A Long Story Short' was perfect for the era. 'Chant #1' upped the funk quotient and reached number three, after which successive singles flopped. It was only when Trevor Horn remixed 'Instinction' that their chart credibility was restored, and they became deadly rivals to Duran Duran. The two groups faced off in a Mike Reid-hosted celebrity pop quiz. Dagger insisted that Spandau revise beforehand, but they still lost. They had the compensation of a worldwide smash with 'True' and the stylistically similar 'Gold'. Such songs, argues journalist Paul Morley, revealed the band as old-fashioned medallion men rather than new romantics. 'Through The Barricades' was typically stylised. 'As a recording and a vocal performance, I thought it was one of the most complete things

Tony Hadley: 'People eventually become nostalgic and go back – "Bloody hell, those guys were actually really good, great songs, great playing, great singer." And people reflect on that. Good. Justice.'

we did,' says vocalist Hadley. By the mid-eighties, their relationship with their label soured. Hadley went solo while the Kemps took starring roles in *The Krays*; Martin subsequently joined the cast of *EastEnders*. Spandau's final appearance together, however, came in court, royalties the source of the dispute. Gary Kemp successfully defended the action against former members Hadley, Keeble and Norman.

2/Adam & The Ants
Points: 370

Definitive single: 'Prince Charming' (1981) ● 12 Top 20 singles ● 5 Top 20 albums

Before turning into a nationally famous fop, Stuart Goddard was a veteran of the punk wars. Adam paid Sex Pistols manager Malcolm McLaren to advise him, only to see his entire band abandon him to form Bow Wow Wow with McLaren. Perhaps that's where Adam got the idea for highway robbery from. Club owner Phillip Salon remembers seeing

Adam dissolved in floods of tears after being given the heave-ho. He kept the name and McLaren's concept of exploring Wild West imagery and using tribal drumming. Ant developed the idea with new songwriting partner Marco Pirroni and producer Chris 'Merrick' Hughes, one of two percussionists the group employed. 'Dog Eat Dog' broke through in October 1980, followed by 'Antmusic'. Ant claimed at the time that the famous white line across the nose (rather than up it, as is rock 'n' roll custom) marked his declaration of war on the music biz. Antmania swept the nation, but not everyone in the band was satisfied, including Pirroni, who remembers them bemoaning the fact that despite being the biggest band in England, they had little luck with the ladies. The truth was, the heroic anti-

Chris 'Merrick' Hughes: 'You could tell it was going to go places just by Adam's attitude. He was absolutely ... adamant.'

hero roles Adam was playing, be they pirates, highwaymen or his enduring characterization of Prince Charming, appealed to pre-pubescents rather than groupies. Financial disputes arose following 'Ant Rap'. Adam kept Pirroni, and Hughes as producer, and embarked on a solo career. 'Goody Two-Shoes', a reply to critics who thought he was too pious and clean living, went straight to the top of the charts, before he returned to his acting career.

1/Duran Duran
Points: 438

Definitive single: 'Rio' (1982) ● 15 Top 20 singles ● 6 Top 20 albums

Taking their name from a character in sci-fi fantasy *Barbarella*, Duran Duran were formed by John Taylor (bass) and Nick Rhodes (keyboards), who grew up on the same housing estate in Birmingham. They worked through a series of temporary musicians until Roger Taylor was recruited as drummer. Andy Taylor, the third unrelated group member with that surname, became their guitarist. Simon Le Bon was recruited principally because he was the first aspirant singer to turn up with his own lyrics. After touring with Hazel O'Connor, the band's debut 'Planet Earth' went Top 20 in 1981, and the ball was rolling. Their self-titled debut album reached number three and was followed within a year by *Rio*, which housed a string of successful singles – 'Save A Prayer', 'Hungry Like The Wolf' and the title track. Their first number one came with 'Is There Something I Should Know' in March 1983. Each was accompanied by a lavish video. 'Rio' introduced the boats, beaches and birds image with which they're still associated. Accusations of decadence engulfed them, a claim that Le Bon emphatically denies. John Taylor reckons in this business, 'you're either morally sound or you're not. Well, we were. Whether you like it or not.' As the biggest pop band of the mid-eighties, they got to record a James Bond theme song, 'A View To A Kill', before embarking on breakaway projects Arcadia and Power Station. Prior to 1986's *Notorious* Andy and Roger Taylor quit. Still, Duran Duran found it hard to escape the eighties ghetto. Reduced to a trio, Le Bon admits they were heading for a slump at that point. Guitarist Warren Cuccurullo, a Former Frank Zappa

Nick Rhodes: 'When it came to the end of the eighties, there were a lot of people rubbing their hands together. Right, that's the end of the decade. We're going to lock the door, and by the way, make sure Duran Duran are in there.'

associate, stepped in and 'Ordinary World' became a Top 10 hit in 1993, but shortly thereafter John became the third and final Taylor to exit. The trio of Le Bon, Rhodes and Cuccurullo continue as Duran Duran.

Romo No-Nos – Close But No Hatstand

Kajagoogoo: 'Too Shy' (1983)
Howard Jones: 'New Song' (1983)
Classix Nouveaux: 'Is It A Dream' (1982)
Toyah: 'It's A Mystery' (1981)
Bow Wow Wow: 'Go Wild In The Country' (1982)
A Flock Of Seagulls: 'Wishing (If I Had A Photograph Of You)' (1982)
Thompson Twins: 'Doctor Doctor' (1984)
Associates: 'Club Country' (1982)
Heaven 17: 'Temptation' (1983)
Marilyn: 'Calling Your Name' (1983)

Progressive Rock

Abandon hopes of brevity, all ye who enter here. Where its rock 'n' roll ancestor in the fifties and sixties had been an adrenaline rush of youthful excitement, progressive rock was contemplative and studied, steeped in the cult of the musician as 'artist'. Diminished sevenths, time changes, costume changes, and pretension of biblical proportions, all were essential ingredients. Where else could you find musicians who pursue a policy of booking airline tickets for their guitars, forty-foot inflatable pigs that cause air traffic control to re-direct international flights, or music considered so beyond the pale, US armed forces played it at South American dictators in order to root them out of their bolt holes? These are the catacombs of rock music wherein reality and fantasy become blurred concepts. Ah, yes, concepts. They had a few, this lot. In keeping with the nature of progressive rock, this chapter is longer than all the others in the book, hence leaving no room for trivia sections. That stuff's for pop fans.

10/Camel
Points:47

Recommended album: *Mirage* (1975) ● Weeks on UK album chart: 47

These ships of the desert were formed in 1971 in Guildford, led by guitarist and vocalist Andrew Latimer, who has remained in the saddle throughout their existence. In search of a more expansive sound, Latimer placed an advert for a keyboard player. Pete Bardens was the only one to reply. Drummer Andy Ward came up with the name Camel. Their first album for Decca subsidiary Gama was 1975's *Mirage*, which used a Camel cigarette packet on its sleeve. The band weren't happy about this commercial compromise, particularly Ward. Camel executives came to the studio and suggested they write songs themed on tobacco. The association was stubbed out, though their manager begged them to reconsider. With their sponsorship money up in smoke, Latimer decided to write a concept album inspired by a children's book. Label executives were aghast when informed it was to be devoid of anything approaching a conventional song. *Snow Goose* went on to sell 3 million copies.

> **Andy Ward:** 'It's not a very good association, is it? Music and lung cancer.'

Apparently Decca's publicist attempted to coerce the band into wearing gold leotards, or at least claiming to be involved in hard drugs. But, perhaps showing a capacity for obstinacy rivalling that of the animal that named them, the band was not for turning. Like many progressive rock outfits, Camel suffered from the emergence of punk. That didn't stop them releasing concept albums, 1984's *Stationary Traveller* wrestling with seemingly unreconcilable themes of the Cold War and transsexuality. In the mid-eighties Decca dropped the band from its roster and Camel went into extended hibernation. Latimer became embroiled in a legal dispute with his former manager. 'I was left with nothing, really,' he says. 'Just a name, no band, nothing. And the name, at that time, was a curse, too.' He eventually moved to California and hired session musicians to record *Dust And Dreams* in 1991. Since then he has become master of his own destiny, marketing Camel albums via the internet.

9/King Crimson
Points: 74

Recommended album: *In The Court Of The Crimson King* (1969)
Top 10 albums: 2 ● Weeks in UK album chart: 54

According to their biographer, Sid Smith, King Crimson were purveyors of music that 'stomps you into the ground, kills your dog, and throws you out of your house'. He's exaggerating, of course. They started as a trio entitled Giles, Giles & Fripp (drummer Michael Giles, bass player Peter Giles and Robert Fripp on guitar and mellotron). After Pete Giles left, Fripp recruited Ian MacDonald on saxophone and schoolfriend Greg Lake on bass. After just twenty gigs, the band secured a support slot to the Rolling Stones in Hyde Park, playing in front of 650,000 in July 1969. Their music, meanwhile, was branching into jazz and classical textures. They were at their most challenging on *In The Court Of The Crimson King*, which subverted some of the air-headed optimism of the sixties and ushered in darker musical sentiments. Fripp hired and fired musicians with frequency, and with a new line-up including Bill Bruford (from Yes) he cut King Crimson's next landmark album, *Larks' Tongues In Aspic*. The title came directly from the answer percussionist Jamie Muir gave when asked to describe King Crimson's music. The stage shows rapidly got wilder, Muir cavorting as a caveman and various members climbing PA stacks and throwing chains at 'tuned' Domestos bottles. After Muir left for a Tibetan monastery in Scotland *Red* was recorded as a trio of Bruford, bass player John Wetton and Fripp. It was an album that many rate highly, not least Nirvana's Kurt Cobain. But by 1974 Fripp was ready to throw in the towel, and disappeared to a spiritual retreat for reflection. On his return to recording in 1978 he moved to New York and worked on David Bowie's *Heroes*. In 1981 King Crimson returned, initially under a new guise, Discipline, with singer Adrian Belew. Fans were confused, not least by the absence of Fripp's distinctive mellotron sound. In 1986 Fripp married pop singer and TV personality Toyah, fond of hosting late night TV programmes and talking about how to have a mutually rewarding sex life. Fripp and King Crimson, in the meantime, keep ploughing their furrow.

8/ Hawkwind
Points: 121

Recommended album: *In Search Of Space* (1971)
Top 10 singles: 1 ● Top 10 albums: 1 ● Weeks in UK album chart: 101

'There will be bleeding from orifices and an ache in the pelvic region' they promised gig-goers, and they weren't wrong. Formed in the late sixties, Hawkwind pioneered a spacey take on hard rock, or, if you prefer, a heavy take on space rock. With lyrics steeped in science fiction and apparently, an appetite for pharmaceutical consumption that would jaundice other bands, Hawkwind has persevered as a cult act, the loyalty of its fans matching that of the Deadheads, fanatical followers of America's Grateful Dead. According to long-standing wind instrumentalist Nik Turner, the name came about due to 'my rather objectionable habits of coughing and spitting and farting.' As for their central inspiration,

Danny Baker: 'You went to see Hawkwind because Stacia took her clothes off. And when that top came off she was a big girl.'

bass player Lemmy (one of a bewildering array of contributors) says 'Everything in Hawkwind was drug related. When we relaxed, that was drug related too.' Turner spiced things up by introducing the band to Stacia, 'an Amazonian German fertility goddess' he'd met on the Isle Of Wight. The rest of the band agreed to let her dance, provided she was naked.

Hawkwind registered their prog rock credentials with second album *In Search of Space*, a concept piece apparently about space travellers who land on Earth and become two-dimensional pieces of vinyl. 'Silver Machine' was their only hit in a thirty-year career that's left a legacy of 120 albums and counting. The story goes that they let Lemmy sing it because no-one else worked out. The follow-up, 'Urban Guerrilla', was unfortunately released at the height of an IRA bombing campaign. The next thing Nik Turner knew, security forces were ripping up his floorboards looking for plastic explosives. In 1975 Lemmy was arrested on the Canadian border for drug possession. 'The only reason they got me out of jail,' he says, 'was because my replacement couldn't show up early enough.' He was fired at four in the morning after the gig. Darlings of the free festival circuit, Hawkwind soldier on to this day, with Turner and singer/guitarist Dave Brock still at the helm. And who says you can't teach an old dog new tricks? Their thirtieth anniversary gigs saw Lemmy dueting with Samantha Fox on backing vocals.

7/Rush
Points: 178

Recommended album: *2112* (1976)
Top 10 albums: 8 ● Weeks on UK album chart: 98

Beloved by drummers everywhere as one of the tiny number of commercially successful rock bands to let their tub-thumper write lyrics, Canada's Rush owed a substantial stylistic debt to Led Zeppelin. The band were formed at school by Geddy Lee (vocals/bass) and guitarist Alex Lifeson. They recorded their debut album in 1974 but lost original drummer John Rutsey. The replacement was lyric-writing whizzkid Neil Peart, though the first time Alex and Geddy saw him, he was selling farm equipment in a small town an hour from

Toronto. 'Geddy and I were the cool city guys, with long hair, platform shoes, we were really hip. This guy looked dorky, we thought. Don't know if he'll work out.' Peart set up his drum kit and started playing a series of purring triplets (whatever they are). Alex and Geddy purred in response, and Rush set out on tour with Kiss and Aerosmith. However, Rush's own brand of earnest hard rock failed to ignite audiences, and, in 1976, they changed tack. They emerged with a lavish sword-and-sorcery concept set in the year 2112. The group thought it would be their last record. Instead, it turned them into prog rock superstars. 'We were all reading *Lord Of The Rings*, Isaac Asimov and so on,' admits Geddy, sensitive to criticism that Rush were responsible for turning rock music into a preserve for consumers of fantasy literature. The band arrived in Britain just as punk upped the ante.

Geddy Lee, on touring with Kiss and Aerosmith: 'They taught us how to behave properly on the road. They were nice, polite gentlemen and they never acted untoward and it was a very wholesome environment.'

They weren't impressed. 'That scene instantly legitimized us as musicians,' reckons Geddy. 'Overnight, we went from being rather crude hard rock musicians to virtuosos by comparison.' As the eighties dawned Rush retreated to a more formulaic adult rock sound (as on hit singles 'Spirit Of Radio' and 'Tom Sawyer') and became one of the most successful touring bands ever. And they're still going, though they've put the elves and hobbits to bed for now.

6/ELP
Points: 215

Recommended album: *Brain Salad Surgery* (1973)
Top 10 singles: 1 ● Top 10 albums: 7 ● Weeks in UK album chart: 135

A band who, some argued, never really knew the meaning of restraint, Emerson, Lake and Palmer, progressive rock's first supergroup, became so extravagant in the seventies that they toured with the names of each member painted on top of their individual trucks. Keith Emerson, having played in the Nice, had a vision for a new band based on a similar three-piece format featuring keyboards, bass and drums. He set out to recruit the best instrumentalists he could find – Greg Lake from King Crimson on bass and vocals and drummer Carl Palmer, formerly of Atomic Rooster. The format required Emerson to front the band. 'It's very difficult to be a frontman with a 350-pound Hammond organ,' he sighs. He did his best, however, routinely wrestling keyboard furniture into submission during the band's garish live sets; he routinely ended gigs by stabbing his Hammond organ with ceremonial knives. The unholy squeal of feedback that resulted would close gigs, punters sauntering away believing such indulgence had embellished a good night's entertainment. Palmer wisely had his drum kit erected with gongs down one side to shield him from the possibility of ricocheting knives. Poor old Greg Lake had to compete somehow. So he bought himself a £2,000 Persian carpet. To stand on. Albums such as *Tarkus*, *Trilogy* and *Brain Salad Surgery* confirmed ELP as leaders of the prog rock hierarchy. In 1977 came *Works*, a double album featuring three solo sides and one

Carl Palmer: 'If you looked up the word pretentious in the dictionary, you could possibly see a picture of Emerson, Lake and Palmer.'

collaborative side, comprising 'Pirates' and 'Fanfare For The Common Man'. The latter was a high watermark for prog rock indulgence. Then along came punk to kick their sorry carcass. Palmer was aghast. 'There was this DJ, John Peel, he said something really stupid like, "Emerson Lake and Palmer is a waste of talent and electricity". He must be eating his words now.' ELP had a much higher calibre of fans. The members of ELP, meanwhile, unsurprisingly went on to become solo artists. No-one knows if they got to keep the trucks.

5/Yes

Points: 323

Recommended album: *The Yes Album* (1971)
Top 10 singles: 1 ● Top 10 albums: 10 ● Weeks in UK album chart: 213

The longest-living prog rockers of those who remained committed to their original vision, Yes were formed in 1968 when Accrington farm worker Jon Anderson (vocals) met up with former choirboy Chris Squire (bass/vocals) while cleaning glasses at a London club. The band they put together found itself at odds with the prevailing psychedelic pop movement, but did secure a support slot at Cream's 1968 farewell show. Though their debut album introduced Anderson's distinctive falsetto, it failed to sell. It was only when they recruited guitarist Steve Howe and wunderkind keyboard player Rick Wakeman that they primed themselves for global success. *Fragile* (1971) and *Close To The Edge* (1972) sold millions. But Anderson wanted to experiment further. Specifically, he wanted to record the next album outdoors. 'The compromise was that we'd be in town but try to make it countrified,' says Wakeman. They converted the studio into a farmyard, with white trellis fencing serving as paddocks around different pieces of equipment, and wooden chickens and a cardboard cow with a mechanical udder. The resulting double album *Tales From Topographic Oceans* featured just a single song on each side. Wakeman became disenchanted while touring the record. 'I also felt the audience were bored rigid. It was thunderingly boring to play.' So bored was he, he put in a takeaway order one night to his keyboard roadie. The roadie returned with the curry mid-set. Anderson nonchalantly wandered over and helped himself to a popadom. That wasn't the end. Steve Howe actually bought a seat on Concorde for his guitar. In 1974, Wakeman went solo and apparently tried to whip up some press publicity by phoning Chris Welch of *Melody Maker* with accounts of what would take place at his upcoming gigs. He said he was going to use real horses... on ice. Brent Council and the RSPCA put a halt to that, and he had to use actors on hobby horses instead. Still, it's the thought that counts. Wakeman eventually returned to Yes, whose line-up fluctuated through the eighties and nineties. It's fair to say it will doubtless continue to do so long into the next millennium.

Steve Howe, on reserving a seat on Concorde for his guitar: 'It is so important to me, it is unique, it is possibly the best guitar in the world.'

4/Jethro Tull

Points: 326

Recommended album: *Aqualung* (1971)
Top 10 singles: 3 ● Top 10 albums: 6 ● Weeks on UK album chart: 236

Of all the prog rock bands, Jethro Tull took themselves least seriously. But as Iain Anderson confirms, 'It's OK for me to take the mickey out of Jethro Tull, but if anyone else tries it, they'll get a punch on the nose.' Jethro Tull broke in 1969 when 'Living In The Past' reached number three in the British charts. At the folky end of the progressive spectrum, Anderson attempted to use the flute in the same way Eric Clapton or Jimi Hendrix might use their guitars. Conversely, while some thought Anderson was the epitome of drugged out indulgence on stage, he was the straightest man in rock. Lead guitar Martin Barre says most gigs would see bags of dope thrown on to the stage. The band would kick them straight back, in disgust. Given such abstinence, it was ironic they ended up touring with Led Zeppelin. 'Martin and I used to race downstairs and take TVs that they'd thrown into the swimming pool out again before we all got into trouble,' admits Anderson.

Ian Anderson: 'Yes, I took to the codpiece. It was sort of a demi-bra for men. Exactly the same purpose, just to create a pleasing but not too obvious shape. A certain amount of uplift and control, just what a bouncing boy needs when dressed in tights on stage.'

They also denied that their 1971 magnum opus *Aqualung* was a concept album. 'I said emphatically at the time and still maintain to this day, that three or four songs do not a concept make,' Anderson says. Right, he thought, we'll give them the mother of all concept albums – *Thick As A Brick*. Apparently no-one seemed to realize it was a send-up and it went to the top of the American charts instead. Where did the money go? Not sex and certainly not drugs. Instead, Anderson invested in salmon farming. He was voted Scottish businessman of the year 1997 after winning the contract to supply Sainsbury's. Since 1967 he's hired and fired thirty-seven members, had five Top 10 albums and three hit singles and can still stand on one leg and play flute like no-one since… well, anyone, really. Anderson (almost) single-handedly toppled a dictator, too. When General Noriega sought sanctuary in the Vatican embassy in Panama City, US troops besieged the embassy with Jethro Tull music.

3/Moody Blues

Points: 435

Recommended album: *Days Of Future Passed* (1967)
Top 10 singles: 3 ● Top 10 albums: 8 ● Weeks on UK album chart: 325

This Birmingham outfit started out as an R&B group who topped the charts with 'Go Now' in 1964, at which time they were considered part of the 'British Invasion'. By late 1966 they had disbanded and reformed with Justin Hayward (vocals) and John Lodge (bass) joining existing members Mike Pinder (keyboards), Ray Thomas (harmonica) and Graham Edge (drums). But the odd single release aside, nothing was happening. 'One night we came home from a gig', recalls Hayward, 'and said it's just not working. Let's try and do all our own stuff.' Decca wanted an LP to promote its 'Deramic Stereo' and picked the Moody Blues to record a version of Dvořák's New World Symphony. However, as soon as the band got into the studio, they locked the doors and insisted on recording their own material. They convinced conductor Peter Knight to indulge them, with *Days Of Future Passed* the result. The album stayed on the US charts for two years and produced two massive hit singles – 'Tuesday Afternoon' and 'Nights In White Satin'. A work of genius? The truth was, LSD was a big factor in the creative process, the group having dropped tabs together for the first time during recording. The Moody Blues went on to be a cornerstone of the sixties psychedelic soundtrack, at one point they had five albums in the US charts in one week. Acting out their rock star fantasies, they chartered a 707 to fly them around and bought a string of record shops. However, by then they'd long since stopped talking to each other, and their efforts spilled into outside projects – Hayward memorably sang on Jeff Wayne's *War Of The Worlds*. As the eighties rolled by, the band's influence retreated. However, they had the comfort in knowing that, while others talked about space rock, they were the rock band played in space. Astronaut Hoot Gibson told the band their greatest hits had been the tape of choice on several NASA missions. Nights in white spacesuits, indeed.

2/Genesis

Points: 735

Recommended album: *The Lamb Lies Down On Broadway* (1974)
Top 10 singles: 8 ● Top 10 albums: 17 ● Weeks in UK album chart: 485

Having met at Charterhouse public school, Tony Banks, Peter Gabriel and Mike Rutherford came up with the modest challenge of translating the Bible into song. Gabriel freely admits that the band never lacked ambition, although he also concedes that attempting to cover the Bible in forty minutes may have been pushing it a bit. Fellow Charterhouse old boy Jonathan King persuaded them to take the name Genesis, and encouraged their initial recordings (with original drummer Chris Stewart). Another drummer came and went before Phil Collins finally turned up for auditions. 'We went to the back garden where there was a swimming pool,' remembers Collins. 'There was a piano on the patio. Mike Rutherford appeared in a smoking jacket and slippers, and I thought, this is great.' The addition of guitarist Steve Hackett gave Genesis their glory line-up. *Foxtrot* – which included twenty-three-minute concept song 'Supper's Ready' – hit the UK Top 20 in 1972 and established the band's fanbase. But by the advent of double album *The Lamb Lies Down On Broadway*, the band had tired of Gabriel's costumed eccentricity and lyrical melodramas. 'It just started to take over,' says Banks. 'There wasn't a single review that talked about anything apart from the way it looked.' Gabriel left, leaving Collins to take over as singer. However, 1976's *Trick of The Tale* confirmed Genesis would not expire commercially shorn of their frontman. Still, the audience hadn't changed much. There were still lots of greycoats and fishing hats. 'Never a woman in sight', admits Collins, 'unless she had a greycoat on as well.' Increasingly, Genesis's output began to appeal to straight pop fans. 'We just thought, f**k it, let's sell out,' admits Collins. They racked up a series of four-minute pop hits with efforts such as 'I Can't Dance', while all three members pursued solo careers. Collins, by far the most successful, eventually left in 1986, leaving Rutherford and Banks to recruit Ray Wilson from Stiltskin for the critically slated *Calling All Stations*.

Phil Collins: 'The audience had been used to this maniac running round with big phallic tubes, and I thought all they're going to get is me, what a terrible disappointment.'

1/Pink Floyd

Points: 1057

Recommended album: *Dark Side Of The Moon* (1973)
Top 10 singles: 2 ● Top 10 albums: 16 ● Weeks in UK album chart: 877

Were Pink Floyd progressive rock? Well, they got dogs to sing into microphones at one point. As a young act performing at the UFO club in London, Pink Floyd began to stretch psychedelic pop until it went ping, wrestling, musically and lyrically, with themes of space and time as well as more familiar adolescent yearnings. Roger Waters (bass), Nick Mason (drums), Rick Wright (keyboards) and Syd Barrett (guitar) became pioneers of freakbeat. Barrett was the group's creative engine, but found the fame resulting from hits such as 'Arnold Layne' and 'See Emily Play' difficult to cope with. Together with the enormous quantities of acid he was taking, it saw him leave to become a recluse in Cambridge. Waters took over effective leadership of the band as Dave Gilmour was recruited as replacement guitarist. However, this was never just a regular studio band, as Keith Emerson of ELP remembers. 'Roger Waters was backstage, and I heard them all discussing who was going to be the next one in the studio the next day. I said, "What, you don't go into the studio altogether?" They looked at me like – no, we go in one at a time. It saves arguments.' Despite this, the group's albums sold in huge quantities, culminating in the commercial juggernaut that was 1973's *Dark Side Of The Moon*. Its acoustic presence and vivid realization of modern production techniques dazzled critics and fans alike. It spent 741 weeks on the Billboard charts – some might argue almost twice the length of an ELP drum solo – and remains one of the most enduring rock albums of all time. They followed it with *Wish You Were Here* (which featured a tribute to Syd, 'Shine On You Crazy Diamond') and *Animals*. The sleeve artwork for the latter featured a huge inflatable pig moored over Battersea power station. When it broke free of its moorings, air traffic control had to re-route aircraft through the south west of England. Eventually a farmer rang up saying he'd found it in his field, and would the band like it back? With *The Wall* (1979), Pink Floyd released the last great concept album of the seventies. It had some unlikely fans, including Noel Gallagher of Oasis, who played it so often as a youngster that he now knows the entire thing off by heart. In 1986 they fell out with each other, but a Waters-less Pink Floyd returned to the stage in 1994 to promote *The Division Bell*. It may well not be the last we've heard from them.

Glam Rock

If a thing's worth doing, it's worth doing with glitter dust, spangly pants and big heels. So runs the rationale of glam rock, a peculiarly British phenomenon that emerged in the early seventies and saw lunatic fashion statements gyrating to a tribal 4/4 beat. Glam was an unabashed return to the rock 'n' roll basics of dressing up and boy-meets-girl, an antidote to the relentless prog rock indulgences of groups such as Yes and Emerson, Lake and Palmer. Often the songs merely updated bubblegum pop basics of the fifties, but glam was bold and unselfconscious where the alternatives were precious and self-regarding.

Glam gave birth to some of the most engaging characters of the period, not to mention some of the ugliest. It was a time when men were men, and some men were women too. It's all David Bowie's fault, really. So squeeze into that mauve catsuit and totter over in those oversized platforms to behold our Top Ten of glam, based on singles chart success between 1970 and 1975.

10/Alice Cooper

Glam points: 72

1 No. 1 ● Top 20 hits: 5

Vincent Furnier, aka Alice Cooper, was given his shot at the big time by Frank Zappa when he was invited to come over for an audition. Zappa said he'd see them at seven. The band duly got up at six – in the morning – and made their way to Zappa's chambers, fully uniformed in glitter and make-up, and started playing. Zappa came downstairs, listened to maybe two songs, and hired them on the spot. He probably just wanted to get back to bed. The group moved to Warner Brothers and in 1972 broke through with teen anthem and truant's charter 'School's Out'. Live shows came replete with shock tactics and hammy theatrics. Pyrotechnics, a guillotine and a live boa constrictor were all employed, though Cooper wasn't overly fond of working with the latter and admits drinking a bottle of

whisky to overcome his nerves the first time it was used in a show. The act also featured the wholesale mutilation of dolls, though Cooper insists they never represented real babies, it was only the dolls themselves he hated and that that was why he chopped them up. The band hit tabloid trouble when a chicken met its death at a Cooper concert – though, in fairness, the ghouly one hardly seems to blame for that. He recalls throwing the unfortunate fowl into the audience only to see it being torn apart. And, he points out, the first eight rows of the audience were wheelchair-bound. But it wasn't just chickens that had good reason to fear Cooper. On his first journey to Britain he sat next to an old lady on the plane. They chatted and played gin rummy together. Feeling tired, she asked her new friend to tell the stewardesses not to disturb her when the food came round. When the plane landed, he tried to wake her up. She was dead. The press, awaiting Cooper's arrival, had an instant headline. If I'd have been thinking,' he muses, I'd have put two little holes right in her neck. She was dead, she wouldn't have known. It would have been perfect.'

9/Alvin Stardust
Glam points: 83

1 No. 1 ● 6 Top 20 hits

Before he became the glam juggernaut Alvin Stardust, glam's very own Gene Vincent started out as soppy slowcoach Shane Fenton, who notched up a handful of Top 40 hits in the early sixties before quitting music for management. In 1973 he returned as Alvin Stardust, the name a tongue-in-cheek tribute to Gary Glitter. He also had a new image, sporting black leather, gloves and pasted-on sideburns. But his secret came back to haunt him. Eager to distance himself from his less than glam-orous past, Stardust descended on *Top Of The Pops* with five bouncers, only to be met by Tony Blackburn, that week's presenter, who immediately queried 'Aren't you Shane Fenton?' Faced with an outing, Stardust assumed a moody demeanour and retorted 'Who?' He maintained the sulky stance for the *TOTP* performance, and it became his trademark. His comeback hit was the asinine 'My Coo-Ca-Choo'– the success of which completely exceeded even Stardust's hopes for it. Subsequent hits included a number one with 'Jealous Mind' and he also enjoyed a starring, albeit humiliating role in the Green Cross Code road safety campaign of the early seventies. This belied his carefully cultivated 'bad boy' of glam image, his choice of leather gloves and sneer a homage to Marlon Brando (others suggest the gloves were worn to cover up black hair dye he couldn't wash off). Fenton kept expecting someone, somewhere, to expose the Alvin Stardust persona as a wind-up, but no-one did. After hosting BBC's *Rock Gospel Show*, he's now a reborn rocker, refusing to let old age get in his way.

8/Suzi Quatro
Glam points: 86

2 No. 1s ● 6 Top 20 hits

Impresario Mickie Most first spotted Susan Quatro (yep, that's her real name) while recording in Motown. He immediately hired crack songwriting team Nicky Chinn and

Mike Chapman to write songs for Quatro, then performing as bass player for Detroit progressive rockers Cradle. All they needed was an image. Determined to move away from the floaty, soft femininity of previous female singers, Quatro insisted she wanted leather, and nothing else, though she swears that she wasn't going for the sexual connotations. Chinn recalls that the Detroit rocker had drive and energy in spades and would pester the two of them relentlessly when they were writing material for her. Their tolerance of her spirited enthusiasm was rewarded when 'Can The Can', topped the UK charts. '48 Crash' followed it to number three. Suddenly, Suzi's (ahem) ballsy rock chick image made her an unlikely feminist icon. To illustrate her toughness, she recalls the time she almost clobbered Lynsey De Paul on the set of *Top Of The Pops*. De Paul had been misquoted in an interview as making derogatory remarks about our Suze. At least, that was her excuse when Quatro pinned her against a window. This was one diminutive Detroit dame you don't mess with. Lifelong friend Alice Cooper reckons that not only is she a decent poker player but if you ever needed her in a fight she'd be right there. Despite a guest slot on *Happy Days* as Leather Tuscadero (spot of typecasting there?), Quatro has never stopped touring. She was recently reunited with Mickie Most on a new album, but has also partaken of a little celebrity cooking and appeared on stage in a revival of *Annie Get Your Gun*.

7/Roy Wood & Wizzard
Glam points: 100

2 No. 1s ● 6 Top 20 hits

Something of an anachronism given glam rock's preoccupation with populist boogie music, Roy Wood and Wizzard revelled in layered textures, their 'big' sound bolstered by two drummers, two saxophonists, two cellists, a keyboard player and rhythm section – a distinctly Spector-esque approach. Jonathan King reckons they made interesting and intelligent records. Their costumes became progressively more extreme over the seventies, mainly at Wood's behest. 'We went through a stage of trying to be as outrageous as we possibly could each time we went on *Top Of The Pops*,' the bearded one recalls. 'We didn't want to repeat ourselves, because we were on there quite a lot. During the day at rehearsals, the rest of the band would hide. I'd always hide some costumes for them.' Gorilla suits, angel wings, Teddy Boy outfits – a case of never mind the warlocks, here's Roy Wood and his reluctant fancy-dress clotheshorses. The group peaked during 1973, enjoying successive numbers ones with 'See My Baby Jive' and 'Angel Fingers', preceding the fondly remembered 'I Wish It Could Be Christmas Everyday', which Wood remembers as the most fun of all to record. Despite appearances, it was put together in blazing sunshine in mid-August. The band did their best to make the recording feel seasonal by making the room look cold and wearing overcoats. Wood is back on the road, but with a new show, new band and new songs.

Roy Wood: 'I've had loads of offers to reform Wizzard and do the seventies revival stuff and all that. I'm not really interested. We've done that. It should be left as it was.'

6/Bay City Rollers

Glam points: 139

2 No. 1s ● 8 Top 20 hits

Looking back with an entirely justifiable degree of shame, singer Les McKeown acknowledges 'the Rollers weren't very cool. But we managed to alert the world to our presence, which is more than any other Scottish band had done up till then.' Bassist Alan Longmuir started the group with drumming brother Derek in 1967. Hunting for an American-sounding name, they stuck a pin in a map of the US for a second time (after wisely rejecting Arkansas) and hit Bay City, Michigan. Manager Tam Paton shaped their career, though guitarist Eric Faulkner takes responsibility for 'moulding' the group's image: 'The tartan and the outfits, that was just stuff that I got from the Army & Navy store.' As Rollermaniacs fan club leader Lynne Clarke admits, Paton manufactured the band purely to appeal to teenage girls; their musical development, or credibility, was never a concern. But to the little girls, the Bay City Rollers were John, Paul, George and Ringo in big boots and tartan. Shows were curtailed when frenzied teenagers hung from the balcony to be closer to the objects of their affection. But then came a series of misfortunes, McKeown was implicated in a fatal car accident, a security guard died during crowd disturbances and a fan committed suicide. When Faulkner overdosed on downers it was perceived he, too, had made a suicide attempt. 'I would have left a note,' he reasons, adding, with a mischievous look, 'I would have left my debts to some people.' The internal bickering reached a head in Japan, when McKeown became so paranoid that he bugged his band members' rooms. The group collapsed in acrimony (see Rollers entry in Boy Bands chapter), though fans can still catch at least one touring version of the group.

Eric Faulkner: 'You could actually make one of our outfits for a couple of quid at the Army & Navy store.'

5/Mud

Glam points: 178

3 No. 1s ● 12 Top 20 hits

From Carshalton in Surrey, Mud had worked the circuit for years, even recording a topical debut single called 'Flower Power' before glam opened the door to their family-friendly rock 'n' roll. Dressed in Teddy Boy drapes and drainpipes, they owed their fortune to the pens of Mike Chapman and Nicky Chinn: glam's top songwriting team gave the band their first number one with 'Tiger Feet'. As well as simplicity, the track boasted its own pelvic-twisting, elbow-flaring dance routine. Guitarist Rob Davis, whose long locks and earrings led some to assume he was actually a girl, remembers picking up the idea while touring in the West Midlands. Punters at a club called the Cock Inn would perform the routine with a glass of beer in their hands, which they would throw over each other, or spit, while dancing. Vocalist Les Gray opted for a more serene dance step, stealing the nifty footwork of the Shadows. In the days when the dinosaur prog rock still walked the Earth, Mud were a welcome reminder not to take things too seriously. In short, they were fun. Their second number one, 'Lonely This Christmas', was actually intended as a spoof, and its dedicated

following took Gray by surprise: he hadn't realized the 'two-for-one' element of the song. Nearly thirty years on, Les is showing no signs of quitting and declares that he'll learn to dance in a chair if he has to.

4/Sweet

Glam points: 185

1 No. 1 hit ● 12 Top 20 hits

Sweet, who comprised singer Brian Connolly, bass player Steve Priest, guitarist Andy Scott, and drummer Mick Tucker, didn't start out as hell-raisers. Their first hit, 'Co-Co', actually featured a steel band. Eventually they persuaded their writers, the ubiquitous Chinn and Chapman, to give them room to flex their muscles and record more rock-influenced material. The first such effort was 1972's 'Poppa Joe', followed by 'Little Willy'. The inherent double entendre of the latter led to them being banned from Mecca dance halls. 'Wig Wam Bam' also reached number four; the group promoted it by shamelessly donning American Indian head-dresses and warpaint. Priest in particular employed layers of cosmetics so thick that even an Eastern European gymnast of the day might have found them unbecoming. Dee Dee Wilde of *TOTP* dancing troupe Pan's People remembers Priest looking a bit like a transvestite with his long hair, all-in-one flares and odd make-up and lipstick. In January 1973 Sweet topped the charts with 'Blockbuster', the first of a trio of peerless glam anthems completed by 'Ballroom Blitz' and 'Teenage Rampage'. However, their reckless lifestyle was even then leading them to the point of disintegration – particularly Connolly. Once widely considered a probable solo artist or film star, his prospects retreated with encroaching alcoholism. 'I didn't have the metabolism that was able to take it,' he admits. 'It got the better of me. I had several cardiac arrests before I knew I had a problem.' Connolly died of kidney failure in 1997.

3/Gary Glitter

Glam points: 197

3 No. 1s ● 11 Top 20 hits

Like Shane Fenton, aka Alvin Stardust, failed sixties singer Paul Gadd (aka Paul Raven, aka Paul Monday) reinvented himself in the early seventies – as Gary Glitter. Gadd admits the moniker was only one of several possible contenders, including Horace Hydrogen, Vicky Vomit and George Bean and the Runners. (He probably now wishes he could change names again. His interview was conducted before recent court developments.) Gary Glitter's records were always a guilty treat. After an unsuccessful start to his career, Gadd teamed up with his (late) co-writer Mike Leander on the set of *Ready Steady Go*, where he was the warm-up act. 'I thought, this guy's fantastic,' explained Leander. 'He's better than any of the singers on the show. So we started making hit records.' Their breakthrough came in the summer of 1972 with the rousing 'Rock And Roll (Parts 1 & 2)'. Glitter remembers that they ran out of money and Leander decided to remix it. The song reached number two and won him a songwriter of the year award.

The hey-heys were Glitter's very own idea. Gerry Shepherd, guitarist with the Glitter Band, remembers the temper tantrums that accompanied his rise to stardom, comparing the glittery one to prima donnas such as Joan Collins or Liz Taylor. But, as he admits, that's what makes 'em what they are. Glitter notched up three number ones with 'I'm The Leader Of The Gang (I Am!)', 'I Love You Love Me Love' and 'Always Yours' between 1973 and 1974. His extravagant dress sense and exclamation-mark expression only added to the high camp factor of his records. However, attempting to pass himself off as a martial arts expert in feature film *Remember Me This Way* was considered a woeful mistake by some critics. After he lost money on his similarly grandiose *Gary Glitter's Rock 'n' Roll Circus* venture, Glitter took a backseat. Undoubtedly good entertainment value as he cavorted on stage in ludicrous and ill-fitting costumes, he returned to performing in 1980. Tabloid headlines about his cocaine addiction and attempted suicide interspersed the comebacks. Worse came in November 1999, when he was jailed for four months after pleading guilty to child pornography charges. He was said to have spent his sentence 'cowering' in the hospital wing of Horfield prison, where he was put on suicide watch. He is currently domiciled in Spain. If not exactly a case of how the mighty have fallen, Glitter has certainly fallen mightily.

2/T-Rex

Glam points: 218

4 No. 1s ● 14 Top 20 hits

In the glam rock milieu, many of the hit songs were of a predictable hue – not least because a large proportion came straight off the Chinn and Chapman production line. Undoubtedly, the unique stylist of the glitter generation was Marc Bolan. A prodigiously talented youngster, he released his first single aged eighteen before joining London psychedelic group John's Children in 1967. Later that year he formed Tyrannosaurus Rex, to which he recruited Mickey Finn as percussionist in 1969, replacing Steve Peregrin Took. Finn remembers thinking it was a joke, the next thing he knew, he was up on stage in front of screaming kids: he can't remember what happened in between. The facts escaping Finn include cutting the album *A Beard Of Stars*, shortening the duo's name to T-Rex and enjoying a number two single with 'Ride A White Swan'. With the addition of drummer Bill Legend and bass player Steve Currie, T-Rex topped the charts with both 'Hot Love' and 'Get It On'. In 1971 and 1972 they were the epitome of cool, the biggest-selling act in Britain by dint of Bolan's distinctive, ethereal vibrato. Drummer Legend found Marc prone to impatience, but couldn't help admiring the elfish one's charm and spontaneity, factors which made T-Rex recordings sound genuinely special. Brian Connolly of Sweet found him highly agreeable: 'He put on the real Mr Cutie when he was performing, but in real life, he was the same person.' Finn believes he was driven, remembering him reading music twenty-four hours a day. 'The Groover', released in June 1973, was Bolan's eleventh and final Top 10 hit. He attempted to revive his career in 1977 with the ITV series *Marc*, but died on 16 September when his car, driven by girlfriend Gloria Jones, left the road at a bend on Barnes Common and hit a tree. Bolan's memory is kept alive by a network of dedicated fanzines and tribute bands such as T-Rextasy. On second thoughts, stick to the records.

1/Slade

Glam points: 265

6 No. 1s ● 16 Top 20 hits

Like many of the bands who struck a rich seam in the glam rock period, Slade endured years of strife on the road to the top. It was in July 1966 that the classic and enduring Slade line-up came together in Wolverhampton – Noddy Holder on guitar and vocals, Dave Hill on guitar, Jim Lea on bass and Don Powell on drums. As the 'N Betweens they trawled the Midlands pub circuit playing covers and sporadic originals before relocating to London in 1969. Chas Chandler of the Animals took over their management and had the idea of shaving their hair, dressing them up as bovver boys and changing their name to Ambrose Slade to cash in on the skinhead craze. It didn't work. In altogether different guise they reached the Top 20 in 1971 with a punchy revival of Little Richard's 'Get Down And Get With It'. Noddy, in tank top, cloth cap and sideburns, wouldn't have looked out of place in the Wurzels, although this didn't diminish his attractiveness to the fairer sex. 'Coz I Luv You' was written by Jim Lea and Noddy in his mother's front room in twenty minutes flat. It topped the charts for three weeks and sent the band on its way. Although their spelling never improved, 'Take Me Bak 'Ome', 'Mama Weer All Crazee Now', 'Cum On Feel The Noize' and 'Skweeze Me Pleeze Me' all repeated the feat. Dave Hill, arguably the most unlikely-looking sex symbol in history, was grateful for any attention, and he boasts a unique claim to glam rock fame with his penchant for women's boots. Despite their string of chart-toppers, Noddy concedes that they're best remembered for what Powell calls '*that* record'. We're talking 'Merry Christmas Everybody' (see Christmas Songs) but Hill opines wistfully that he likes to think that some still remember the other Slade number ones. After Noddy hung up his top hat in the mid-nineties, it left Hill and Powell to continue as Slade II. Lea is training to become a psychotherapist. Noddy's just Noddy, actor, TV personality, DJ and all-round top geezer.

Ten Who Missed The Cut

Barry Blue
(One-Hit Wonder with '(Dancing) On A Saturday Night')
Sparks
(Way too scary to be proper glam)
Chicory Tip
(Took 'Son Of My Father' to the top in 1972)
Mott The Hoople
(One of the best bands of the seventies and chums of Dave Bowie)
Cockney Rebel
(They were great before Harley starting dueting with Sarah Brightman)
Glitter Band
(Nailed a few hits of their own when the bacofoil bulge wasn't looking)
Charlie Gorgeous
(Arsenal forward Charlie George offers us 'A Love Song For My Lady'. Ouch)
Jobraith
(First overtly gay star, though he also claimed to be from outer space)
Kenny
(They met in a banana warehouse. Nuff said)
Hello
(Another glam rock wheeze from the Mike Leander stable)

Really Annoying Records

How the following musical miscreants stormed the charts is a mystery, but this collective body of work constitutes a cultural poison that has seeped deep into the fabric of the British psyche. And that stain just ain't coming out. These are tunes that aren't satisfied with making the blood boil, they also require the stomach to contract and the colon to curdle. Awe-inspiringly awful, bereft of redeeming features, these are songs of misanthropic intent, bludgeoning innocent listeners with fake sentiment, be it familial chutzpah (no less than three celebrate grandparenthood) or hopelessly forced bonhomie (see 'Agadoo'). Our countdown of the chronically dire begins with a song from some good Catholic boys and girls who proved they knew a thing or two about original sin.

10/St Winifred's School Choir   Points: 31

Key hit: 'There's No One Quite Like Grandma'
Chart position: No. 1, November 1980 ● 1 Top 10 hit ● 11 weeks in chart

Dressed in lurid pink and oversized collars, St Winifred's School Choir piloted this impossibly sentimental tribute to their favourite wrinkly to the top of the charts in December 1980. It wasn't their first crack at stardom. Previously one-hit wonders Brian and Michael had used the choir on 'Matchstalk Men And Matchstalk Cats And Dogs'. However, without union clearances, the Mancunian urchins were banned from appearing on *Top Of The Pops*, much to their dismay. The record company sent out for stage school replacements, who were rehearsed in the Beeb's corridors by choir leader Miss Foley. Upset by the need to replace the original choir, Miss Foley conducted a rather half-hearted run through, and was not impressed by the youngsters' attempts to sing in what they considered to be 'northern' accents. Guided by Sister Aquinas, they recorded their own hit. As the song hit number one, John Lennon was shot dead, meaning the single enjoyed just a single week at the top. 'Sister came out with something very unholy at that stage,' recalls Miss Foley. Helen White was part of what some saw as the choir from hell, but missed her moment on *Top Of The Pops*, as she was on holiday when the licences finally came through, an oversight that she says she's never forgiven her mother for to this day. The group also appeared in concert with Abba, whom they had knocked off number one; giddy excitement all round. Sister Aquinas was featured on *This Is Your Life*, where she was reunited with leading light Dawn Ralph. The participants brush off any swipes – as Helen White points out, when did their critics last have a number one?

9/Joe Dolce Music Theatre

Points: 32

Key hit: 'Shaddap You Face' • Chart position: No. 1, February 1981
1 Top 10 hit • 12 weeks in chart

Recorded in thirty-five different languages, the song's author, Joe Dolce hailed from Ohio and could speaka-da-very-good-English-anyhows. His pidgin English parable told the sing-a-long story of Guiseppe as his Italian grandmother fretted over his future prospects. 'My dad smashed a hole in my bass drum that he'd bought me when I was about eight, I made a nine-string guitar, he pulled the strings off that and broke it in half. The first time he saw the Beatles on television, he said "they'll last a week". Those were the early musical influences.' When he presented 'Shaddap You Face' to the world, few could detect the Fab Four's influence. The song kept Ultravox's 'Vienna' off the top spot, sending self-important Midge Ure's pencil moustache almost perpendicular, though keyboard player Billy Currie reckons the song's chorus was great. 'Shaddap You Face' horrified other commentators who saw it as xenophobic. 'I remember running down the street in the Italian neighbourhood I used to hang out in', Dolce confesses, 'and apologizing in advance to all my favourite places.' Jonathan King believes the concept of the song to be downright racist, although Dolce strongly refutes that charge. Dolce and Vietnamese comic Hung

> **Joe Dolce:** 'It was basically Caucasians and white Anglo Saxons that had a problem with it, because they were afraid their Italian friends would be insulted by them laughing at this song. But the Italians laughed too.'

Le recorded an anti-racist version in 1998 attacking Australia's One Nation Party. He currently works in Melbourne as a 'performance artist', and can do a pretty dapper Aboriginal version of 'Shaddap You Face' when pushed. However, it's possible his glory days are behind him. 'You've got to understand that "Shaddap You Face" was something that captured the imagination of the public. Where I am now is not capturing the imagination of the public.'

8/Keith Harris And Orville

Points: 36

Key hit: 'Orville's Song' • Chart position: No. 4, January 1983
1 Top 10 hit • 3 other chart entries • 20 weeks in chart

Keith Harris is, thankfully, the only ventriloquist to place a record in the UK Top 10 – the late Rod Hull preferred to keep his hand up Emu's nether regions rather than on the mixing desk. 'Orville's Song' detailed the unfeasibly large green duck's 'broken heart' and instantly caused a clamour to extend the shooting season. Bobby Crush was doing a summer season at the Scarborough Opera House in 1982 when Harris asked him to write something for the nappied mallard. 'I decided to get a recording studio,' recalls Harris. 'The best one was Abbey Road. If it was good enough for the Beatles, it was good enough for this little fella. I financed it, and Bob Barrett produced it. He did a lot of Basil Brush's stuff. So, he was good with animals.' Crush accepted the commission because, by his own admission, he is without shame. 'Orville's Song' reached number four in the charts – it's fair to say it was an

Keith Harris: 'We're cults now. I think that's what they say, it sounds like it.'

inexplicable moment for many. It was then covered by Germany's top ventriloquist Kliby and Caroline the Cow (eerily, also a green dummy). Their version was entitled 'Wo Kommen Die Babies Hier' (Where Do Babies Come From); Crush had unknowingly provided the German-speaking record-buying public with a sex education song. Rumours that Orville would go solo were defused when the verdant follow-up single, 'It's Not Easy Being Green' emerged. That was the stable's final issue of sodden cultural detritus until rave culture hit in the early nineties. A group called DWA had the novel idea of using Orville's squeaky voice above what's known in the trade as 'a throbbing backbeat' and Harris and Orville found themselves playing to rave audiences. The tabloid press claimed the extended use of Orville's 'Eeeeee' on the record was promoting chemical abuse. They were banned from playing in Stoke-On-Trent, which probably inflicted another blow to poor Orville's heart. After which, it was back to panto.

7/Goombay Dance Band
Points: 37

Key hit: 'Seven Tears' ● Chart position: No. 1, March 1982
1 Top 10 hit ● 1 other chart entry ● 16 weeks in chart

Germany's Goombay Dance Band – think Boney M without the class – are led to this day by the truly unique Oliver Bendt. Some will find it hard to believe that was a name he chose, feeling that it was much smoother than his given surname, Knoch. Having achieved a degree of solo success in 1971 in the German charts with 'Oh Marie', Bendt had a hankering for success on an international scale. He relocated to St Lucia, earning a crust as a fire-eating limbo dancer while putting a theatrical cabaret band together. 'Seven Tears' boasted Bendt's hysterical narration and the backing of a band that included his wife Alicia and children Danny and Yasmin. It was recorded in 1980 but became a surprise UK number one two years later. Follow-up single 'Sun Of Jamaica' bombed in Britain, though it was a number one throughout Europe. Bendt has kept the band going ever since, mining the group's popularity in culturally impoverished eastern European towns, with a fluctuating line-up. He's cagey about the future. 'I don't want to talk too much about it, because I want to have the surprise that it's successful. I'm a little bit superstitious that way. So I will just come out with a record, and everyone will hear.' Some of us have our doubts.

6/Renee & Renato

Points: 39

Key hit: 'Save Your Love' ● Chart position: No. 1, December 1982
1 Top 10 hit ● 19 weeks in chart

Arguably the most unlikely duet of all time, Renee & Renato's 'Save Your Love' paired a prim, svelte blonde with a spherical singing waiter from Birmingham on a song that had all the romantic subtlety of those who serenade diners at restaurants. Punters stupid enough to part with their money for the disc casually assumed that the singers were real-life lovers. Renato Pagliari, who also sang the famed 'Just One Cornetto' advert, was flattered. 'No, she was young enough to be my daughter. Nice compliment, but I'm sorry.' Renee, aka Hilary Lester, laughs off the suggestion, pointing out that she was 22 while Renato was... much older, and that he already had a wife and two children. Lester escaped further recognition by refusing to appear in the accompanying soft-focus video, which was notable for rotund Renato's tragic taste in pullovers; a model donned a blonde wig in Renee's stead. 'It was a very romantic song,' explains Renato. 'Maybe [the song] came out at the right time, when there was too many heavy metal, rock, heavy rock... maybe people got fed up with the bang-a-bang in the head and they want something romantic.' When the single went to number one, the hunt was on for the real Renee; Lester discovered newspaper reporters hiding in the bushes outside her parents' home. The mystery was finally solved and the duo appeared live on television for the first time in January 1983. They chanced their arms one more time with what some critics termed as the excruciating 'Just One More Kiss', but the magic, as such, had gone. Renato is indignant at critical swipes at the record. 'My song is go number one for five weeks. I sold a million records. Who's clever? Five critics, or one million?' Today, Lester is a housewife in the Midlands while Renato works the cruise ships.

> **Hilary Lester on the song's success:** 'I'll never be ashamed of it, but at the end of the day, it is a novelty record. You don't always choose the fifteen minutes of fame that comes your way.'

5/Clive Dunn

Points: 48

Key hit: 'Grandad' ● Chart position: No. 1, January 1971
1 Top 10 hit (plus a re-entry) ● 28 weeks in chart

Clive Dunn was already a national favourite via his characterization of befuddled elderly butcher Corporal Jones in *Dad's Army* when he had his first, and only, hit. The idea for a singing career came about after Ronnie Corbett featured on *This Is Your Life*. The guests were invited to dinner by David Frost, and Dunn found himself sitting next to a musician called Herbie Flowers. Later they met in a Barnes chip shop, and hatched a plot to record a single together. The composition took Flowers, a session bassist who later played on Lou Reed's 'Walk On The Wild Side', about five hours to complete. After voicing the track, Dunn was discouraged by Flowers' use of that crazy, hip pop music jargon. 'Herbie said to me, "I think we've got a monster here, Clive." I didn't know anything about the pop world. "I'm awfully sorry", I said, "I sang it as best as I could."' External events impeded

'Grandad's steady ascent to the top. Striking electric unions had shut off the power, meaning that despite massive demand, EMI simply could not manufacture any more records. Don't panic, thought Dunn. 'I was more worried about the political side of it, that people obviously weren't getting paid properly – they had to go to the lengths of going on strike in the autumn, when everyone wants to make some money for Christmas.' Aww. The song eventually beat down the unions, reaching number one in January 1971. For Flowers, its success was a mixed blessing. 'I've never really lived it down. My career skidded to a halt. I lost all my cred. This is over a quarter of a century ago, and I'm still trying to get it back.'

Herbie Flowers: 'We didn't make a lot of money out of it. The way you make money in this business is write a huge hit that twenty people do covers of. Who's going to cover "Grandad"?'

Dunn decided against pursuing a recording career after he received death threats from a madman claiming to be the song's author. Flowers, who some say would have been only too pleased for someone else to take the blame, subsequently played with Shirley Bassey, Marc Bolan, Paul McCartney and David Bowie.

4/Wurzels

Points: 66

Key hit: 'Combine Harvester (Brand New Key)' ● Chart position: No. 1, June 1976
2 Top 10 hits ● 2 other hits ● 28 weeks in chart

With accents and apparel so exaggerated they would shame the cast of *Allo Allo*, the Wurzels were a West Country self-parody that somehow burred its way into the charts. They were originally formed in the mid-sixties by real-life cider brewer Adge Cutler, enjoying a minor hit with 'Drink Up Thy Zider' in 1967 (other rustic epics included 'Champion Dung Spreader'). When Cutler died in a car crash in 1974, lead vocalist Pete Budd, accordionist Tommy Banner and euphonium player Tony Baylis kept the group together. In 1977 they were taken in hand by producer Bob Barrett who convinced them to write comic lyrics to Melanie's 'Brand New Key'. Budd had actual experience of driving agriculture's new-fangled juggernauts and so together they created 'Combine Harvester'. Its unexpected success led to a dozen appearances on *Top Of The Pops*, where the straw-munching yokels shared a stage with Bob Marley among others. However, their request to use the opening bars of 'Satisfaction' at the start of one appearance was vetoed by the Rolling Stones. Barrett wrote straight back to them, as Banner recalls. 'He said, "On no account will the Stones ever be allowed to use anything that the Wurzels have written."' The Wurzels' follow-up was a version of Jonathan King's 'Una Paloma Blanca' retitled 'I Am A Cider Drinker', a theme true to the group's traditions. Their final hit was 'Farmer Bill's Cowman' (an adaptation of Whistling Jack Smith's 'I Was Kaiser Bill's Batman') though they do all right, thank you very much, on the college ball circuit. There, they can imagine they're still pop stars, as Banner elaborates. 'These two gorgeous girls came up to us the other day. "You don't know us," they said. We thought they were chatting us up. "You don't know us, but you know our grans."'

3/Father Abraham & The Smurfs

Points: 95

Key hit: 'The Smurf Song' ● Chart position: No. 2, June 1978
3 Top 10 hits ● 2 other hits ● 48 weeks in chart

Though it might not roll off the tongue, Vader Abraham En Smurfen was a pop star of some magnitude in the Benelux countries long before he sent out his minions – hook-nosed blue gnomes sporting chefs' hats – to conquer the British hit parade. In some people's eyes their presence was enough to produce a streak of xenophobia in the most ardent Europhile. The Smurfs were created by Belgian cartoonist Peyo (Pierre Culliford) in 1958. In the mid-seventies, writer and producer Frans Erkelens was approached by popular Dutch entertainer Pierre Cartner. He'd developed the persona of the beardy Father Abraham, and thought there might be some mileage in a tie-in single, 'Smurfenlied'. When released, the disc sold 400,000, a mighty amount indeed for the Netherlands. The success was duplicated in Britain when the single, retitled 'The Smurf Song', reached number two. Cartner, fazed by the celebrity, jumped ship to return to his career as a mainstream entertainer. To fill the void, Englishman Barrie Corbett, who'd once opened for the Beatles in the sixties with his band the Mustangs, stepped in. Nowadays the Smurfs perform hits of the day in their own unique fashion, as on 1996's 'Our Smurfing Party'. Sadly, Noel Gallagher refused permission for them to sing 'Wonderwall'. 'He said, "I don't want f*****g Smurfs singing our songs,"' recalls Erkelens. 'We made use of it in the newspapers, it was big news at the time, it helped sell the album – Oasis versus the Smurfs.' Maybe they should have gone for a Blur cover version.

> **Frans Erkelens:** 'My favourite Smurf is the Smurfette. She's the luckiest one in the world. Just one Smurfette, and numerous Smurfs, so she must be smiling.'

2/Little Jimmy Osmond

Points: 97

Key hit: 'Long Haired Lover From Liverpool' ● Chart position: No. 1, November 1972
2 Top 10 hits ● 2 other hits ● 50 weeks in chart

With a rhythm track that echoed the theme to *Steptoe And Son*, 'Long Haired Lover', the biggest selling record of 1972, launched yet another of the Osmond brood onto a public that had seemingly gone Mormon crazy. Osmond takes the criticism on the chin, saying that now he's had other careers, he's got over his former embarrassment and likes to keep pictures from that time as mementos. The song was a mistimed attempt to cash in on the Beatles' Mersey connections. After a turgid follow-up, suitably entitled 'Tweedle Dee', the portly pint-pot became the final piece in the Osmonds jigsaw. His brothers cruelly poured him into an Elvis bacofoil jump suit and made him perform a sweaty version of 'Heartbreak Hotel' which some felt made 'Long Haired Lover' sound like the work of God. Forced to play two shows a day in Las Vegas in stifling heat, he pigged out on ice pops and grilled cheese sandwiches before puking his little guts out over the audience. With Donny's solo career taking the limelight, a toothy power struggle ensued as the

brothers jostled for position, but nowadays they're back playing happy Mormon families and are proud of their accomplishments. While his brothers still perform, Jimmy devotes most of his energy to the string of successful entertainment businesses he runs.

1/Black Lace

Points: 122

Key hit: 'Agadoo' ● Chart position: No. 2, June 1984
3 Top 10 hits ● 6 other hits ● 82 weeks in chart

Black Lace were formed in Leeds and started out with ambitions to be a legitimate rock band. Their 'Mary Ann' was Britain's 1979 Eurovision Song Contest entry, though neighbouring Yorkshire pop band Smokie sued, believing it was a shameless copy of their 'Oh Carol'. Plagiarism is the least of Eurovision's problems, and Black Lace finished seventh in Israel. They returned to the Yorkshire club scene, though the occasional hostile audience member was frequently on hand to remind them what he thought of them. An image change was required, obviously. Trimmed to a duo of Colin Routh and Alan Barton, they employed new manager John Wagstaff, who knew a commercial party tune when he heard one. Holidaying in Majorca, Wagstaff heard 'The Birdy Song', recognized its hit potential, brought it back and presented it to Black Lace. Unsurprisingly, the duo dillied and dallied over recording it, and by the time they had the thing in the can, it was someone else's hit. Undeterred, he brought another sure-fire winner to Routh and Barton; this time, they snapped it up. 'Superman (Gioca Jouer)' was an instant smash, but the duo feared they were destined to become one-hit wonders. So they ill-advisedly attempted a 'serious' song, 'Hey You', apparently styled on Kajagoogoo. It bombed. Then Wagstaff stumbled on the big cahuna, 'Agadoo', originally recorded by the Saragossa Band – who hailed from Germany as it happened. Critics of the time bemoaned the fact that a song they saw as repetitive and idiotic struck an immediate chord with the Great British Public. Adopted by Club Med as their theme song, it ensured sun 'n' sex holidaymakers would forever associate the song with cheap booze and drunken shenanigans. However, the group's royalties disappeared when the distribution company went bankrupt the week they were due to be paid. Shame. Follow-ups such as 'Do The Conga' and 'Gang Bang' (memorably featured on the film *Rita, Sue And Bob Too*) were merely mediocre when compared with the unforgettable status of 'Agadoo'. Roadie Rob Hopcraft was promoted to replace Barton in 1991. In a bizarre twist of fate, Barton joined Smokie, but died in a tour bus crash in 1995. Hopcraft and Routh can still be found entertaining clubs the country over, pushing their pineapples and, doubtless, shaking trees.

Some Other Cultural Atrocities

Kids From Shame
Neil Reid: 'Mother Of Mine' (1972)
Krankies: 'Fan' Dabi' Dozi' (1981)
Grange Hill Cast: 'Just Say No' (1986)

Animal Tragic
Wombles: 'The Wombling Song' (1974)
Rick Dees And His Cast Of Idiots: 'Disco Duck (Part One)' (1976)
Muppets featuring Robin: 'Halfway Down The Stairs' (1977)

Total Balls
England Football Squad: 'Back Home' (1970)
Kevin Keegan: 'Head Over Heels In Love' (1979)
Gazza: 'Geordie Boys (Gazza Rap)' (1990)

Soap Duds
Anita Dobson: 'Anyone Can Fall In Love' (1986)
Stefan Dennis: 'Don't It Make You Feel Good' (1989)
Amanda Barrie and Johnny Briggs: 'Something Stupid' (1995)

Bad Lieutenants
Telly Savalas: 'If' (1975)
Billy Howard: 'King Of The Cops' (1975)
Dennis Waterman: 'I Could Be So Good For You' (1980)

Easy Listening

Easy listening does exactly what it says on the tin, being a musical statement so demure and attention-shy, it's designed to complement other activities rather than necessarily secure the listener's attention. This is music as non-stimulus, with the accent on mood, with lush instrumentation accompanied by simple lyrical epigrams. However undemanding it may be on the ear, and however many critics have turned their noses up at its very premise, a number of capable songwriters have worked in the field – from Martin Denny to popular music's greatest writer, Burt Bacharach. Other occasional exponents include Frank Sinatra and Elvis Presley (whose 'Wooden Heart' exemplifies the genre's traits).

Easy listening tunes (other interchangeable appellations include middle-of-the-road and mood music) generally comprise orchestrated arrangements of standards or newer material that harks back to the sentimental romantic songwriting of the forties and fifties. Its singers merge with that music to produce a seamless whole – so as not to distract from the matter at hand, be it decorating, an intimate meal with a loved one or shampooing the dog. The following ten artists are those who performed the trick most successfully, based on UK singles and album sales.

10/Tony Bennett

Points: 358

Biggest UK chart hit: 'Stranger In Paradise' (No. 1, 1955)

Although he's equally at home working alongside jazz musicians, notably through the auspices of his musical director and pianist since the fifties, Ralph Sharon, Bennett's real virtues are as a balladeer. Born Anthony Benedetto, he worked as a singing waiter as a teenager growing up in the big band era. Bob Hope spotted him in New York in 1959 and booked him as his support act at the Paramount Theater. His rendition of 'Boulevard Of Broken Dreams' led to a contract with Columbia Records. The partnership yielded a run of singles successes, including 'Rags To Riches' and a pop interpretation of Hank Williams' country standard 'Cold, Cold Heart', both of which topped the US charts, aided by Bennett's easy-going charm. As friend Marty Mills notes, the man is a consummate professional easily capable of wrapping an audience round his finger. Bennett kept most of his jazz forays for his albums, working with Count Basie's Orchestra and Stan Getz amongst others. His other major pop hits included 'I Lost My Heart In San Francisco', before the notion of pop changed altogether. In 1965 his marriage ended and Bennett plunged to an all-time low. Beatlemania saw him shoved further into the sidelines, and his substance intake accelerated. In 1979 he almost drowned in the bath after a cocaine overdose. After a few excursions on his own label and two duet albums with jazz great Bill Evans, he was left without a contract until 1986. The resurrection of his career is attributable to son Donny taking over as his manager and agent. After several well-regarded albums back at Columbia, covering both the jazz and pop spectrums, Bennett performed an *MTV Unplugged* spot that opened up a brand new audience for him, one he has subsequently courted with great success. An appearance at Glastonbury was particularly notable. He is also an accomplished painter who has exhibited in Paris and London as well as America.

9/Dionne Warwick

Points: 629

Biggest UK chart hit: 'Heartbreaker' (No. 2, 1982)

Burt Bacharach and Hal David's chanteuse of choice, Warwick's emotive but disciplined vocals were heard to astonishing effect across some of the songwriting duo's most thrilling work between 1963 and 1974. As personal secretary Marie Byers recalls, when the diminutive young Warwick first emerged, everyone who heard or saw her was knocked out; New York loved her. Warwick came from a musical family and as a child sang in gospel choirs, alongside her recording artist sister, Dee Dee. Her first hit came in 1963 when she broke free of the New York backing singer milieu to record 'Don't Make Me Over', having been spotted by Bacharach at a Drifters recording session.

Dionne Warwick on Cilla Black's cover version of 'Anyone Who Had a Heart': 'If I had coughed in the middle of a lyric, Cilla would have coughed. It was verbatim.'

Bacharach and David married Warwick's soul fizz to elegant, emphatic songwriting, moulding her into a mainstream pop diva. The melodic guile of their material suited her expressive, teasing vocals perfectly, and massive hits including 'Walk On By' and 'I Say A Little Prayer' followed. 'We did rely upon each other's talents,' admits Warwick, 'and trusted each other's talents.' UK artists such as Sandie Shaw, Dusty Springfield and Cilla Black desperately sought to replicate her sound without ever getting in the same postal code. However, when Bacharach and David fell out, Warwick was hurt at only finding out about it by reading the newspapers. All three former partners sued each other, and paid out a lot of money before eventually kissing and making up. Ironically, Warwick's first pop number one came in 1974 after she broke away from Bacharach and David, cutting 'Then Came You' with the Detroit Spinners. Thereafter, the odd duet aside, her career petered out, despite an ill-fated attempt at disco. She did reunite with Bacharach for the 'That's What Friends Are For' Aids celebrity benefit single. In the nineties she's

become an advocate of censorship (railing against what she sees as anti-women lyrics in rap) and a spokesperson for the Psychic Friends Network, regularly intoning: 'For over five years now we've brought you quality psychic readings at a price we know you can afford.' Warwick insists she doesn't regret it for a moment.

8/Dean Martin   Points: 837

Biggest UK chart hit: 'Memories Are Made Of This' (No. 1, 1956)

Dino Paul Crocetti was arguably the coolest rat in Hollywood's legendary pack, and certainly the most handsome. He grew up in Ohio the son of an Italian barber. After leaving school (where he was bullied for his pidgin English) he worked in local coal mines and steel mills and fought amateur boxing bouts. He also delivered bootleg liquor and found a job as a croupier at a local speakeasy. Modelling himself on crooners such as Bing Crosby, he issued his first single in 1946 ('Which Way Did My Heart Go?'). His showbiz break came when he partnered comic Jerry Lewis on stage in Atlantic City, playing the straight man to Lewis's hyperventilating clown. By the end of the forties they were a hugely popular double act, their reputation enhanced by a sequence of successful comedy films for Paramount before their relationship soured in 1956. Martin's first success as a singer came with 1953's debonair 'That's Amore', which typified the singer's detached, regal presence. In 1958 *The Dean Martin Show* aired on NBC. Hits such as 'Volare' followed, but Martin was just as celebrated for his hell-raising behaviour as his records, often in tandem with soul brother Sinatra, and fellow Rat Pack members Sammy Davis Jr and Shirley MacLaine. Their pooled charisma was exploited in a trio of films: *Ocean's Eleven* (1960), *Sergeants 3* (1962) and *Robin And The Seven Hoods* (1964). Martin became noted for his drinking exploits and his extravagant showbiz bashes. Friend Eddie Fisher recalled that the parties were meeting places for the great and the beautiful, but that Martin himself would always be away from the action, usually watching TV. Ex-Capitol president Alan Livingston states that of the whole Rat Pack, only Martin refused to be at Frank Sinatra's beck and call. Sinatra liked to stay up and chew the fat into the wee hours; Martin would simply get up and leave when he'd had enough. Legendarily he'd also call the police about his own parties so he could get some sleep and put in a round of golf the next morning. Eventually, however, his philandering caught up with him and his wife walked out on the father of seven after twenty-three years of marriage. Thereafter he was pictured escorting a twenty-five-year-old Miss America around town. The arrival of the Beatles cast a dark shadow over the careers of many long-in-the-tooth crooners, but somehow Martin escaped the cull. Indeed, in 1964 he knocked the Beatles off the top of the US charts with the saccharine 'Everybody Loves Somebody'. He went on to another round of celebrity-studded TV specials, before his health began to fail in the late seventies. When his son Dean Paul died in a plane crash in 1987, it was a blow from which Martin Sr never recovered. Livingston remembers seeing Martin at his favourite restaurant every time he went there, sat in a corner, drinking alone. Dean Martin died, a recluse, on Christmas Day 1995.

7/Dusty Springfield

Points: 895

Biggest UK chart hit: 'You Don't Have To Say You Love Me' (No. 1, 1966)

Considered by many to be the finest white female singer of her generation, Springfield's recording career has outlasted the vagaries of pop music fashion – conquering genres from R&B to country to pop ballads, disco and beyond. Born Mary O'Brien in 1939, as a child Springfield modelled herself on Peggy Lee. After convent school she joined vocal trio the Lana Sisters, who recorded fleetingly for Fontana, before forming family group the Springfields in 1960 with brother Dion. Hits including 'Island Of Dreams' and 'Say I Won't Be There' brought them Top 5 chart placings, but Dusty eventually opted for a solo career. Her debut single 'I Only Want To Be With You' was another Top 5 hit, before she embarked on a rewarding partnership with Burt Bacharach and Hal David. Next to Dionne Warwick, Springfield was the duo's favourite singer. 'Anyone Who Had A Heart' and 'I Just Don't Know What To Do With Myself' were typically distinctive Bacharach compositions, their insistent hooklines belying the musical complexities beneath the song's surface, Springfield caressing them into tender romantic enchantments. She also shared her writers' perfectionism, and would insist on retakes should she suspect a single breath was out of place. Bacharach remembers that she didn't want anyone, even him,

Friend Pat Rhodes: 'Musicians were frightened of her because she knew her music back to front. They'd say, oh, she's a bitch to work for. She wasn't, she just knew what was right and what was wrong.'

around during a playback. By the mid-sixties Springfield was one of British pop music's brightest stars. Her appearance – beehive haircut and Panda-thick black eyeliner – helped to define the decade visually. She also had a mind of her own. Her 1964 tour of South Africa was aborted when she refused to play in front of segregated audiences. On her return she delivered her most elegant performance yet, 'You Don't Have To Say You Love Me'. Yet contemporary singer Sarah Cracknell of Saint Etienne reckons 'she seemed to be filled with self-doubt all the time, constantly putting herself down'. Springfield responded ambiguously to questions about her sexuality. 'Whatever anybody else says,' reckons friend Pat Rhodes, 'I still say Dusty was bisexual.' With the advent of the summer of love, it seemed her moment had passed. Instead, she upped sticks to Memphis and recorded the sublime, soul-inflected *Dusty In Memphis*. It housed the international smash 'Son Of A Preacher Man', yet neither the album nor the Kenny Gamble and Leon Huff-produced follow-up *A Brand New Me* remedied her commercial decline. The seventies were lost to drug-related problems and suicide attempts. The Pet Shops Boys contacted her in 1987 and invited her to duet on their worldwide hit, 'What Have I Done To Deserve This?' As ever, Springfield moved on to new pastures, and her 1995 album *A Very Fine Love* was recorded in Nashville with country musicians. It was during the sessions for the album that she was diagnosed as suffering from breast cancer, an illness from which she died in March 1999. Just a few days later she was inducted into the Rock and Roll Hall Of Fame.

6/Engelbert Humperdinck

Points: 1,097

Biggest UK chart hit: 'Release Me' (No. 1, 1967)

The would-be enigma of easy listening, Humperdinck was born Arnold George Dorsey in 1936 in Madras, India. One of ten kids raised in Leicester, he took up the saxophone before becoming a ballad singer with local dance bands. Despite TV appearances and tours with Marty Wilde, the singer's career faltered and in 1963 he contracted tuberculosis. It took the intervention of manager and former roommate Gordon Mills (a songwriter for early British rock 'n' roller Johnny Kidd and manager of Tom Jones) to reinvent him. Rechristening him Humperdinck (after the German composer) he structured a whole new image, shrouded in mystery, and maintained by his disappearance after every show. Quite rightly, to this day Dorsey sees it as quite an achievement on his part to conjure a romantic image out of the name Engelbert Humperdinck. Though some would label the act pure corn, it worked, aided in no small part by Humperdinck's velvet larynx and the well-chosen material, particularly his signature song 'Release Me'. His chance came when he stood in as a last-minute replacement on *Saturday Night At The London Palladium* and sang the song to a spellbound TV audience of millions. It kept the Beatles' 'Penny Lane'/'Strawberry Fields Forever' off the top, thereby ending the moptops' sequence of ten successive number ones. The breakthrough was sustained with songs such as 'There Goes My Everything', 'The Last Waltz' and 'After The Lovin'' and a clutch of platinum albums. Indeed, he was the biggest-selling British artist of 1967, and his splendid sideburns bristled from the covers of a thousand pop mags. He became best chums with Tom Jones, his only serious rival in the late sixties crooner stakes until they fell out after Humperdinck left their shared management. Thereafter the singer disappeared into the cabaret circuit, though his fanbase has hardly dwindled – it's estimated that some eight million people, mostly women of a certain age we must assume, are members worldwide. It's also allowed him to buy a nice piece of real estate – Mrs Humperdinck Patricia Dorsey relates that the garden is of such a size that her hubby uses a dog whistle to call her if he doesn't know where she is. She's forgiven him for fathering two illegitimate children and remains his number one fan. 'I'll go into the dressing room, and he's always very nervous. As soon as he puts his black pants on, I call them his magic pants, the tummy goes, and there's this gorgeous guy. And he walks out on stage and that's Engelbert, that's the star. That's not my husband, that's the star.'

5/Carpenters

Points: 1,553

Biggest UK chart hit: 'Yesterday Once More' (No. 2, 1973)

Karen and Richard Carpenter formed this enduring sibling duo – whose angelic melodies and kooky innocence masked deep personal unhappiness – in the mid-sixties. They won a 'battle of the bands' show at the Hollywood Bowl in 1966 (singing 'Dancin' In The Street') but a projected recording contract with RCA fell through. Herb Alpert at A&M was the first to respond to their demos, resulting in a minor hit with a version of the Beatles 'Ticket To Ride'. Another cover version, Burt Bacharach's '(They Long To Be)

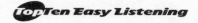

Close To You', previously sung by Dionne Warwick, gave them their breakthrough in 1970. The song served to highlight the duo's innate harmonic majesty, while Jack Daugherty's understated production gave the record a clarity of sound that was almost sepulchral. The wholesome hits continued to flow through the seventies, a mixture of covers (such as Leon Russell's 'Superstar', Neil Diamond's 'Solitaire' and the Marvelettes' 'Please Mr Postman') and celestial originals from Richard and co-writer John Bettis (including 'Only Yesterday'). In all they hit the UK Top 40 sixteen times during the seventies, and Karen became a major star. Which annoyed Richard somewhat, particularly when he was referred to as 'Karen Carpenter's brother'. He apparently also hated the image that had been concocted on their behalf; the British press nicknamed them 'goody four-shoes'. They travelled to London in 1976 to pick up twenty-one gold discs but were forced to leave them behind at Heathrow because they were too heavy for excess baggage. Concerns for Karen's health began in November 1975 when she was hospital- ized, weighing only 90lbs. Richard's advancing addiction to quaaludes also undermined their success. The group attempted to expand their reference points, notably on a cover of Canadian rock band Klaatu's 'Calling Occupants Of Interplanetary Craft', but in truth they rarely messed with the sonic template (Richard nixed an attempted 'raunchy' solo album by Karen in 1979). And all the time Karen was becoming more ill. Richard main- tains that no-one knew about anorexia or bulimia at the time; no-one seemed to recognize the problem, even Karen herself. Singer Petula Clark recalls giving Karen a hug and feeling as if she was embracing a bag of bones. In 1983, Karen was rushed to hospital after being found unconscious at her parents' home. The coroner's verdict was that death was caused by anorexia nervosa. Richard maintains to this day that he's hurt that his sister should be remembered as a girl that died from an eating disorder and not as one of the world's best singers, let alone as a truly nice person.

4/Andy Williams
Points: 1,629

Biggest UK chart hit: 'Butterfly' (No. 1, 1957)

Williams (born Howard Andrew in 1928) is a thoroughbred of easy listening; ever- smiling, relaxed in demeanour, but always immaculately turned out and the perfect host. He began by singing in church in his native Iowa, before forming a quartet with his broth- ers. They moved to Los Angeles and backed Bing Crosby on 'Wishing On A Star' in 1944. Williams' solo career began in 1952 as a regular on Steve Allen's *Tonight Show*; he secured his first recording contract with Cadence Records four years later and scored his first US Top 10 hit with 'Canadian Sunset'. 'Butterfly', an old Charlie Gracie rockabilly number released the following year, took him to number one. Further hits included 'Are You Sincere' and 'Lonely Street', before he moved to Columbia Records. His conversa- tional singing style had matured after an early fascination with Presley; by his own admis- sion Williams loves singing ballads, and attributes his approach to singin' 'em like he talks 'em. The best example was his enduring version of Henry Mancini's 'Moon River'. Considered the definite reading of the song, it was never actually released as a single at the time. However, the hits dried up post-Beatles. Undeterred, Williams concentrated on

TV work (his long-running show is to be credited for giving us the Osmonds). Anxious about his height, Williams would always be shot from a low-lying camera, and be given the tallest stool in any interview or duet situation. He aimed for a laid-back Cary Grant-esque style on TV and adopted a very conservative wardrobe, including jumpers reminiscent of English actor Rex Harrison. The show was live and often the time-out buzzer would necessitate a hasty exit. Williams' album releases of the time were based variously around Broadway musicals and film themes. All were highly successful, though his TV show was eventually cancelled in 1971 (the same year he hit with the theme from *Love Story*) after a hugely successful fourteen-year run. Thereafter his success was limited to the UK, where 'Solitaire' was a Top 10 hit in 1973. Williams continued to broadcast Christmas specials with his wife Claudine despite their 'amicable' separation in 1976. When she was subsequently charged with shooting her new boyfriend to death on a skiing holiday, Williams supported his ex-wife in court (she was found guilty of manslaughter). In 1992 he established his own entertainment complex in Branson, Missouri, from where he still issues the occasional album. The 'emperor of easy' was back on the charts in 1996 when a car commercial used his signature song 'Music To Watch Girls By' and brought him back to the chat show circuit, a career boost that he compares to taking Viagra.

3/Nat King Cole

Points: 1,656

Biggest UK chart hit: 'When I Fall In Love' (No. 2, 1957)

Born Nathaniel Adams Coles in Alabama in 1917, the son of a Baptist minister, Cole formed an amateur group with his brothers before taking solo engagements as a pianist. Forming his own bebop group with guitarist Oscar Moore and bass player Wesley Prince, the Nat King Cole Trio's engaging, Earl Hines-informed jazz style soon became popular on America's West Coast, resulting in a hit single with 1942's 'Straighten Up And Fly Right'. His conversion to vocalist was partially at the behest of Capitol's president Alan Livingston, based on a vocal that Cole performed for an album. Cole himself didn't think he was a singer and had to be talked into stepping behind the microphone on a more regular basis. He subsequently toured with jazz giant Benny Carter and popped up in a series of films. His popularity was confirmed when 'Love You (For Sentimental Reasons)' became his first chart-topper in 1946. Between the years 1944 and 1964 he averaged three hit singles a year, including definitive renditions of 'The Christmas Song', 'Nature Boy', 'Mona Lisa' (which he hated on first hearing), 'Too Young', 'Unforgettable', 'Pretend' and 'Stardust'. Wife Maria, whom he married in 1948, attributes the stream of romantic ballads to their relationship and reveals that he often took up her suggestions for ballads to record. Bongo player Jack Costanzo played with Cole from 1949 to 1953 and confirms that Maria was the impetus behind many of Cole's song choices; he adds that the rest of the band quietly resented this, as more ballads meant they got to play less swing numbers. His vocal approach, a languid, unhurried delivery cushioned by the warmth of Cole's personality, was beloved of jazz and pop fans, and he was an acknowledged influence on everyone from Chuck Berry to Elvis Presley. He was also a gifted and inventive jazz pianist in his own right. Dubbed 'the sepia Sinatra' by some, Cole's success came in the face of racist oppo-

sition, including a beating at the hands of the White Citizens Council at a 1956 concert. He also faced the wrath of some in the civil rights movement who accused him of being too eager to make compromises when he didn't condemn the attacks. When he moved to a plush Los Angeles neighbourhood, Maria remembers having to scrape off the words 'nigger' from their steps. He also had a TV show pulled because of hostility from white sponsors; Max Factor famously complained they couldn't sell their lipstick on a show presented by a black person. Cole prospered despite music's sixties revolution, cheekily adding the Noel Sherman song 'Mr Cole Won't Rock And Roll' to his live sets. The hits continued, notably 'Ramblin' Rose' and 'Let There Be Love'. He died from lung cancer in 1965 doubtless caused by his heavy smoking, and is succeeded in the industry by his daughter, Natalie. A version of 'Unforgettable' with Cole's vocals dubbed on to duet with those of his daughter was a Top 20 hit on both sides of the Atlantic in 1991.

2/Burt Bacharach
Points: 1,957

Biggest UK chart hit: too numerous to mention

A man who ranks alongside George Gershwin and Irving Berlin as one of the twentieth century's greatest songwriters, Bacharach was born in Kansas City in 1928. By the time his father's journalistic career had transplanted him to New York, he was already an accomplished pianist, percussionist and celloist, though he hated taking the piano lessons. Bacharach played in a series of jazz bands in the forties, inspired by Charlie Parker and Dizzy Gillespie, while studying music theory and composition, before army service intervened. On his return from Germany he placed his first songs with the Ames Brothers, Patti Page and Steve Lawrence. Marty Robbins gave him his breakthrough hit in 1957 with 'The Story Of My Life', which went Top 20 in America. It was the first successful collaboration with songwriting partner, lyricist Hal David, with whom he would also compose the theme song to sci-fi film *The Blob*. The pairing topped the UK charts in 1958 with Perry Como's 'Magic Moments'. Bacharach then wrote material for the Drifters (with Bob Hilliard) before renewing his association with David in 1961. Drifters backing singer Dionne Warwick was recruited as the perfect conduit for the pair's songs in the early sixties. Between 1962 and 1968 she scored fifteen major hits, while Cilla Black, Sandie Shaw and the Walker Brothers all achieved UK number ones with Bacharach/David material. His film scores included *What's New Pussycat?*, *Alfie* and 1969's *Butch Cassidy And The Sundance Kid*, which won two Oscars. Their winning formula? Bacharach provided an acute melodic sensibility to David's romantic statements, without resort to sentimental kitsch or obviousness – Warwick's defiant, empowering 'Walk On By' is arguably the supreme example. Bacharach doesn't deny his reputation as a demanding perfectionist for a moment. While Bacharach recorded himself infrequently, he did score one notable hit with 1965's 'Trains And Boats And Planes'. The transition from the sixties to seventies stymied this prolific writer (though the Carpenters' version of Warwick's '(They Long To Be) Close To You' hit number one in the U.S. early

Dionne Warwick:
He was and still is a taskmaster. It was like taking an exam every time you sang one of his songs.'

in 1970). Thereafter his relationship with David ended, his marriage collapsed and the hit well ran dry as he sojourned in his beach hut for the best part of a decade. He returned in 1981 with the Oscar-winning 'Arthur's Theme', written with Carol Bayer Sager (whom he later married) and Pete Allen. Warwick returned in 1985, reaching the top of the US charts early the following year alongside an all-star cast featuring Elton John, Gladys Knight and Stevie Wonder with 'That's What Friends Are For'. A duet by Patti LaBelle and Michael McDonald ('On My Own') repeated the feat later the same year, but otherwise his Midas touch deserted him. Bacharach has retained his popularity with today's pop icons, however, including Noel Gallagher (Bacharach's image featured on the cover of Oasis's *Definitely Maybe*), All Saints and Elvis Costello (with whom he recorded 1998's *Painted From Memory*).

1/Frank Sinatra
Points: 2,952

Biggest UK chart hit: 'Strangers In The Night' (No. 1, 1966)

Frank Sinatra was almost as famous for his lack of humour as he was for his vocal excellence, which adorned what many consider to be the best examples of recorded sound in the twentieth century. But with Sinatra it was always more than just a voice. While others had arguably more impressive techniques, the Sinatra package came with such depth and charismatic presence that the finished product was irresistible. The fact that Sinatra never escaped his reputation for fraternising with America's underworld only added to the intrigue and sense of occasion on his records. A major film star as well as recording artist, Sinatra left school aged sixteen to pick up occasional gigs as a wedding singer, marrying sweetheart Nancy a year later. Prior to the outbreak of World War II he doubled as a waiter and singer at the Rustic Cabin roadhouse in New Jersey. After working with Harry James he was spotted by bandleader Tommy Dorsey, with whom he began to record in the early forties (on records including 'I'll Never Smile Again', 'Delores' and 'There Are Such Things'). Their success allowed him to buy out his contract and, inspired by Bing Crosby, try to establish himself as a solo artist; a brave step in an era dominated by bandleaders. His appearances at the Paramount Theater saw modern pop fandom born – his army of Bobbysoxers (so titled after the prevailing foot fashion of the era) were the first to employ unreconstructed screaming to signal their appreciation. Actress Janet Leigh states for the record that while she never got the chance to tear at ol' blue eyes' clothes, she's certain she'd have done so if the opportunity had presented itself. Sinatra appeared in a run of successful films and was involved in various political campaigns, though his anti-racist stance and visits to Cuba also saw him farcically accused of Communism. After marrying second wife Ava Gardner in 1951 his career began to stall, though he secured an Oscar for his portrayal of Maggio in *From Here To Eternity*. He was said to be devastated after Gardner left him and twice attempted suicide. His musical output revived as he switched to Capitol, with whom he recorded thirteen albums that all reached the US Top 5 between 1954 and 1961. At the time, Alan Livingston's decision to take him on was considered ill-advised. Livingston recalls telling a roomful of Capitol biggies that he'd just signed Sinatra, to be met with horror-struck faces. But Livingston regarded Sinatra as the best

popular singer of all time and he felt duty-bound to try to bring the man back. For many, 1956's *Songs For Swingin' Lovers* was his finest hour, its string-laden backing tracks shedding further radiance on Sinatra's stellar performances, exemplified by the definitive version of Cole Porter's 'I've Got You Under My Skin'. He also continued to appear as a 'straight' actor in films, notably in 1955's *The Man With The Golden Arm* and 1962's *The Manchurian Candidate*. His first directorial credit came with war film *None But The Brave* in 1965, while musical films included *Young At Heart*, *The Tender Trap*, *Guys And Dolls*, *High Society* and *Pal Joey*. After initially dismissing rock 'n' roll as 'degenerate', he embraced Elvis Presley before 'retiring' in the early seventies. In between, he married wife number three – nineteen-year-old actress Mia Farrow. His tetchy persona left collaborators and friends alike nervous of his mood swings. Livingston is one of many who have gone on record to confirm that, if you crossed Sinatra, he'd destroy you if he could. In the eighties and nineties Sinatra was venerated by a new generation of fans, not least through the enduring popularity of songs such as 'New York, New York' and, particularly, 'My Way'. Both were dismissed by purists as being pure schlock, but try telling that to your dad after he's hammered the Christmas Scotch. Though he recorded less frequently thereafter, Sinatra's 1993 *Duets* collection paired him with Tony Bennett, Barbra Streisand, Bono and others (but unsurprisingly not Sinead O'Connor, whom he publicly rebuked for her Pope photo-burning outburst). Since his death in May 1998, there has been conjecture about his link with the assassination of Kennedy; specifically that he was key to 'persuading' Chicago to vote Democrat and the Mafia were outraged at the incoming president's lack of gratitude for their efforts. The truth may never come out, but Sinatra remains impeccably qualified for the sobriquet 'larger than life'.

Some Other Easy Listening 'Greats'

Perry Como
Demis Roussos
Liberace
Percy Faith
Lawrence Welk
Des O'Connor
Max Bygraves
Mantovani
Henry Mancini
Richard Clayderman
Julio Iglesias
Barry Manilow
Ray Conniff
Jackie Gleason

Eighties Soul

Our look at eighties soul features fewer iconic artists, Prince aside, than either of its generational forerunners. There was no Otis, Marvin or even mavericks such as Sly Stone or George Clinton to give the genre lift-off as traditional soul singers faced unprecedented competition from a myriad of spin-off genres co-existing within the 'black music' enclave. However, while the Brit-funk boys described below (Linx and Imagination) moved relatively few records on a global scale, they did shift consciousness, providing Britain with its own indigenous soul ethic for the first time. They prepared the ground for Soul II Soul, the real innovators here, to expand R&B's sonic template in the late eighties.

In America soul artists were overshadowed to a greater or less extent by the emerging hip hop and 'urban' R&B revolution, though the more versatile stars (such as Chaka Khan) adapted and co-opted the upstart movements. While the eighties provided an elephant's graveyard for traditional soul mores, one or two straight balladeers, Vandross and O'Neal in particular, managed to carve out a niche without adapting their sound. The following list is based on UK singles and album sales.

10/Cameo   Points: 97

Recommended album: *Word Up* (1986)

Cameo's origins date back to 1974 when Julliard School-trained vocalist (and erstwhile drummer) Larry Blackmon put the New York City Players together. Following their name change in 1976 they embarked on a frenetic touring schedule. Alongside Blackmon, vocalists Nathan Leftenant and Tomi Jenkins were backed by a musical ensemble of up to thirteen members. They picked up some beefy funk tips as support act on George Clinton's Funkadelic Mothership tour and released their first charting album, *Cardiac Arrest*, in September 1977. Like all their records, it was produced by Blackmon. A succes-

sion of gold albums followed, exploiting the group's distinctive hybrid of energetic funk and soul. These drew on what Blackmon describes as the 'raw power' of their stage shows. However, it was only with 1984's 'She's Strange' that they began to enjoy crossover singles success. As the decade progressed and the band slimmed, they spiced the funk mix with shrieking rock guitar leads. Cameo's first UK Top 20 hit came in 1985 with 'Single Life'. The group's signature song, 'Word Up', followed. An aggressive marriage of hip hop, rock and funk threads, it reached number three in the UK charts, though the threads of Blackmon's stage-gear garnered as much attention as the song. Blackmon had been handed a red codpiece (designed by Jean-Paul Gaultier) to wear. 'I had no idea what it was,' says Blackmon. 'I opened it a little bit, said, "Oh, shit, what is that?"' The rest of the band encouraged him, he recalls: '"Oh, man, Larry, that's balls out! Go, man!"' For their *Top Of The Pops* appearance, the first run-through was performed waist-up as BBC executives fretted over showing the nation Larry's crimson crotch. Blackmon also worked extensively with other artists, including comic Eddie Murphy, as part of his Atlanta Artists studio. Leftenant had departed by the advent of 1992's *Emotional Violence*, and thereafter Cameo split from Warner Brothers and Blackmon took his enterprise independent. They have continued to perform as part of sundry old school funk package tours. As Blackmon admits, 'We're not trying to be any different. But we're not trying to be, period. For us, the way it falls out of the shoot, it's a Cameo product.'

9/Linx
Points: 230

Recommended album: *Intuition* (1982)

Linx were standard-bearers for the short-lived Brit Funk movement of the early eighties, alongside Imagination, Freeze and Light Of The World. Singer David Grant and bass player Sketch (aka Peter Martin) grew up in East London on a diet of Motown and funk records, as well as domestic rock and pop influences. When they couldn't interest any record labels in their new soul project they formed their own production and publishing companies, hoping to satisfy a ready-made audience among a growing club scene that had yet to be recognized in mainstream media outlets. Recruiting accompanists Bob Carter (keyboards/production) and Andy Duncan (drums), they cut a 1,000-copy pressing of debut single, 'You're Lying'. It sold out within a week, and Chrysalis Records came knocking on their door, along with several other labels who had sniffily dismissed them out of hand previously. 'If the industry isn't working for you the way you want it,' says Sketch, 'you've got to do things to work around it and change it. A lot of the time you won't be able to change it by just beating at it, but it's so full of holes, you can get in easily.' Re-released, the single became a Top 20 hit and brought an appearance on *Top Of The Pops*, though Grant's enjoyment of the experience was spoiled by his decision to wear dark glasses, rendering him unable to follow the sightline of any BBC cameras. On their first tour they introduced backing singer Junior Giscombe, who would score solo success himself as the Brit Funk movement went overground. 'You're Lying'

David Grant: 'I come from Basildon, I don't come from Brooklyn. So I'm going to do it my way, and me and my boys are going to have our thing.'

also reached the US R&B charts. But Grant maintains that the idea was never to simply replicate the US soul tradition. Further hits included 'Intuition', their landmark single, which employed a prominent calypso backing. They also drew on more unlikely sources, including rock, trying their hand at Alice Cooper's 'School's Out'. Apparently, Sketch wants to know where the footage is, if only to destroy it. However, after second album *Go Ahead* in 1982, he left the band, Grant continuing as a solo artist, achieving one notable hit in tandem with Jaki Graham ('Could It Be I'm Falling In Love' in 1985). He's currently singer for United Colours Of Sound. Sketch, now a member of 23 Skidoo, feels Linx's full potential was never realized, not through any fault of their own, but due to a complete absence of support systems and media for a group of Linx's type.

8/Luther Vandross

Points: 281

Recommended album: *The Best Of Luther Vandross... The Best Of Love* (1989)

R&B balladeer, the king of the slow-jam, Vandross came from a musical family; his father a crooner, his mother a gospel singer and his sister a member of doo wop outfit the Crests. After learning the piano aged three he put his first band together at high school in the Bronx. That act, Listen My Brother, went on to appear on Sesame Street. However, with little interest from record labels the group broke up, and Vandross took up a succession of day jobs until Listen My Brother's former guitarist Carlos Alomar called in 1974. He was working with David Bowie on his *Young Americans* album. Soon Vandross was arranging the vocal parts on the record and contributing a song, 'Fascination'. Vandross supported Bowie on the subsequent tour, also working with Bette Midler, and becoming a prolific session singer (for Burger King, Kentucky Fried Chicken and Miller Beer, as well as Quincy Jones, Chic and Sister Sledge). By 1980 he had a solo contract for a second time, this time with Epic Records. His debut album *Never Too Much* reached the US Top 20, the title-track subsequently topping the R&B charts. In 1983 he recorded 'How Many Times Can We Say Goodbye', a duet with Dionne Warwick, the artist whom he once claimed 'formed his whole life' after seeing her in concert aged thirteen. Released in 1986, 'Give Me The Reason' confirmed his commercial prowess by reaching the UK Top 30, leading to a succession of hit singles during the eighties including 'I Really Didn't Mean It' and 'Stop To Love' (arguably his best song) totalling eight Top 40 entries during the decade. Throughout he also kept up his output as a collaborator and producer, working with Diana Ross among others, and also singing live at the wedding of a New York couple who 'won him' in a 'wedding-of-a-lifetime' contest. He also ballooned to a 54-inch waist before getting back in trim via a crash diet. By his own admission, he has gone 'up and down like Oprah' ever since. In 1992 he sued his record label Sony and joined with Janet Jackson on 'The Best Things In Life Are Free', a UK number two hit. It was the first of several distinctive duets, including 1994's 'Endless Love' with Mariah Carey. If music be the food of love, Vandross's silky tenor remains a

Luther Vandross on collaborating with David Bowie: 'He said, "Can I change the lyrics?" I said, "Of course. You're David Bowie; I live with my mother. Of course you can change the lyrics."'

candlelit dinner next to the fast food of modern R&B. 'I want to sing when I'm seventy,' he confides. 'I've been singing since I was three. I was singing at the beginning, why not sing towards the end, because I plan on being here much past seventy.'

7/Imagination
Points: 297

Recommended album: *Imagination Gold* (1984)

Alongside Linx, Imagination held up Britain's end for eighties soul exhibitionism. Comprising Leee John, Ashley Ingram and Errol Kennedy, the group were formed by John (real name John McGregor) after a youth spent in America, where he sang backing vocals for the Delfonics and Chairman Of The Board (Ingram played bass for both bands). Thereafter, John returned to Britain and enrolled at the Anna Scher Theatre School to study drama. The trio was formed in London in 1981 and hooked up with producer Tony Swain, who remembers them setting out to tackle everything that other bands would never have touched. A series of soul-inflected pop hits started with debut single 'Body Talk', an old Swain composition discovered by John on a demo tape. He added lyrics one night on his mum's kitchen table and produced a song that took them on to *Top Of The Pops*. 'I had this thing called a soiree, it looked like a nappy,' recalls John. 'Ashley was wearing these tights and Errol was wearing these really tight trousers. But they weren't wearing what they call… a dancer's belt. Basically, it looked like we were

Leee John: 'Everybody thought we were from America, "They're really outrageous." As soon as they found out we were British – "Oh, they're really camp!"'

showing our knobs. So they gave everybody BBC jock straps. Unfortunately, they're padded, so you look twice the size!' Further success arrived with 'Just An Illusion' and 'Music And Lights', each accompanied by ever more outlandish costumes. John got his own chat show on LWT, but slowly the hits petered out and in 1984 he returned to acting work (he'd appeared in the *Doctor Who* story 'Enlightenment' a year previously). The band regrouped in 1986, switching to RCA Records, scoring one further minor hit, 'Instinctual', two years later. Though they never made an impact beyond Britain's shores, echoes of Imagination's light funk approach and heavily syncopated vocals can be identified in subsequent musical threads such as deep house. Leee remains philosophical about his pop past: 'Sometimes it works, sometimes it doesn't. There were some funny moments.'

6/Chaka Khan
Points: 301

Recommended album: *I Feel For You* (1984)

Yvette Marie Stevens, a good old-fashioned beltin' diva for the eighties, was raised in Chicago and originally rose to prominence as part of R&B group Rufus. Before that she had formed the Crystalletes at the age of eleven, then went on to tour alongside Motown's Mary Wells as part of the Afro-Arts Theater. Politicized by the Black Panthers during the late sixties, she took the name Chaka Khan. She moved through a number of bands before alighting at Rufus, where she piloted several funk-based gold and platinum albums during the seventies. Khan turned solo in 1978 and her self-titled debut album was a smash, thanks to the inclusion of 'I'm Every Woman', later reprised by Whitney Houston. It was the first big hit from Khan's collaboration with famed 'diva' producer Arif Mardin, who recalls the song's recording: 'We were in the studio cutting a song, and it arrived by messenger. We played it, and said, we have to stop what we're doing and do this song right away.' However, she was still contracted to Rufus, and returned occasionally to perform with the band until 1982. It's fair to say they felt a little betrayed by her decision to record solo, as keyboard player Kevin Murphy recalls: 'We were her big brothers, we looked out for her. We wanted to see her succeed to the nth degree. But we'd have liked to have been with her when it happened.' She demonstrated her versatility in 1982 by recording an album of jazz standards, *Echoes Of An Era*. Two years later she revived her pop career with *I Feel For You*, a platinum record boosted by a Prince-written title-track that featured cameo appearances from Melle Mel and Stevie Wonder (a long-time fan, Wonder had written Rufus's 1974 smash 'Tell Me Something Good' specifically for Khan's voice). 'I Feel For You' won her a Grammy award, though Mardin insists that the repetition of Chaka's name at the track's outset was accidentally caused by his uninitiated foibles with a sampler. 'I was not very happy at all,' claims Khan, on first hearing the results. 'I said, "What did you do to this song?" He said, "Don't worry, my dear, it will be a hit."' Not only was it a hit, but one that Khan never equalled in her subsequent career. By the end of the eighties she'd relocated to Europe, winning a further Grammy in 1990 for her duet with Ray Charles, 'I'll Be Good To You'. Thereafter, the nostalgia circuit beckoned. 'I'm a real fighter,' insists the woman who's done for more leopard-skin than *Coronation Street*'s Bet Lynch.

5/Shalamar

Points: 321

Recommended album: *The Greatest Hits* (1986)

Shalamar was formed in 1977 by producers Dick Griffey and Simon Soussan as the ultimate pre-fab fab three. Griffey insists he 'could take a great song and make a hit with a mediocre artist. Or a chicken.' The production duo had scored a hit with a disco medley of five old Motown standards recorded by session singers, 'Uptown Festival'. When it became a hit in both the UK and US they hired Jody Watley (a former dancer on the *Soul Train* TV show and goddaughter of Jackie Wilson), Jeffrey Daniel and Gerald Brown to promote the subsequent album. The trio was kept together thereafter, with the substitution of Howard Hewett for Brown, who apparently asked for too much wonga. Hewett remembers his first meeting with his prospective employer. 'Dick is just a big, gruff cat. He says, "Sing something for me."' 'He sang about eight bars of "Feel The Fire" by Peabo Bryson,' Griffey recalls. 'I said, "That's enough." I went and bought him a topcoat and gave him $500.' By the following Monday Hewett was lip-synching on national TV to the song. After teaming them with producer Leon Sylvers

Jeffrey Daniel, on reactions to his body-popping: 'People thought a rope was pulling me. They thought there was oil on the floor, that I had wheels on my shoes. Anything. They didn't understand what was going on.'

III, Shalamar's biggest American success came in 1980 when 'The Second Time Around' reached the Top 10. They switched focus to Britain thereafter and were rewarded with a run of three consecutive hits in 1982; 'I Can Make You Feel Good', 'A Night To Remember' and 'There It Is'. Watley was pregnant and therefore unable to promote the records. Griffey sent over Daniel, who'd married and divorced singer Stephanie Mills, instead. He brought the hip hop dance innovation, body-popping to British audiences via *Top Of The Pops*, and was subsequently invited to demonstrate the noble art on *Jim'll Fix It*. 'Michael Jackson's act is Jeffrey's Daniel's,' reckons Griffey. 'The military jacket, the cap, the white socks. He's the one that taught all of that to Michael Jackson.' Daniel, magnanimously, reckons he 'never had a problem' with the King of Pop allegedly half-inching his act and renaming it the moonwalk. Daniel would leave the group in 1984, after bickering between Watley and Hewett reached 'separate limo' proportions, to become the host of the UK version of *Soul Train*. He also starred in Andrew Lloyd Webber's preposterous *Starlight Express*. Watley's solo career produced 'Looking For A New Love' (1987) and 'Real Love' (1989), both reaching number two in the US charts. Hewett recruited Delisa Davis and Micki Free to keep Shalamar going, but he too was gone by 1986, with former LA Rams football player Sidney Justin his replacement. Shalamar's chart career was over by 1986. Ten years later the original reunited to perform vocals on Babyface's 'This Is For The Lover In You', which hit the US Top 10.

4/Alexander O'Neal

Points: 324

Recommended album: *The Best Of Alexander O'Neal* (1995)

O'Neal was briefly a member of Minneapolis R&B group and prince protégés Flyte Time until he was kicked out for alleged arrogance. Other unproven stories suggest Warner Brothers refused to sign him because he was 'too black'. He released a solo single, 'Playroom' in 1980, but then hooked up with Flyte Time graduates Jimmy Jam and Terry Lewis, who had secured a deal for their own label with CBS. They liked him for being an 'old-fashioned soul singer', someone who got up on stage and sweated it out without worrying too much about the effect on his personal grooming. Jam and Lewis wrote and produced O'Neal's 1985 debut album, which proved most successful in Britain, where it spawned a series of hits (including his duet with Cherrelle, 'Saturday Love'). Most commentators put its success down to the production team, and even O'Neal admits it was 'a great working relationship', but merit should also be attributed to O'Neal's fantastic vocal range. There was also the 'persona'. Bringing a double bed on stage, on which to throw some startled but enthusiastic lady audience member, was perhaps over-egging the lurve cake. Little wonder he'd be showered in knickers and bras during each performance. O'Neal, sensibly, refrained from picking the undergarments up, 'because I never knew where they'd been'. Within a year of his initial breakthrough, O'Neal was admitted to a Minnesota clinic suffering from acute alcohol and

Alexander O'Neal, on his stage-wear: I'm not going to not wear my suit because it's hot. I'm not going out there in a jogging suit, because people come to see a show. They don't want to see someone who's dressed just like them.'

cocaine addiction. 'I had a big entourage of guys,' he says, 'everybody was just having fun. We would just enjoy the ladies, and they enjoyed us. We tried to have a good time.' His success, in Britain at least, continued unabated, with 'Criticize' (which he co-wrote with Jellybean Johnson) reaching the UK Top 5. By 1988 he was sufficiently popular in the UK to release a Christmas album – *My Gift To You*. In the nineties, after splitting from Jam and Lewis following *All True Man*, O'Neal's career nosedived. Despite signing with Motown and relocating to London, some critics believe he has wasted his undoubted talent on largely inadequate material. A shame for a man whose voice was once variously compared to those of Marvin Gaye, Bobby Womack and, most regularly, Otis Redding.

3/Kool & The Gang   Points: 464

Recommended album: *Everything's Kool And The Gang: Greatest Hits* (1988)

Kool & The Gang were originally formed in 1964 in New Jersey by Ronald Bell and bass-playing brother Robert 'Kool' Bell. Over three decades they adapted their sound to the zeitgeist with tuneful precision. In the late sixties they played gritty funk and R&B, before becoming one of the touchstone acts of the disco years. At which time Ronald, always effectively the group's leader, moved into production, as the band recruited vocalists Earl Toon Jr and, most significantly, James 'J.T.' Taylor. They also began working with jazz arranger Eumir Deodato, establishing a sequence of hits between 1979 and 1982 (including disco staples 'Ladies Night' and 'Celebration'). 'They were taking away all the big horn arrangements and all the real funky street sounds and placing it around this unknown voice,' argues Taylor. Then again, of course, there was the credibility question. 'I didn't think about selling out, I didn't understand what that meant, until "Celebration", with the yahoos and stuff,' recalls Taylor, remembering the reaction from the band's long-term fans: 'What are you guys? Country cowboys or something? Brothers don't do that.' After Deodato left they continued to score with singles such as 'Joanna' and 'Cherish', though Taylor also left the group, mid-performance, in 1986. 'That night I called home and called my family and said that's it. I can't take it.' He undertook a brief solo career while the mother group, despite a succession of replacement singers, sank into the obscurity of the nostalgia circuit.

Trevor Nelson: 'Real pop disco that they got down to a tee. The catchiest songs you've ever heard in your life. And the cheesiest, to be quite honest.'

2/Soul II Soul   Points: 510

Recommended album: *Club Classics Volume 1* (1989)

The beauty of Soul II Soul lies in their appreciation and credible utilization of several diverse musical strands, while never neglecting their primary calling as a soul band. Jazzie B (Beresford Romeo) started out in music as a sound system operator, alongside friend and multi-instrumentalist Philip 'Daddae' Harvey. By the mid-eighties, Soul II Soul, as

Harvey had named them, were the hottest warehouse rave organizers in London, attracting the attention of Nellee Hooper, formerly of Bristol's nascent Massive Attack family. The trio, part of a huge and ever-expanding 'soul collective', began a Sunday night residency at Covent Garden's Africa Centre, where Trevor Nelson was a DJ. Their profile was further bolstered via Jazzie B's slot on Kiss-FM (then still a pirate station). After recording a demo of 'Fairplay', the group secured a contract with Virgin Records' subsidiary 10, signed by Mick Clarke for the princely sum of £500, and embarked on a long-incubated but rapidly realized streak of success. After Rose Windross and Do-reen provided vocals on their first

> **DJ Trevor Nelson:** 'Every venue they did, they transformed it into some planet. No-one was doing that at the time.'

two singles, the franchise was completed with the addition of Caron Wheeler. Jazzie had told a disbelieving Trevor Nelson he'd found 'the British Anita Baker', but he was proved right when 1989's 'Keep On Movin'' took them into the UK Top 5. Its spacious, shuffling rhythm and rich grooves borrowed liberally from soul, reggae and hip hop idioms, a composite sound that was frequently imitated on both sides of the Atlantic. Follow-up

> **Mick Clarke, on 'Keep on Movin'':** 'It was instantly clear to me that this was the most important British black record that had been made, ever. It was just so compelling.'

'Back To Life (However Do You Want Me)' sailed to the top of the UK charts and became a global blockbuster. 'We were just basking in the sun', recalls Jazzie, 'every time we walked into a hotel, we were no longer put into mouldy, scabby, smelly hotels. We were in "suites" now.' America embraced them, bestowing two Grammys on the band, but they fared less well in their own backyard. Nominated for three Brit Awards in 1989, they won nothing, losing out to Lisa Stansfield. Neneh Cherry was so outraged she broke her trophy in half and gave one part to Jazzie.

By the end of the decade, Wheeler had moved on to a solo career, and Jazzie B and Hooper were concentrating on production work (including Sinead O'Connor's 'Nothing Compares 2 U'). It's fair to say the band's profile has diminished subsequently, but for a brief time in the late eighties Soul II Soul did what no other British act had done before, and opened new doors for the future of R&B.

1/Prince   Points: 838

Recommended album: *Sign O' The Times* (1987)

Tricky customer, our purple friend, who variously goes by the name The Artist, the Artist Formerly Known as Prince and, with the effect of irking layout artists the world over, a symbol. Born Prince Roger Nelson, the son of a jazz pianist, Prince taught himself the piano, drums and guitar. His first recordings came as part of Minneapolis soul collective Grand Central. Among its cast of members was Andre Anderson, a close friend whose parents had adopted Prince after he'd fallen out with his stepfather. He secured a solo contract with Warner Brothers in 1977 after a studio audition, and began to chart a series of testosterone-fuelled funk singles, culminating in 1979's R&B chart-topper 'I Wanna Be Your Lover'. Schooled on the James Brown (whom he'd seen in a pivotal experience as a ten-year-old) work ethic, Prince and his ever-changing backing band the Revolution began to sock it to American audiences. They toured with the Rolling Stones. 'We were meat to the lions,' reckons drummer Bobby Z, 'that audience just looked at us like it was a freak show, and reacted accordingly.' The Revolution were forced to dodge bags of chicken, Jack Daniel's bottles and even a grapefruit from the unappreciative Stones audience. As if that wasn't enough for them to contend with, their leader refused to confirm set lists until the moment he went on stage. Prince also began pet projects such as The Time, from whence came production whizz kids Jam and Lewis, and girl group Vanity 6. It was with the release of *1999* (in 1982) and its MTV-plugged single, 'Little Red Corvette', that Prince finally reached the mainstream, with which he subse-

Sheena Easton: 'According to the press he bought me an apartment, which then became a mansion, because that was an even bigger story, in Paris, which was even more glamorous. And how our affair ended was telepathically. I think that speaks for itself.'

quently enjoyed a fitful but durable relationship. Celluloid next, and the *Purple Rain* film. The soundtrack produced a US number one in 'When Doves Cry', arguably Prince's most poignant song. The bombastic title-track, which recalled Jimi Hendrix as much as James Brown, reached number two. By the mid-eighties Prince was established as the new superstar of black music through singles such as 'I Would Die 4 U' (as was his custom, taking liberties with spelling), 'Raspberry Beret' and 'Kiss'. A second film, *Under The Cherry Moon*, followed, before Prince changed tack impressively for the urban warning of 'Sign O' The Times' in 1987 – proving there was far more to his artistic range than romantic and sexual topics. A year later he returned to the hardcore funk of his roots with the *Black Album*, before nixing its release at the last minute (ensuring it became one of the most famous bootlegs of all time). He issued a typically bizarre press release to explain the change of heart, insisting that his bad side, Spooky Electric, was responsible. He was the man who was behind the revival of Sheena Easton's career, whose saucy and subversive 'Sugar Walls' (written by Prince) got her into a slanging match with near-miss First Lady Tipper Gore. It was often suggested that his collaborations with female artists were of a personal nature, conjecture which gives our Sheena the hump. He also worked alongside Madonna and George Clinton (paying part of the latter's tax bill to get him back on his feet). Prince closed the decade by composing the theme to the new Batman film ('Batdance'). In the nineties he unveiled a whole new backing group (The New Power Generation) and continued his progress with platinum albums *Graffiti Bridge* and *Diamonds And Pearls*. Thereafter chart returns dwindled somewhat, a situation doubtless exacerbated by confusion over his name (he became 'the Artist formerly known as Prince' in 1993). He married dancer Mayte Garcia (their son died aged one week in October 1996) and fell out big-style with record label Warner Brothers. For a while he insisted on not answering questions in interviews (even televised interviews, which was a bit bizarre) and wearing the legend 'Slave' on his forehead at awards ceremonies, an act famously punctured by Blur's Dave Rowntree, who had 'Dave' embossed on his bonce in felt-tip. Having secured his freedom from a major label, several critics remain unconvinced he has yet found the best means of utilizing it.

Some More Quintessential Soul Albums Of The Eighties

Atlantic Starr: *All In The Name Of Love* (1987)
Change: *Glow Of Love* (1980)
Randy Crawford: *Randy Crawford* (1980)
Terence Trent D'Arby: *Introducing the Hardline According to Terence Trent D'Arby* (1987)
DeBarge: *All This Love* (1982)
Force M.D.'s: *Love Letters* (1984)
Gap Band: *Gap Band VI* (1984)
Nona Hendryx: *Female Trouble* (1987)
Al Jarreau: *Breakin' Away* (1981)
The Time: *What Time Is It?* (1982)
Ashford & Simpson: *Solid* (1984)

Stadium Rock

S tadium rock is an increasingly pejorative term applied to those groups who ply their trade with an introductory 'We love you, Philadelphia', throw hissy fits if their backstage rider doesn't feature aubergine fajitas hand-rolled by virgins, and conclude their performances with a signature song that invariably has adoring couples nuzzling together like oversexed grizzly bears.

It all began with the Beatles in 1964, who had to book a baseball arena, Shea Stadium, to house their legions of fans. In the seventies the Americans caught on, to the benefit of a declining cigarette lighter industry, those with a preference for manes rather than conventional hairstyles, and manufacturers of unfeasibly large amplifiers. The following acts, who have sold more than 350 million records between them, have three things in common. They're American, they rawk, and they do it in cavernous auditoria. They have no place in their hearts for subtlety or cadence, and for an hour and a half, not only do they want to be adored, they insist on it. Whatever excess you care to name, they've been there, and they've sold us the T-shirt. They may even have a lucrative sideline selling videos of their sexual encounters with celebrity girlfriends. Our results are divvied up, in a fantastically opaque manner, on the basis of record sales and the relative carnage associated with each act.

10/Kiss

Recommended album: *Destroyer* (1976)
Gratuitous Rock Star Act: Simultaneously releasing four eponymous solo albums

In the mid-seventies Kiss had Middle America's parents running scared, though at heart they were always pantomime dames. Vaudevillian rockers Paul Stanley, Gene Simmons, Peter Criss and Ace Frehley took Alice Cooper's schlock Gothic humour, added copious layers of greasepaint and became comic book rock heroes. Guns N'Roses' guitarist Slash pays tribute to Kiss's preconceived idea of a corporate business model for being 'as commercial as you can get for a rock 'n' roll band'. Released in 1975, *Alive!* built on a growing live reputation and turned them into superstars, but they were already super-savvy business operators. Gene Simmons copyrighted the dollar symbol as his label's logo. Neil Jeffries, former editor of metal mag *Kerrang!,* believes that merchandising in rock effectively began with Kiss. Their fanbase, the Kiss Army, numbering millions, snapped up anything associated with the band. This product line included, but was by no means limited to, dolls, models, toy guitars, dustbins, comics, sheets, pillow covers, Christmas tree decorations, telephones, golf balls, pool cues, blankets, full latex rubber suit costumes and toilet paper. In 1983, with interest in the band declining, Kiss did the unthinkable, appearing on stage unmasked. Retaining only Simmons and Stanley from the original line-up, they enjoyed the biggest hit of their career with 1987's 'Crazy Crazy Nights'. Despite proclamations that they'd never daub themselves in warpaint again, in 1996 the slap was reapplied for a nostalgic and lucrative worldwide tour. But don't suggest to them they're only in it for the money. 'The idea is not to have any limitations at all,' says Simmons. 'Not to have any limited dreams of what a band can't do and won't do. We make our own rules and live by them. Whether someone gets it or not? It's too bad.' A tongue-wiggling touché from the towering Mr Simmons.

9/Heart

Carnage points: 25

Recommended album: *Greatest Hits* (1998)
Gratuitous Rock Star Act: Double-dating your guitarist and manager, also siblings

Seattle, prior to becoming the grunge capital of America, once resounded to that most despised of musical entities, the power ballad. Heart, steered by sisters Ann and Nancy Wilson with sundry male accompanists, started out as a folk rock group, who made their debut in 1976 with the well-received *Dreamboat Annie*. However, they didn't appreciate the way their record company marketed them. 'They made it look like two sister lesbian lovers,' cringes Ann. 'There was a little byline that said it was only our first time. It was supposed to be titillating.' A move to Capitol in 1985 brought about an image re-evalua-tion. They were recast as 'the female Led Zeppelin', though their hits were exclusively power ballads. But as the arenas filled out, so did Ann. Rock photographer Ross Halfin remembers being banned from taking pictures in the mid-eighties, while videos for songs such as 'Alone' routinely featured Ann in soft focus. 'Ann's image got to be a big deal,' admits Nancy. 'The feeling then was – I was always trying to protect her, always standing in front.' The arrival of grunge was a final nail in the coffin for the overblown rock ballad.

Nancy Wilson: 'The roaring eighties. It's pretty funny when you see that stuff now. God! My hair was... tall. My clothes were tight. My feet hurt just looking at those videos now.'

'Thank God for grunge, man,' exclaims Nancy. 'It kicked the whole thing. It cleared the decks.' Nowadays, unsurprisingly considering some of the poisonous comments aimed at Ann by fellow professionals (as if male middle-aged rock stars always maintain uniform waistlines) the Wilson sisters enjoy a lower profile, writing and singing together in acoustic project Lovemongers. They're even back living at their parents' house.

8/Poison

Carnage points: 32

Recommended album: *Greatest Hits 1986–1996* (1996)
Gratuitous Rock Star Act: Rider included 876 boxes of condoms. At each venue

As preposterously pouty as pomp rock gets, Poison used enough hairspray to accelerate global warming by a decade. Perhaps their quest for glamour and decadence had something to do with humble origins in Mechanicsburg, Pennsylvania. They were certainly hungry for any party action going. While most stadium bands fantasized about having their pick of the Baywatch babes, lead singer Brett Michaels actually 'boffed' (to use Beavis and Butthead's expression) Pamela Anderson in a home-made blue movie. The group's breakthrough came with 1986's *Look What The Cat Dragged In*. Although it spent over 100 weeks on the US album chart, not everyone was impressed. Megadeth's Dave Mustaine thinks it should have been called 'what the cat stepped in'. In 1988 their ballad-by-numbers, 'Every Rose Has Its Thorn', topped the American charts for three weeks; as Twisted Sister singer and DJ Dee Snider points out, exasperatedly, it's only one chord... Their success soon diminished, as did their legendary partying. While Michaels' diabetes ensured a little restraint in his corner, best friend and guitarist C.C. DeVille was taking living for the moment to new extremes. 'I don't think there's five years of his life he could recount,' notes Michaels. 'I knew that I was going to lose my best friend, but I couldn't save him. He was just gone.' It ended up in a fist fight in 1992. De Ville walked out, after which the band declined further. Michaels became a movie mogul and actor in partnership with Charlie Sheen. Then he got the phone call from C.C. 'He said, "I'm sober and I'd like to come back and try and make it work again." Probably one of the best days of my life, because it just felt awesome.' They set out on tour again in 1999, predictably falling out with each other just a few weeks later.

7/ZZ TOP

Carnage points: 41

Recommended album: *Eliminator* (1983)
Gratuitous Rock Star Act: In 1985 Hill was shot in the stomach – his girlfriend was trying to yank his boots off at the time, and his gun fell on the floor and went off

Three hombres who looked like they'd walked straight out of a spaghetti western, doubt-less leaving a deal of broken furnishings behind. Famous Texan rockers ZZ Top toted an infectious blend of revved-up southern boogie. Their fanbase included, by their own admission, topless dancers, rodeo clowns, midgets, rednecks and celebrity wrestlers. Jimi Hendrix once called Billy Gibbons the finest guitarist of his generation, though Gibbons himself stresses his approach was rudimentary, arguing that he only knows three chords. The hirsute trio was completed by bassist Dusty Hill and drummer Frank Beard – the one without a beard – authenticating the fact that, unlike their arena-friendly peers, ZZ Top had a sense of humour. The popularity of their heavily amplified contemporary blues was initially limited to the south. They became an act of national standing in 1977 when they promoted *Tejas* by recreating parts of Texas on stage courtesy of buffaloes and buzzards, cacti and sand. Yes, really. Eventually MTV awoke to their visual potential after the

release of *Eliminator*. That album boasted a slicker, though still quantifiably ZZ Top-honed sound, and three classic videos for 'Gimme All Your Lovin'', 'Sharp Dressed Man' and 'Legs'. The imagery of fast cars and informally attired ladies led to sales of 10 million copies, a feat repeated by 1985's *Afterburner*. ZZ Top are still hanging in there in the 21st century – the cyber cowboys paid in advance to ensure they're the first band to play in space, with bookings on NASA's Space Shuttle.

6/Mötley Crüe

Carnage points: 57

Recommended album: *Decade Of Decadence – '81-'91* (1991) ● Gratuitous Rock Star Act: In 1988 their manager was convicted of importing 40,000lbs of marijuana

The distilled essence of hard rock hedonism, Mick Mars, Tommy Lee, Vince Neil and Nikki Sixx, by their own admission, spent most of the eighties drugged to their eyeballs. Photographer Mick Wall reckons he's never met any band 'that was quite as genuinely dangerous and dodgy as Mötley Crüe.' They won their spurs on the LA Strip, rooming together in an apartment above the Whiskey-A-Go-Go decorated with beer cans, hypodermic needles and women's underwear. The band's rationale was simply full-time excess. Biographer Dante Bonutto remembers the band's appetites for carnal indulgence in particular. 'With Mötley Crüe there was always a crossover into the world of porn and strippers. The "Girls Girls Girls" track is kind of a tribute to strippers and striptease clubs the world over.' Vince Neil committed his bedtime antics to VHS, taping a drunken sexual encounter with girlfriend Janine and a 'friend'. 'I wish I could cash in on it,' he opines. 'I didn't own the tape. I'd never had it in my possession. I wish.' Drummer Tommy Lee was obviously enchanted by the home movie idea, and explored the concept with girlfriend Pamela Anderson. Their much-gawped-at encounter allegedly grossed $77 million in sales when distributed on video. But it wasn't all fun and laughter in the Crüe camp. In 1985 Neil was involved in a car accident that killed Hanoi Rocks' drummer Razzle and was found guilty of vehicular manslaughter. Among all the carnage, the records seemed almost irrelevant. Bassist Nikki Sixx was hanging out with Steven Adler and Slash

Vince Neil: 'We'd go in, smoke some heroin, bring in some girls, we'd have porno sh*t hung up all over the place.'

of Guns N' Roses in Hollywood in December 1987 when he overdosed. He was pronounced dead at the scene but was revived via injections of adrenalin. Neil remembers his bandmate's considered response to his malaise: 'He hitchhiked home and shot up more heroin.' Not to be outdone, in 1998 Lee was jailed for spousal battery as Pammy sued for divorce.

5/Bon Jovi

Carnage points: 62

Recommended album: *Slippery When Wet* (1986) ● Gratuitous Rock Star Act: As if he would ever mess with that hair by being arrested

New Jersey's second-generation Sicilian rockers – named after poster-boy frontman Jon Bon Jovi aka John Bongiovi – used family connections to get themselves off the ground.

Cousin Tony Bongiovi, was a record producer who'd worked with Talking Heads, Gloria Gaynor and the Rolling Stones at his studio, the Power House, where Jon occasionally swept the floor. Honouring his father's wishes, Tony did his best to cut his young cuz some studio time. However, the resulting session was hardly what his protégé had hoped for. He was invited to supply vocals to 'R2D2 We Wish You A Merry Christmas' on the *Star Wars* Christmas album. Doubtless grateful for this introduction to the 'big time', Jon went his own way and broke big in 1986 as singles such as 'Livin' On A Prayer' became MTV staples. But slowly the truth dawned: Bon Jovi were more pop than metal. They became stadium overlords and pin-ups, neatly marketed across musical constituencies and generations. Jon and writing partner and guitarist Richie Sambora put their shoulders behind a New Jersey band called Skid Row. They enjoyed short-lived success until a fall-out over royalties, the vast majority of which were retained by Bon Jovi. Jon reckons he barely recouped his investment, though Sambora eventually returned his share of royalties. Jon is now an actor, self-celebrated as an 'all American hero'.

4/Van Halen

Carnage points: 74

Recommended album: *Van Halen* (1978) ● Gratuitous Rock Star Act: Eddie Van Halen insisted on backstage bowls of M+Ms, with the brown ones removed

Eddie Van Halen stretched the possibilities of guitar sound, reshaping the context of rock musicianship by playing flange-fingered trebly metal solos at unearthly speed. The band's combination of craftsman and showman was completed by singer Dave Lee Roth – lending the group an edgy dynamism, but also a built-in schism. Additionally comprising Michael Anthony on bass and Alex Van Halen on drums, the group's self-titled 1978 debut jack-knifed rock out of its post-Black Sabbath and Deep Purple trough. For the first time in years, hard rock was fast and exciting rather than ponderous and bloated. Writer Dante Bonutto remembers seeing Eddie backstage before their performance at Donnington in 1984. 'He was doing press-ups in the backstage area, warming up. It was like watching Muhammad Ali about to go into the ring.' For his part, Roth loved the lifestyle. He had a 'special' pair of trousers made entirely from pieces of women's underwear thrown at him on stage. Eddie subsequently played with Michael Jackson, but after the group's hyper-successful *1984* album, Roth departed. Sammy Hagar was recruited as replacement, but the fans weren't sure about the new boy. To the surprise of many, it was the Van Halen act that prospered, while Dave Lee Roth's descent into self-parody saw him slowly disappear from the charts. Many yearned for that original Van Halen line-up. When Roth performed guest vocals on a new track in 1986, leaving Hagar to storm off in a huff, many thought that would be the case. Much to Roth's disgust, the band opted to recruit Gary Cherone of Extreme instead. It seems the guitar's the star in this group.

Mick Wall: 'Whoever you name, Dave Lee Roth was undoubtedly the most over-the-top, larger-than-life rock star you could ever hope to meet.'

3/Guns N'Roses

Carnage points: 81

Recommended album: *Appetite For Destruction* (1987) ● Gratuitous Rock Star Act: On a South American tour in 1992, managed to get arrested in three separate countries

The most self-destructive act in rock 'n' roll, Guns N'Roses rose stratospherically before crashing to earth in a drug-induced tailspin. Led by good-looking reprobate William 'Axl Rose' Bailey (his stage-name, famously, is an anagram for something really quite rude) and Stoke-On-Trent-born guitarist Slash, Guns N'Roses attempted to weld punk attitude to hard-rock power chords. Axl's Mid-West friend Izzy Stradlin on rhythm guitar, LA rocker Steve Adler on drums and punk rocker Duff McKagan from Seattle completed the line-up, who were courted by a clutch of record companies. 'To us, it was great,' reckons McKagan. 'It was a free lunch. We were poor, man, we were dirt poor.' Slash reckons that all that attention certainly helped them support their other hobbies. 'A couple of us had these little drug dependency things. So we had, like, free petty cash when we could get it.' They opted for Geffen and in 1987 they released *Appetite For Destruction*, which eventually reached the top of both the UK and US charts. Thereafter the fireworks started, with the band being accused of sexism, homophobia, drug promotion and plain stupidity. The drug problem was particularly bad. Steven Adler left in 1990 to be replaced by Matt Sorum. In July 1991 Axl assaulted a member of the audience who was taking photos of him. Fifty people, including fifteen police officers, were injured in the resulting riot. Axl, who apparently by now was firmly of the impression that the world was out to get him, attempted to turn Guns N'Roses into a 'mature' rock band. *Use Your Illusion 1* and *2*, released on the same day, were the fastest-selling albums in rock history and it seemed that Guns N'Roses were destined to be the Led Zeppelin of the nineties. Unfortunately, narcotics and egos got in the way. An album of punk covers, *The Spaghetti Incident?,* came out, but that was it. Axl systematically kicked everyone out of the band and then produced – nothing. The world is still waiting to see what he comes up with next.

2/Metallica

Carnage points: 100

Recommended album: *Metallica* (1991) ● Gratuitous Rock Star Act: Hetfield receiving third-degree burns in 1992 after a stage prop exploded

A brutal, stripped-down answer to the hairspray bands of America's West Coast, Metallica started out as a Motörhead copy band, invented thrash rock, and finished the millennium working with symphony orchestras. Their roots, however, are purely blue collar. Drummer Lars Ulrich grew up in Denmark, the son of a tennis pro, before electing to travel to the UK on a musical pilgrimage. Spending time with bands such as Iron Maiden and Lemmy's aforementioned lot, he decided to opt out of the pro-tennis world – wisely, in retrospect. Relocating to Los Angeles, he teamed up with singer and guitarist James Hetfield. Dave Mustaine also played guitar with the band from 1982 to 1983. Hetfield remembers Mötley Crüe coming to check them out. The meeting quickly dissolved into a scuffle. Ulrich remembers the odds being fairly imbalanced as everyone in Mötley Crüe were well over six feet five – it ended up being more of a chase than a fight. Their thunderous 1983 debut, *Kill 'Em All*, completely defied heavy metal convention (the same year bass player Cliff Burton died in a tour crash), though it wasn't until 1986's *Master Of Puppets* that the group began to reap commercial rewards.

Metallica became an underground institution, their progress only impeded on the occasions Hetfield injured himself skateboarding. Their 1991 eponymous effort topped the UK and US charts and confirmed them as the biggest names in hard rock – although they were now also penning ballads such as 'Nothing Else Matters'. They'd

Dave Mustaine: 'We'd just go to rehearsal, play a bunch of cover songs, get super stoned and super drunk. See who fell asleep first and then wrote on their face.'

begun to take themselves too seriously for some, and many were outraged when they attacked internet site Napster for unlicensed distribution of their music. They simply claim they've moved on, though Hetfield admits the suggestion of recording with the San Francisco Philharmonic would have prompted him to raise one of his fingers, had it been suggested back in their thrash rock days.

1/Aerosmith

Carnage points: 109

Recommended album: *Toys In The Attic* (1975)
Gratuitous Rock Star Act: Record company CBS legendarily complained when the band requested royalty cheques be paid directly to their drug dealers

A band whose consumption of heroin and cocaine made even their most showy peers look like lightweights, in the mid-seventies Aerosmith were taken to heart by millions of American kids who just wanted to 'rock out'. As singer Steven Tyler's ex-wife Cyrinda Foxe Tyler points out, the band had no political or social statements to make; they simply wanted to get stoned. As such, they came to define American arena rock. Formed in 1970 in Boston, Tyler and guitarist Joe Perry gave the band their hard-rocking, hard-consuming image, backed by Brad Whitford (rhythm guitar), Tom Hamilton (bass) and Joey Kramer (drums). Their breakthrough record, 1975's *Toys In The Attic*, only served to accelerate a burgeoning reputation for on-the-road indulgence. Writer Dante Bonutto reckons that if they had to walk ten yards from a dressing room to the stage, they'd order a stretch limo. Noddy Holder of Slade once supported the band in Kansas City, and recalls the promoter being forced to send out for white towels at ten in the evening, because the band didn't like the colour of the ones provided. Obstreperousness aside, Tyler and Perry's appetite for drugs saw them dubbed 'the toxic twins'. Tyler's ex-wife recalls that scarves tied to his microphone stand had hollowed pockets created by his seamstress to keep pills and large quantities of cocaine inside. Photographer Ross Halfin remembers one occasion when Tyler worked his way through five grammes of cocaine mixed with heroin before a show – halfway through he simply slid down an amplifier and passed out. Bebe Buell was pregnant with Tyler's daughter Liv when she 'bailed out'. 'I ran for my life, quite frankly. Pregnant, I ran for my life.' By the mid-eighties the toxic twins had successfully extinguished their stash. With everyone preparing obituaries, no-one predicted their rebound on the back of Run DMC's hip-hop remake of 'Walk

This Way'. With its groundbreaking video it put Aerosmith back on track, and they have retained their position at the head of American rock's hierarchy since. More impressively, both the toxic twins have detoxed.

Ten Hard-Rocking Live Albums

MC5: *Kick Out The Jams* (1969)
Lynyrd Skynyrd: *One More From The Road* (1977)
Aerosmith: *Live Bootleg* (1978)
Cheap Trick: *Live At Budokan* (1978)
Blue Öyster Cult: *Some Enchanted Evening* (1978)
Ted Nugent: *Double Live Gonzo* (1978)
Kiss: *Alive!* (1985)
Metallica: *Live Shit: Binge & Purge* (1993)
Van Halen: *Live, Right Here, Right Now* (1993)
Anthrax: Live: *The Island Years* (1994)

Heartbreakers

What distinguishes a heartbreaker from a common-or-garden love song? One essential ingredient. They must be capable of communicating the subject's emotional devastation at the loss of not just their latest flame, but the love of their life. There are two basic types. Many of the most successful ones ostensibly 'shield' their pain from observers, an emotional device that only emphasizes the depths of hurt ('Walk On By', 'The Tracks Of My Tears'). Others simply bask in the emotional torment that's been left behind ('The Sun Ain't Gonna Shine Anymore', 'Love Don't Live Here Anymore'). Note the repetition of the final word (technically, of course, it should be two separate words, but pop writers never were big on spelling) in those song titles. It's no coincidence, more a convenient way of signalling the absolute end of a relationship. These, the musings of the desolate dumped and emotionally bereaved, are the ten greatest heartbreakers of all time, based on the UK chart success of the numerous recorded versions.

10/'The Sun Ain't Gonna Shine Anymore' Tearjerking total: 200

Weeks in chart: 14 ● Weeks at No. 1: 4 ● Number of covers: 1

There's no doubt who performed the definitive version of this immortal, towering ballad – the wonderful Scott Walker. As Stuart Maconie points out, 'Scott Walker could sing you anything and you'd drop to your knees and *weep*.' The song stormed the charts in 1966, credited to the Walker Brothers. As John Walker admits, 'It's the first time I walked out of the studio knowing for sure that not only was it going to be a number one, it was going to stay there. And it did.' The Walker Brothers were Scott Engel, John Maus and Gary Leeds. They were actually not brothers at all, and had formed in Los Angeles in the mid-sixties before moving to London to dodge the Vietnam draft. Within a couple of years they'd scored hits with 'Make It Easy On Yourself' (a UK number one) and 'My Ship Is Coming In'. 'The Sun Ain't Gonna Shine Anymore' was written by Bob Crewe and Bob Gaudio. They specifically had crooner Frankie Valli in mind for the song, having written virtually all of his hits. Bob Crewe remembers Valli hearing it for the first time. 'Frankie

walked by our little writing room in the Atlantic building in New York. He popped his head in and said, "That song goes nowhere, it's mine."' However, when Valli's version flopped, the pair offered it to the trio. The Walker Brothers' version, emboldened by Ivor Raymond's orchestra, topped the UK charts, cementing their status as teen phenomena – Scott and John were treated for concussion after being mobbed in Chester, while Gary was kidnapped by Harrow Technical College students as part of their rag week. The song was legendarily playing while East End gangster Ronnie Kray killed George Cornell in the Blind Beggar pub. After shooting Cornell through the head, Ronnie was heard to remark, 'the sun ain't gonna shine for *him* any more.' The Walker Brothers soon splintered, Scott and John heading for solo careers. Gary became a motorcycle courier. In Essex. Their signature song has subsequently been covered by David Essex and Cher.

9/'All By Myself'
Tearjerking total: 220

Weeks in chart: 20 ● Number of covers: 1

'All By Myself' was written and recorded by Eric Carmen, a veteran of Midwest American groups including the Raspberries. A year after that group broke up in 1975 he released this wrist-slashing epic, which he'd written after returning from the Raspberries' final tour. Carmen was sitting in his tiny apartment and, by his own admission, feeling sorry for himself. One of his favourite classical pieces was Rachmaninov's second piano concerto. 'I thought, there's so many people that will never even hear this because it's a classical piece. Maybe I could adapt this little piece stolen from it….' A dramatic ballad inspired by his love of strong melodies but equally by his lack of a girlfriend, by three o'clock in the morning he had the basic tune and lyrics written. He played the song to Clive Davies of Arista, who immediately offered Carmen a deal. 'I thought, what wonderful taste this man has,' blushes Carmen. The song has endured via numerous cover versions, with everyone from Babes In Toyland to Celine Dion chipping in. Carmen takes great pride in his contribution to the human condition. 'A lot of people came up to me and said, "I was getting divorced when that record came on the radio, and it just about pushed me to suicide."' Well, that's good. That was the desired effect.' Carmen himself enjoyed two further US hits, but that was it. Still, he's not all by himself again. He's got the royalties from Celine Dion to count, though he blew some of it on Wall Street investments. It's fair to say the Babes In Toyland royalties look less promising.

8/'If You Leave Me Now'
Tearjerking total: 230

Weeks in chart: 18 ● Weeks at No. 1: 3 ● Number of covers: 1

Chicago first got together in 1967 in the city that gave them their name. Before becoming kings of middle-of-the-road pomp rock, they were widely considered to be avant-garde rockers, playing opening sets for Jimi Hendrix and Janis Joplin. Thereafter they became a byword for moribund, soppy US rawk music. When punk happened in 1976, they

responded by offering up this treacly ballad, written by singer Peter Cetera and arranged by Jimmie Haskell. It was written 'from the heart', according to trombonist James Pankow, over Cetera's fear of losing his current amour – making it one of the few 'present tense' heartbreakers. It also announced Cetera's singular falsetto style. His ability to sing with seemingly no facial movement was a legacy of the group's rock origins. On an earlier tour Cetera was put into intensive care after four Marines took objection to his long hair at a baseball game. His jaw was wired shut for months, leading to a 'gottle of geer' singing style that even Rod Hull couldn't match. In the nineties, with boy band producers scurrying around for anything that was vaguely memorable that hadn't been filleted by rivals, several would-be moguls stumbled on the song once again. Upside Down were the worst offenders, taking their version of the song into the Top 30 in 1996. As the singer of that version, Giles Kristian, admits: 'If you're going to do a cover, it's got to be better, or it's got to be very different. I can honestly say ours wasn't better, and it wasn't an awful lot different. If I was going to listen to the song again now, I'd play the original.'

7/'Cryin''

Tearjerking total: 250

Weeks in chart: 20 ● Weeks at No. 1: 3 ● Number of covers: 1

Allegedly one of Elvis Presley's favourite songs, 'Cryin'' was co-written by the man who popularized it, Roy Orbison, and Joe Melson. Orbison, the famously shy Texan with the big dark glasses and honeyed larynx, had first come to prominence at Presley's old haunt, Sun Records, but his greatest successes came with the help of friend and producer Fred Foster of Monument Records. 'Cryin'' was written after a chance meeting with his ex-girlfriend that left him in 'an emotional puddle'. Significantly, as Orbison later confirmed, 'When that song came out, I don't think anyone had accepted the fact that a man should be able to cry when he wants to cry.' Foster remembers hearing the composition for the first time. 'When he came in and sang me "Cryin'"', I said, "OK, I'll book the session." He said, "What are you talking about, man, aren't you gonna change it?" I said, "No, nothing there to change. That's perfect like it is."' How right he was. Orbison had a run of successful singles and albums, but his career was dogged by tragic personal circumstances. In 1966 his wife was killed in a motorbike crash. Both his sons then died in a house fire two years later while he was touring. He subsequently married German-born Barbara Wellhoener in England in 1969. She argues that her late husband possessed rock 'n' roll's most romantic voice, adding that there was always hope in that voice somewhere to balance the heartache. A subsequent version of 'Cryin'' was released by Don McLean, topping the UK charts in 1980, before Orbison re-recorded the song as a duet with k.d. lang for the soundtrack to *Hiding Out*. Though the film bombed, their duet won a Grammy. The Canadian songstress remembers the experience of sharing the same microphone with Orbison fondly. 'At one point, our cheeks touched. His skin was softer than mine. It was so gentle. It was like electricity.' Since Orbison died from a heart attack aged fifty-two in December 1988, the song has passed into lang's custody.

6/'The Tracks Of My Tears'

Tearjerking total: 290

Weeks in chart: 23 ● Number of covers: 3

Smokey Robinson's definitive work, hurt but defiant, remains one of the gems of the
Motown catalogue. 'The Tracks Of My Tears', first released in 1965, is a beautifully
packaged composition, its braying trumpets and close-knit harmonies accentuating
Robinson's masterful vocal. Of the song's genesis, Robinson recalls that out of nowhere
one day, he suddenly started to think about someone crying so much that their tears literally made tracks on their face. The resultant song spoke of intense, irrevocable heartbreak,
a failed relationship haunting a protagonist who welled up in sympathy with the song's
sublime arrangement. Of course, it was only one of Robinson's classic lyrics, but it's his
most enduring effort, making sense in whichever context it finds itself – such as the
jukebox favourite of the troops in Oliver Stone's Vietnam epic *Platoon*. While Robinson
has enjoyed mixed fortunes over the years, his greatest song has been sullied by arguably
less worthy hands, some more unworthy than others. Paul Young offered a contemporary
big band version with Q Tips. 'That era was when punk was still hovering around',
reckons Young, 'so it was quite unusual to do love songs. But, if you're in a soul band,
what else do you do?' Undoubtedly the best non-Smokey attempt was Linda Ronstadt's
1976 country-inflected hit. A minimalist version came from the Zombies' former frontman
Colin Blunstone in 1982, in collaboration with Pete Bardens of progressive rockers
Camel. Bardens believes that he probably made the song keyboard-heavy, although he
admits that it's all a bit of a hazy memory today. Go West also offered a version in 1993.
Their treatment added a new arrangement, because, as the band's Peter Cox admits, they
weren't attempting to improve on the original, because nobody could. And last, but by no
means least, Bryan Ferry of Roxy Music had a pop. Ferry was particularly impressed by
the way Robinson wrote so intelligently about human feelings in the song – as Smokey
says, he writes about love because it's the never-ending subject.

5/'Love Don't Live Here Anymore'

Tearjerking total: 310

Weeks in chart: 27 ● Number of covers: 2

Rose Royce, an eight-piece R&B band formed in Los Angeles, first hit in the seventies via
the soundtrack for the film *Car Wash*. It saw them welcomed into the disco fold, but the
group always recognized that ballads were the key to career longevity after disco had
finished burning up the dancefloor and burned itself out. 'Love Don't Live Here
Anymore' proved their point, rising to number two in the UK charts in 1978, powered by
a distinctive, plaintive vocal from lead singer Gwen Dickey. They were furnished with the
track by songwriter Miles Gregory after some particularly unhappy domestic developments. 'Miles Gregory had been in the studio with us on one of our marathon sessions',
remembers Dickey, 'and when he went home, his wife said she didn't believe he'd been
in the studio for three days. She said to him, "If this happens again, I won't be here when

you come back." A couple of weeks later it happened again. He went home, and when he opened his front door there was nothing in his house. And where their bed used to be, she'd written in lipstick, "Love Don't Live Here Anymore".' Nowadays the song is dated somewhat by the intrusive syn-drum sounds. According to Dickey, percussionist Terral Santiel was tuning his bongos and it ended up on the tape by accident. Madonna covered the song on *Like A Virgin*. 'It is an honour for Madonna to record one of my songs,' says Dickey, diplomatically, but she won't offer an opinion on the results. Have-a-go pop hero Jimmy Nail had a go in the mid-eighties, the melancholy nature of the song clearly striking a chord. He put his version together with Roger Taylor of Queen, who remembers Nail insisting he'd only run through it a maximum of three times in the studio. They never worked together again. In the nineties, Double Trouble decided to make a quasi-spiritual house number out of it. Their version included a modish backbeat, prominent flutes and a regulation sultry soul vocalist. 'The video tried to capture different scenes of places in London', remembers Leigh Guest, 'old houses, people on park benches – love don't live here anymore. I wanted to inject a little more meaning into the song.' Those images of a heartless society were rendered piercingly true when his former Double Trouble partner Michael Menson was killed in a racist attack, for which his murderer was eventually sentenced to life imprisonment in 1999.

4/'I'm Not In Love' Tearjerking total: 400

Weeks in chart: 32 ● Weeks at No. 1: 2 ● Number of covers: 3

10cc's Graham Gouldman and Eric Stewart were evidently in a state of what the Americans love to call 'denial' when they penned this understated, though somewhat tongue-in-cheek ballad. Despite its title, the song's subtext spoke volumes about the singer's emotional condition. It was the pinnacle of a string of seventies hits by the Mancunian quartet, who were named after 'the average volume of a male ejaculation' by Jonathan King. Their highly developed and very English pop sensibility had already secured number one status with the prison-break romp 'Rubber Bullets'. The ballad was Stewart's idea. 'I thought, I am in love, how do I get this across in another way?' Once I had the idea of saying *not* in love, I could give you all the reasons why I was still totally in love with this person.' Lol Creme (who completed the band along with Kevin Godley) was initially less than impressed with what he thought was a 'slushy ballad'. The track's densely harmonic opening notes were based on a total of 256 voice tracks featuring three voices recorded 16 times each. Creme had the idea of adding a female vocal to perform the voiceover line. Their secretary, Kathy, was nearest at hand, and got the job. Although the group were reticent about releasing it as a single, extensive radio play soon forced their hand and the song shot to number one in June 1975. Several other artists have since tried to improve on it. 'I'm really flattered that some people think they can do the song in another way,' says Stewart, with perhaps a slight note of scepticism. He reckons he knows of over fifty cover versions, the worst of which critics believe is possibly an upbeat disco stomp by Petula Clark. While Godley and Creme subsequently forged a career as a duo, then directed a series of successful promo videos, Stewart and Gouldman reunited the

band in 1991. Four years later they agreed, to the lament of many, to release a new, acoustic version of the song that was promoted on daytime TV. That aside, the song's provided an excellent pension plan for Stewart, but sadly not Creme, who regrets that of all the material he penned for 10cc, their biggest hit escaped his writing credit.

3/'Smoke Gets In Your Eyes'   Tearjerking total: 460

Weeks in chart:39 ● Weeks at No. 1: 1 ● Number of covers: 3

Despite appearances, Jerome Kern's 'Smoke Gets In Your Eyes' was not an anti-smoking tract. Instead, it started the tradition of great ballads documenting the excuses employed by emotionally aggrieved lovers for their inability to control the waterworks ('The Tracks Of My Tears' and 'Walk On By' are both direct descendants). The Platters, a US vocal group created by vocal coach Samuel 'Buck' Ram, were the first to pilot this enduring number to the top of the UK charts in 1959. Ram found the group a contract with Mercury and added personnel from other acts he managed (included Zola Taylor, a rare female in the vocal group milieu) to the existing line-up. However, the band continued to feature Tony Williams on lead vocals – a man whose headstrong delivery and emotionally involving performances distinguished the Platters from the welter of vocal groups boasting similar technical ability. 'Only You' became an R&B number one in 1955, serving as a prelude to another Ram-composed smash, 'The Great Pretender', memorably reprised in Alan Freed's film *Rock Around The Clock*. The Platters were thus the first black act to crack the mainstream *Billboard* charts in the rock 'n' roll era, and by the time they recorded Kern's classic 'Smoke Gets In Your Eyes', were the acknowledged kings of doo wop. Kern had written the song for his 1933 Broadway show *Roberta*, with lyrics from Otto Harbach (a film version was issued two years later). A succession of cover versions of the song has ensued, including chart efforts by Blue Haze and Bryan Ferry and just about every mainstream jazz and cabaret pop act you care to mention. Some of them include Thelonious Monk, Liberace, Earl Bostic, Glenn Miller, Mantovani, Tommy Dorsey, Dinah Washington, Serge Gainsbourg, Stephane Grappelli and even Robert Maxwell (sadly, not *that* Robert Maxwell).

2/'What Becomes Of
The Broken Hearted?'   Tearjerking total: 570

Weeks in chart: 51 ● Weeks at No. 1: 2 ● Number of covers: 2

'What Becomes Of The Broken Hearted?' was originally recorded by Motown 'hard man' Jimmy Ruffin in 1966. He stole it from under the Detroit Spinners' noses and managed to revive his career just as it was beginning to look as if he'd live to regret turning down a place in the Temptations. Written by Jimmy Dean, Paul Riser and William Witherspoon, Ruffin gave the song bucketloads, turning the composition into an instant R&B standard. His edgy, empathetic version has, needless to say, never been surpassed. However, that hasn't stopped

a legion of imitators from trying. One of these came from housewives' favourites Robson and Jerome. Newly liberated from roles in TV's *Soldier Soldier*, they'd just hit with a similar re-run of 'Unchained Melody' (or 'unbridled opportunism' as some wags re-named it). 'What Becomes Of The Broken Hearted' was chosen to capitalize on their breakthrough. And what was in it for our acting pals? Filthy lucre. The song sold nearly 1 million copies and stayed at the number-one spot for three weeks. As Jimmy Ruffin himself points out, those who try to improve classics can come a cropper. However, he has a soft spot for Dave Stewart's 1981 effort, which featured guest vocals from ex-Zombie Colin Blunstone, primarily because the duo hadn't tried to meddle too much with it. Oh, and Paul Young's had a go, placing his version on the soundtrack to *Fried Green Tomatoes*. So what does Ruffin think is the song's timeless message? 'Go on with your life, have a great life. Forget about the piece of whatever that did this to you, forget about what you did to yourself in the name of love, and move on, and say, hey, there's got to be something better than this.'

1/'Walk On By' Tearjerking total: 600

Weeks in chart: 50 ● Number of covers: 5

When Gwen Dickey thinks of Dionne Warwick's original version of Hal David and Burt Bacharach's immortal song, she's reminded of the Sistine Chapel: 'It doesn't get any better than that.' A perfect meeting point between a supreme lyricist, a divine composer and a staggering voice, 'Walk On By' is the peak of three separate and laudable careers. 'I knew Burt would write a great melody,' says Warwick. 'I knew Hal would write fabulous lyrics, and they both relied on me to get that message across to the listening ear.' 'Dionne, from the very beginning, knew how to get out of the lyric what the lyric writer meant,' says David. Of course, as was standard for a Bacharach-David song, there was the usual protracted recording session for her to negotiate first: 'I don't think there was ever a session that we did that we didn't do at least thirty takes on the song,' says Warwick. 'Ninety-nine per cent of the time after the thirtieth take they went back to the third one and took that.' Released in 1964, the single topped both the UK and US charts. The cover versions flowed thereafter, including a verbatim Cilla Black effort and one from David Essex. Others to chance their hand include 'funkiest white men in soul' the Average White Band and, more recently, Gabrielle. However, there are two other versions of the song that really stand the test of time. One came from old punk sweats the Stranglers, who added spittle to the song's original sentiment, as well as an astounding instrumental detour. As Hugh Cornwell remembers, the song came about from early gigs which they secured on the premise of being a covers band. 'If we played too many of our own songs, the promoter who booked us would come up and complain. "Walk On By" was really well known, it's a great song, and we thought we could have some fun with it.' Cornwell himself believes the definitive take on the song was included on Isaac Hayes's *Hot Buttered Soul* album; Bacharach also rates Hayes's treatment of the song, particularly for the way Hayes came up with a tone and then just s-t-r-e-t-c-h-e-d it over twelve magical minutes. But as Warwick says, 'No matter how many times it's recorded, and by whom, it's still my song.' She believes it 'will outlive all of us', and she's probably right.

How Much Emotional Grief Can You Take?
Ten Other Heartbreakers

Aztec Camera: 'We Could Send Letters' (1981)
Bob Marley: 'No Woman No Cry' (1975)
Dawn Penn: 'You Don't Love Me (No, No, No)' (1994)
Elvis Presley: 'Heartbreak Hotel' (1956)
Jim Reeves: 'There's A Heartache Following Me' (1964)
Lou Rawls: 'You'll Never Find Another Love Like Mine' (1976)
Bonnie Raitt: 'I Can't Make You Love Me' (1991)
Lou Reed: 'Caroline Says' (1973)
Randy Vanwarmer: 'Just When I Needed You Most' (1979)
Sinead O'Connor: 'Three Babies' (1990)

Guitar Heroes

The guitar has been the dominant instrument underpinning most of the post-war rock 'n' roll movement. Henry VIII plucked a lute string or two, a few centuries before Robert Johnson mortgaged his soul to the devil in return for his mythical guitar technique. His innovations informed subsequent blues (B.B. King) and jazz artists (Django Reinhardt), leading the way to contemporary rockers, notably Chuck Berry. To many, such as anthropologist Desmond Morris, the body of the guitar is a metaphorical scrotum, the neck an extension of the male appendage. Noel Gallagher isn't having that. It's a plank of wood with six strings, and that's all he's admitting to.

We've restrained our discussion so as not to dwell too heavily on chord progressions, effects pedals and string selection (all of which are probably very important indeed and none of which this writer understands). We've focused instead on the contribution each has made to the musical milieu in which they evolved. These Marshall-stacked, plectrum-wielding virtuosos (sixpence-wielding in Brian May's case) have provided the impetus to some of popular music's most treasured moments. Our selection, based on UK and US chart positions with bonus points for innovation, has thrown up a purist's selection. Each is a highly individual and distinctive stylist, though not all have consistently graced good records. But a glance at their definitive recordings underscores their importance as midwives to some of the great songs of the last thirty years.

10/Johnny Marr   Points: 220

Definitive performance: 'How Soon Is Now?'

For many, the Smiths were incontestably the best band of the eighties. They had a potent rhythm section and a fantastically charismatic and articulate frontman of course, but their songwriting ultimately hinged on the supremely imaginative guitar playing of Johnny

Marr. Anyone in any doubt about his contribution need only glance at the pages of Morrissey's solo career – the story of a man at sea without the right musical collaborator. Born in Ardwick in 1963, Marr had played in a clutch of local Manchester bands when manager Joe Moss told him to sound out local scenester Morrissey. Marr duly knocked on Morrissey's door and the two started working together almost immediately. The addition of bassist Andy Rourke and drummer Mike Joyce completed the band. The press was instantly drawn to Morrissey's eloquent obsessions with British cultural iconography and a contract with Rough Trade saw debut single 'Hand In Glove' top the independent charts. The Smiths' subsequent run of distinctive singles was dominated by Marr's guitar imprint.

Bernard Butler (former Suede guitarist): 'I spent most of my time once I'd got the Smiths albums sitting in front of the video watching live tapes. That was the only romance I was getting at the time, that's for sure. But that's all I needed or wanted.

Able to empathize with the group's alternately strident ('Rusholme Ruffians' was an acknowledged heir to Presley's 'His Latest Flame') and despondent material, Marr's musical affinity for Morrissey's lyrical mood swings forged an irresistible creative bulkhead. When *Meat Is Murder* entered the UK charts at number one in 1985, the Smiths' adoring following went overground. Marr applied his trademark red Gibson to the Smiths' broader canvasses with equal dexterity. While other 'indie' bands of the period used a similar 'jangly' aesthetic, Marr's work boasted greater clarity and precision and made every note count. Despite Morrissey stating that rumours of an imminent Smiths split would result in the whisperers being 'severely spanked' with a wet plimsoll, it was Marr who broke the group up, although he maintains that tensions had been building for months. While Morrissey embarked on a solo career, Marr became a gun for hire (an expression he hates), working with Paul McCartney, Talking Heads, the Pretenders and, most intriguingly, Matt Johnson's The The. He then formed Electronic with New Order's Bernard Sumner (and, initially at least, Neil Tennant of the Pet Shop Boys), a combination that has enjoyed some chart success since the late eighties. In the late nineties Joyce and Rourke sued Marr and Morrissey over unpaid monies from the Smiths' career, a state of affairs Rourke likens to a messy divorce. Marr is currently piloting his own band, and singing for the first time, with the Healers.

9/Ritchie Blackmore   Points: 280

Definitive Performance: 'Smoke On The Water' (dah-dah-dah, dah-dah-DAH-DAH…)

We've tackled Ritchie's Deep Purple and Rainbow careers elsewhere (see Heavy Metal). What can we add to the story of the ruthless old perfectionist? Here's a couple of insights. Former bandmate Ian Gillan thinks he's an outstanding player with a stunning sound that distinguished him from his peers. Rock author Malcolm Dome pays tribute to Blackmore's talent but also acknowledges the man's moodiness and unpredictability. Blackmore started out with the late Screaming Lord Sutch and recalls being unnerved at the sight of his employer emerging from a coffin on stage at the start of the act. Sutch was giving him a lift home after the show and Blackmore wasn't entirely sure whether they'd be travelling by car, hearse, or spaceship. Seeing Robert Plant of Led Zeppelin

convinced Blackmore that his band, Deep Purple, wouldn't prosper without their own braveheart screamer. Enter Ian Gillan and hits such as 'Black Night' and 'Strange Kind Of Woman'. Then, exit Ian Gillan, as Blackmore warmed to his revolving door personnel policy. In came David Coverdale. He didn't last either. Blackmore openly admits to having favoured the sulk-and-sack-'em approach to the let's-sit-down-and-talk-this-over tack. He huffed his way into Rainbow, or Ritchie Blackmore's Rainbow, just to make the point about who was boss here. Cue new singer Ronnie James Dio – for a while, anyway. Graham Bonnett did a quick stint. Joe Lynn Turner was next up and next out. Thereafter Blackmore reformed Deep Purple, lured by a £2-million fee. Apparently, meeting Frank Sinatra finally helped Blackmore put everything into perspective. Old Blue Eyes greeted the Purple plank-spanker with 'Who are you?' when they met, whereupon Blackmore realized that it was time for him to seek pastures new. Or in his case, pastures old: he has laid down his Stratocaster and now plays mediaeval music.

8/Carlos Santana

Points: 290

Definitive performance: 'Black Magic Woman'

Born in Mexico, the son of a mariachi violinist, Carlos Santana learned his craft in the strip joints of Tijuana. He put together the Santana band in San Francisco in the late sixties after quitting his dish-washing job, combining his own Latin traditions with electric blues and R&B. Drummer Michael Shrieve and keyboardist Gregg Rolie hailed from the suburbs, but were playing alongside a Puerto Rican, a militant black, a Nicaraguan and a Mexican (Santana himself). Shrieve saw the ensemble as more street gang than hippy combo, but with music as their weapon. They captured the public's imagination after appearing at Woodstock ('Soul Sacrifice' featured on the attendant film and album) and debut album *Santana* spent two years on the US charts, partly as a consequence. Follow-up *Abraxas* spent six weeks at the top and produced a major hit in a cover of Fleetwood Mac's 'Black Magic Woman'. Santana's guitar lines, framed by driving percussion, congas and timbales, dominated the group's sound. Observers considered him the most emotionally authentic guitarist post-Hendrix; Santana argues that if the performer doesn't *feel* it, the audience won't either. Eventually he fought with percussionist Mike Carabello, a disagreement put down to a 'clash of chemical influences'. After they both stormed out in 1971, Shrieve was forced to put together a band to fulfil a Madison Square Garden date. A makeshift percussionist was recruited from the audience who eventually completed the band's tour of South America. Santana rejoined the band and continued to cut albums, the prevailing influence shifting from blues to jazz. He also cultivated a groaning trophy cabinet, and in 1998 was given a star on the Hollywood Walk of Fame and inducted into the Rock 'n' Roll Hall of Fame. But the best was yet to come. In 1999 he employed a younger generation of collaborators (including Lauryn Hill and Everlast) and long-term fan Eric Clapton to record the album *Supernatural*. A phenomenal success, with sales of over 21 million copies, it housed US number ones 'Smooth' and 'Maria, Maria'. He swept the boards at the 42nd Grammy Awards in February 2000, winning nine categories. Just rewards for a man who's played

in front of audiences totalling more than 13 million – and hired almost as many backing musicians. He's also turned down gigs with the Pope, Fidel Castro, and Bill Clinton (four times). As Shrieve says, the man can't be bought.

7/The Edge

Points: 300

Definitive performance: 'I Still Haven't Found What I'm Looking For'

U2's sound conceptualist, David Evans piloted the good ship U2 from sweeping late seventies post-punk brashness (he might as well have called himself 'the Echo') through to the panoramic acoustics of million-sellers such as *The Joshua Tree*. More recent albums have somewhat devalued his currency as a guitarist, but he's remained central to the construction of U2's increasingly diverse output. Early songs such as '11 O'Clock Tick Tock' marked him out as the most theatrical guitarist of his generation, an extravagance reined in over successive recordings. U2 was

> **B.B. King:** 'The [U2] rhythm section consists of four people. The Edge is all four.'

formed with singer Bono (who gave The Edge his nickname because of his 'sharp mind'), bass player Adam Clayton and drummer Larry Mullen Jr at a mixed-religion Dublin school in 1976. At first, they were a bit rough around the edges, but they got their break when they lied to a TV producer and said the Ramones songs they were playing were their own. Manager Paul McGuinness also spotted the Edge's talent, noting that whereas other punk groups played chords, the Edge dealt uniquely in single notes. Moreover, he played a Gibson Explorer, a very flash instrument to be touting around in the days of punk. Clearly, McGuinness reasoned, the man had bottle. By November 1980 U2 had completed their debut album, *Boy*, which announced the group's emotive, anthemic rock style. Their breakthrough song was 'New Year's Day', which patented the Edge's alternately sparse and overdriven, effects-laden guitar sound. Their American popularity was cemented by their bravura performance at Red Rocks, released as *Under A Blood Red Sky* in 1983. Some of that raw bluster was refined by producers Daniel Lanois and Brian Eno on *The Unforgettable Fire*, the first U2 album to gain significant exposure in America. The Edge's first solo venture, a soundtrack album with Sinead O'Connor, was released in August 1986. He also composed music for a Royal Shakespeare Company production of *A Clockwork Orange 2004* (though author Anthony Burgess criticized the score for being 'neo-wallpaper'). In between those projects, *The Joshua Tree* topped both the British and American charts. The nineties saw U2's sound expand beyond conventional rock parameters, and the Edge's contributions, though still significant, shifted axis (he co-produced 1993's dance music-informed *Zooropa*). He has frequently been characterized as an 'anti-guitar hero', and he's certainly less self-important than most. He enjoyed himself on the band's 1997 *PopMart* tour, out-tapping Spinal Tap by performing karaoke renditions of 'Sweet Caroline', and he has increasingly worked as a lyrical as well as musical collaborator with Bono.

6/Pete Townshend

Points: 320

Definitive performance: 'Won't Get Fooled Again'

Backtrack to the mid-sixties, when Townshend's band were trying to change the world. A celebration of youth, exuberance, Englishness and the rejection of authority, the Who were also inherently contradictory – and so much more exciting because of it. Born in 1945 in Shepherd's Bush, Townshend was hooked on imported American R&B records while at art college. He started out playing banjo in a Dixieland band with bass player John Entwistle before both joined Roger Daltrey's Detours. As the High Numbers, they recruited eccentric drummer Keith Moon, and quickly endeared themselves to the style-conscious Mods populating London's trendier venues. Renamed the Who, the quartet's fiery brand of R&B (they christened it 'maximum R&B') hit the charts in 1965 with 'I Can't Explain'. Their popularity mushroomed, particularly in front of live audiences (they are officially the loudest band of all time), with Townshend's ritual demolition of guitars at the close of shows a particular highlight (though Moon's offstage antics made as many headlines). Their commercial pinnacle came with Townshend's ambitious *Tommy* album in 1969 (for some reason described by DJ Tony Blackburn as 'sick'), which stayed in the US charts for nearly two years. *Quadrophenia* in 1973 was Townshend's second 'rock opera', this one a tribute to the Mod scene that first embraced the group. In that period they worked successfully in both pop and rock idioms, Townshend perfecting a balance between aggression and vulnerability as both writer and guitarist. He never lost his mastery of the brutal, broad brush-stroke rock song, but he was also equal to the task of layering detail into every canvas (for an early example see masturbation eulogy 'Pictures Of Lily' from 1967). Despite many quarrels between Townshend and Daltrey, the Who maintained the same line-up until Moon the Loon's death in 1978 which painfully reminded his band members of the consequences of the rock 'n' roll lifestyle. Townshend went on to a solo career, then threw himself into campaigning against hard drug use. There were also several farewell Who tours. For sheer musical attack the Who were peerless in the late sixties, and only the Beatles had a more lasting influence.

5/Brian May

Points: 390

Definitive performance: 'Bohemian Rhapsody'

Enough jokes about the hair and clogs, already. Brian May served as musical sounding board to Freddie Mercury, providing a banquet of pop, ballad and hard rock for popular music's biggest showman to ham out on. May built his first guitar aged sixteen, hand-crafted from an old fireplace and embossed with shelf-edging. Although May displayed early talent, he was equally successful academically, achieving ten O-level passes and three A-levels. But during studies in astronomy and physics, he decided to pursue music. He formed Smile with Queen drummer Roger Taylor in 1967 after he'd had enough of his professor encouraging him to continually redraft his thesis. Taylor knew Mercury from their shared stall at Kensington Market. As May recalls, Mercury attended their gigs and

added lots of suggestions, but they thought he was all talk until he offered to sing for them. With the addition of bass player John Deacon, the group, renamed Queen, played its first set in June 1971. Its first hit came three years later with 'Seven Seas Of Rhye', a product of what May describes as the 'kitchen sink approach'. The *Sheer Heart Attack* album followed, its sales buoyed by the performance of attendant single 'Killer Queen'. An ideal introduction to May's guitar style, 'Killer Queen's semi-operatic interludes and beefy riffing anticipated the group's defining moment, 'Bohemian Rhapsody'. A seven-minute rock opera, it was played pre-release fourteen times over one weekend by band friend DJ Kenny Everett in November 1975 and sure enough, on Monday the kids were a-thronging the record stores. Featuring one of the first promotional videos (directed by Bruce Gowers and costing a paltry £5,000), the song defied conceptions of what the pop single could aspire to. Thereafter Queen became bona fide global rock stars, their status cemented by a memorable appearance at Live Aid (the fact that they'd recently played Sun City in apartheid-riven South Africa was glossed over). The band was dominated by Mercury's personality. May, the principal songwriter, just occasionally made the tabloids by dint of dating soap star and parallel-permed paramour Anita Dobson though, to his credit, he admits to being fashion-blind. Even after Freddie's death, he's remained a workaholic. Step forward boy band Five, who wanted to cover an 'anthemic rock song'. They chose 'We Will Rock You'. The band asked to sample May's guitar; he replied that he might as well play on the track himself. Cue another entry on a long chart CV.

4/Hank Marvin

Points: 440

Definitive performance: 'Apache'

Marvin's spacey guitar leads propelled the instrumental magic of the Shadows; that he could manage a few tasteful dance steps only augmented the package. Born Brian Rankin, Marvin is an unlikely guitar hero in retrospect, bespectacled librarian looks and Jehova's Witness beliefs notwithstanding. Yet his instrumental leads powered the Shadows' melodrama of sound, his technique augmented by adroit studio effects and exquisite timing. Cliff Richard's manager, whom Marvin met in a Soho club in the late fifties, confessed he needed a lead guitarist for a forthcoming tour. Marvin agreed to the invitation, providing he could bring friend Bruce Welch along. They caught a bus to the council house the former Harry Webb shared with his parents. Richard remembers that they gelled personally and musically right from their first 'jam' together. Marvin, along with Welch (rhythm), Jet Harris (bass) and Tony Meehan (drums) became the Drifters and backed Cliff Richard on 'Livin' Lovin' Doll', a hit in early 1959. They changed their name to the Shadows at Harris's suggestion after being sued by the American Drifters. Most of the great records that ensued were composed on Marvin's Fender Stratocaster, one of the first models to elude an import ban. When it arrived, the group took it out of the case and simply stared at it in blissful awe. As Richard admits, Marvin's guitar invented the Shadows' sound. Their first major hit came with 'Apache', recorded at Abbey Road and written by Jerry Lordan. It took root at number one for six weeks in August 1960 and set the trend for a series of instrumental smashes, such as 'Wonderful Land' (1962) and

'Atlantis' (1963). It also became 'the national anthem of hip hop' when DJs discovered the instrumental break (via the Incredible Bongo Band's version) some fifteen years later. The Shadows augmented their own career by supporting Cliff Richard on record and in pantomime, and even showed up as puppet likeness in the *Thunderbirds Are Go!* movie. Crowds of screaming fans followed them everywhere, resulting in scenes of hysteria that pre-dated Beatlemania by a few years. But while the girls loved Cliff, Hank was the subject of adoring male affection. As success dwindled in the late sixties, Marvin recorded solo and became a Jehova's Witness in 1973. BBC boss Bill Cotton Jnr persuaded the Shadows out of retirement in 1975 to represent Britain in the Eurovision Song Contest in Brighton, where they finished second with 'Let Me Be The One'. Later Marvin moved to

> **Bruce Welch:** 'All the guys wanted to be in the Shadows. They were all wearing horn-rimmed glasses with no glass in, because they wanted to be like Hank.'

Australia. In 1996 he was honoured by a tribute album featuring reverential interpretations of his work from artists including Ritchie Blackmore, Peter Green, Mark Knopfler and Brian May. Even some of the punks of '77 loved the 'king of the twang'. Marvin recalls talking to some young punks who'd turned up at one of their concerts and finding, to his surprise, that they admired the economy of the Shads' two guitar, bass and drums line-up. They felt it was a primitive approach and, as such, had much in common with punk's back-to-basics approach. Who'd have thought it?

3/Jimmy Page

Points: 480

Definitive performance: 'Stairway To Heaven'

Prior to providing Led Zeppelin with the sonic ballast behind its trailblazing seventies success, Page had made his TV debut as part of a child skiffle group. When asked then if he wished to pursue a musical career, he instead pledged his future to biological research. However, by the sixties he had become a prolific session musician, appearing on landmark recordings by artists including Them, Lulu and the Who, as well as numerous *Top Of The Pops* cash-in albums that featured studio recreations of recent hits. He spent 1966 to 1968 as a member of blues-rock greats the Yardbirds. When that band sundered he recruited John Paul Jones on bass and keyboards and singer Robert Plant (who put him in touch with drummer John Bonham) to fulfil contractual obligations as the New Yardbirds. Their first live set as Led Zeppelin – the name adapted from a remark variously attributed to the Who's Keith Moon or John Entwistle – came in October 1968. The accent was on hard-driving blues riffs, which suited Page's demonstrative, earthy style perfectly. The most arresting example was 'Dazed And Confused', a song Page had kept from his Yardbirds days, which featured an extended solo section in which he extemporized using a violin bow. On an early American date, headline act Iron Butterfly were so unsettled by their audience's ecstatic reaction to the unsung support band, they refused to go on. Despite manager Peter Grant's insistence that the band should not release singles in Britain, and a consequent lack of radio and TV exposure in their home country, Led Zeppelin's self-titled debut album became a Top 10 success in May 1969. Baroness Von Zeppelin was so flattered by the use of her name that she visited the band at a TV date in Denmark.

However, when she heard them play, she immediately contacted her lawyers. By the end of the year, follow-up *Led Zeppelin II* had topped the US charts on the way to sales of over 8 million. The carnage quota rocketed through the seventies as Led Zeppelin proved they could take on all-comers for party hi-jinx, a long list of drug and groupie anecdotes peppering the headlines (the best of which were later recounted in gory detail in the quintessential rock book, *Hammer Of The Gods*). However, there was more to the group than simple-minded rock bombast and hedonistic mythology, and Page's guitar work, which always betrayed a debt to revered acoustic guitarist Bert Jansch, began to explore folk traditions and nuances. That influence was captured in the group's most enduring composition, the eight-minute-plus 'Stairway To Heaven'. Though never released as a single, some religious die-hards took exception to Page's praise of Aleister Crowley and accused the song of 'backward masking'. John Bonham was found dead in September 1980 after choking in his sleep and his death knocked the stuffing out of the band. Led Zeppelin's break-up was confirmed by the end of the year (though they reformed, with Phil Collins on drums, for Live Aid). Page went on to form the Firm, and composed the soundtrack to *Death Wish II* for his neighbour, director Michael Winner who describes his new-found lovey's contribution as 'spectacular'. Further collaborations involved David Coverdale (Whitesnake) before Page rejoined Plant for 1998's *Walking Into Clarksdale* project. The same year he also scored his biggest solo success by reviving Zep classic 'Kashmir' on Puff Daddy's 'Come With Me' from the soundtrack of *Godzilla*.

2/Eric Clapton
Points: 500

Definitive performance: 'Layla'

Though it's possible he isn't actually divine, as his fans and supporters once suggested (mid-sixties London was daubed in graffiti insisting 'Clapton Is God'), he is still the supreme white interpreter of the blues. Contrary to suggestions otherwise, he's more than repaid any debt owed to that tradition. By the time of his self-titled 1970 debut album, Clapton was a veteran of several celebrated groups, including the Yardbirds, John Mayall's Bluesbreakers and Cream. As Jack Bruce of the latter band notes, 'from the first few notes with Eric, it was pretty obvious he was… ahead of everyone in a big way.' He also played on the Beatles' *White Album* and was an occasional member of John Lennon's Plastic Ono Band. His reticence at pursuing a solo career continued with the Derek & The Dominos' album, which housed arguably his greatest composition, 'Layla'. Famously, it expressed his love for Patti Harrison, who just happened to be married to someone else. A Beatle. Nevertheless, the woman in question passed between the two rock stars with a minimum of ill feeling, and all three remained friends. Clapton had long since established a reputation for the warmth of his Stratocaster-based sound, which some critics called 'woman tone' (this was the sixties, after all). However, his playing owed as much to J.J. Cale (whose 'After Midnight' he covered on his debut solo album) as the Delta blues greats, and he continues to cite both as pivotal influences. The early seventies were quiet but he made a comeback in 1973,

B.B. King: 'To me he's a genius. He has me doing things that it's hard for my lady to get me to do.'

encouraged by Pete Townshend. *461 Ocean Boulevard* followed in 1974, topping the charts and spawning a number one cover version of Bob Marley's 'I Shot The Sheriff'. His output thereafter relied increasingly on ballads, which frustrated fans and critics alike. The commercial returns rendered such arguments academic.

The best example was 1977's *Slowhand*, titled after the nick-name Yardbirds' manager Giorgio Gomelsky gave him. Featuring a successful blend of straight blues and pop, it housed the hit singles 'Lay Down Sally' and forty-somethings' favourite 'Wonderful Tonight'. In 1991 Clapton's four-year-old son Connor died in a fall, a tragedy he later documented in 'Tears In Heaven'. Nowadays he maintains an annual pilgrim-

> **Eric Clapton:** 'You don't fall in love with the wife of a Beatle. It's the last thing you do in the late sixties or early seventies. It's not good form if you want to survive.'

age to the Albert Hall and has set up his own 'tough love' rehab clinic on a Caribbean island. He also fulfilled a lifetime's ambition by working with B.B. King, who offers this tribute: 'In my opinion, he's the number one rock 'n' roll player. And he plays blues better than most of us.'

1/ Jimi Hendrix

Points: 580

Definitive performance: 'Crosstown Traffic'

The one guitarist who always played with heart and soul, in alliance with a master's (some would say an alien's) technique, there remains a mystique about Hendrix that no other musician can touch. Sensing possibilities that others did not, he executed them with a raw, intuitive ability that was sometimes masked by his equal gifts as a showman. While to many he symbolized the drugged-out narcissism of the sixties, he was also a softly spoken, intrinsically shy man (though this being the sixties, it didn't stop him from allegedly getting it together with as many as seven groupies a night if circumstance afforded him the opportunity). Hendrix, who played left-handed but used an 'upside

> **Chas Chandler, ex-Hendrix manager:** 'You just sat there and thought, this is ridiculous. Why hasn't someone signed this guy up? How come he's loose?'

down' right-handed guitar rather than have the strings realigned, served a tough apprenticeship. He was in his early twenties before deciding to pursue music as a full-time career (and, as recounted elsewhere in this book, it took the Isley Brothers to lend him money to buy his guitar back out of hock). Chas Chandler of the Animals spotted him playing at a show in Greenwich Village. Shaken and

stirred by what he'd seen and heard, in 1966 Chandler invited him to England and hooked him up with bass player Noel Redding and drummer Mitch Mitchell. The Jimi Hendrix Experience quickly made its mark on London's 'swinging' club scene, capitalizing on their burgeoning live popularity with the singles 'Hey Joe' and 'Purple Haze', both of which were UK Top 10 hits. However, it took an appearance at the Monterey Pop Festival in 1967, at which Hendrix climaxed the set by setting fire to his guitar, to export their appeal back to America. Some fans lament the fact that Hendrix was increasingly associ-ated with such extravagances – playing behind his back or with his teeth – rather than his true innovations with feedback and acoustic dynamics, but it's easily possible to enjoy both elements of the man. Touring feverishly, the trio followed 1967 debut album *Are You Experienced?* with *Axis: Bold As Love* then the double album *Electric Ladyland*, both in 1968. Thereafter Hendrix was beset by management problems and an increasing reliance on hard drugs. Both Chandler and Redding quit, and Hendrix took to the stage at Woodstock with a new line-up – which nevertheless performed a gravity-defying, era-defining version of 'The Star Spangled Banner'. Britain's take on Woodstock was the Isle Of Wight Festival. Hendrix came to the stage at two in the morning. Lemmy, his guitar roadie, could sense that all was not well. 'I was so used to him being magic, but at the Isle of Wight he was garbage. He didn't want to play there. You could feel it.' Hendrix's death came less than three weeks later, on 18 September 1970. He'd suffocated after taking sleeping tablets and vomiting in his sleep. He was only 27, and his solo career had lasted barely four years.

Boy, Could They Play Guitar
some more six-stringed saints

B.B. King
(still bossing the blues)
Chuck Berry
(where everyone got the idea for rock 'n' roll from)
Eddie Van Halen
(the Stratocaster-wielding-tremelo-dive-bomber par excellence)
George Harrison
(unarguably the talent in the Beatles)
Jeff Beck
(didn't just write 'Hi Ho Silver Lining', you know)
Keith Richard
(has put up with Mick Jagger longer than Jerry Hall)
PJ Harvey
(extraordinary singer, extraordinary guitar sound)
Mark Knopfler
(Dire Straits' somnambulist sultan)
Richard Thompson
(pastoral pugilist)
Rise Kagona
(the Bhundu Boys' magnificent guitarist)
Steve Albini
(destroy all melodies)
Steve Jones
(Sex Pistol who kept it simple, stupid)
Neil Young
(non-careerist old codger permanently chasing new sounds)
Steve Vai
(fret-shredding rock survivalist)
Duane Eddy
(twangster supremo)
Frank Zappa
(good guitarist, even better conversationalist)
Johnny Thunders
(New York Dolls/Heartbreakers genius)
Jonny Greenwood
(Radiohead's perpetually embarrassed guitar hero)